Atlas Hardwood Identification

Ruyan Tian   **Ruling Tian**   **Rusong Tian**

Editor Meng Tian & Ian Herring

Illustrations by Moo Meng

Abstract:

This Atlas consists of a new sanding method that is introduced by the authors.

Readers will learn how-to:

> Sand a piece of wood cross surface under flowing water.
> Capture a micro-photograph with a smartphone and portable microscope.
> Adjust the magnification of a micro-photograph to match the images contained within this book.
> Identify distinctive features that can be seen in a micro-photograph.

With these instructions, readers can obtain high quality wood surface samples and sharp micro-photographs that can be compared with microscopic slides.

The Atlas also contains 278 species of wood with over 800 color images that are included for the reader to reference, including a macro-view, 13X, and 30X cross surface images of each species, many of which are commercially important hardwoods.

This is particularly useful to wood anatomists engaged in automatic identification analysis. Everyone responsible for the verification of wood agents, are involved in the timber trade law enforcement, the CITES inspector, curators of wood repair and cultural heritages, forestry researchers, students of wood anatomy, and wood collectors will find this book is a great help.

Cover photos and inside flap photos: Ruyan Tian
All microphotographs: Ruling Tian
Cover design: Ruyan Tian
Illustrator: Moo Meng

ruyan.tian2021@gmail.com
wanmuren@gmail.com
Youtube: Wood Identification by Microscope by Ruling

Preface

Wood products are everywhere around us. Big things including chairs, tables, and shelves. Little things including chopsticks, clothespins, and spatulas. People make wood products for different purposes according to the distinct characteristics of the wood. For example, a red wine cask must be made of white oak and not of red oak, because a cask made of white oak will not leak. In addition, there are laws in place that can restrict or prohibit the trade and use of endangered timber. Therefore, it is important to identify different species of wood when purchasing and using wood products.

The empirical method of identifying a wood species, is to see, touch, smell, compare grain, texture, color, weight, and discover other characteristics of the wood. This method requires a lot of experience to master and it can contain little information, inevitably involving subjective elements. This can leave the identification range small and result in inaccuracies. Additionally, the public will be unable to learn these methods quickly enough to identify wood in a timely manner.

There is a method that compares the microstructural characters in a wood sample with microscopic slides or photomicrographs of an identified specimen. The results are objective and accurate. Unfortunately, it requires professional equipment, along with the accompanying skills and knowledge to utilize, making this approach difficult for the public to access.

This book introduces a simple and easy-to-learn method to obtain microstructural images. The tools are inexpensive and readily available to anyone interested in identifying wood. Provided within are 834 microscopic images of identified specimens that cover 278 species of hardwood for reference, along with 24 examples of the distinctive features of wood microstructure that have been specifically selected.

The author hopes that this book will help everyone properly identify wood species.

Contents

Guide to Sanding & Shooting

Making wood specimens & taking micro-photographs

Cutting Wood Sample

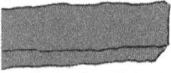

A. Wood

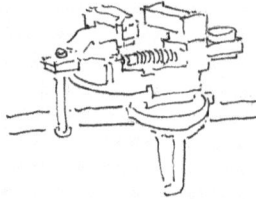

B. Vice

C. Fine Saw

1. Cut 20mm-30mm.

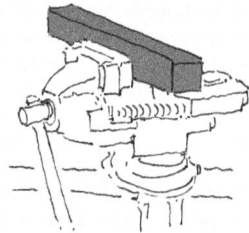

2. Fix specimen in vice.

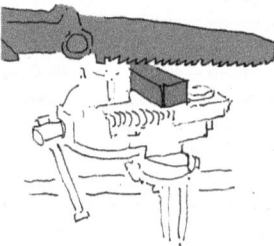

3. Saw vertically.

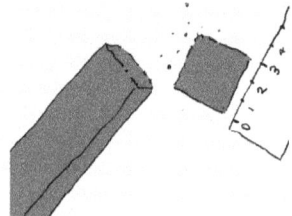

4. Blank specimen.

Sanding Tools

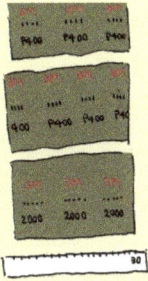

1. Water-proof sand paper

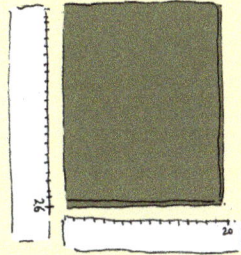

2. Hard plastic plate

3. Fine brush

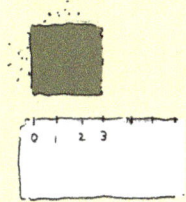

4. Specimen

Sanding Process

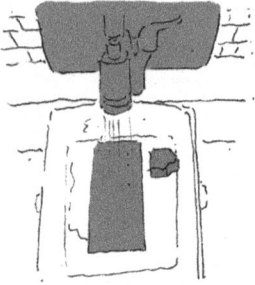

1. Soak sand paper &
specimen with water.

2. Sand specimen under
flowing water.

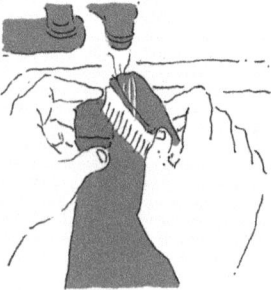

3. Use brush to remove debris.

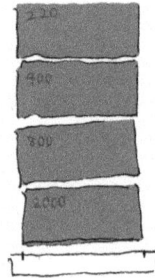

4. 220-400-800-2000
grinding sequence.

Shooting Tools

1. Smartphone

2. Portable Microscope

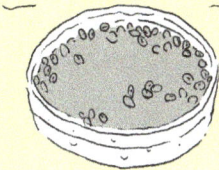

3. Small bowl with mungbeans.

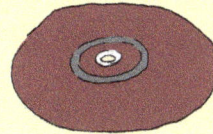

4. Disc

Method of Fixing Specimen

1. Put the wood specimen on top of mungbeans.

2. Put disk on top of the wood specimen.

3. Push disk down to fix specimen horizontally.

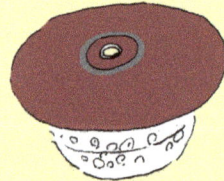

4. Specimen should now be horizontal.

Large specimen without disk.

Small specimen with disk.

Taking a Microscopic Photo

Clip portable microscope onto your phone.

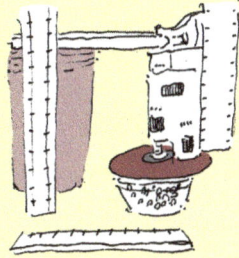

Large specimen
without disk.

Small specimen
with disk.

Examples of Phone Stands

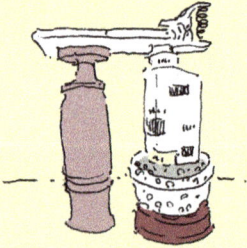

You can use any objects around you!

The phone zooms in directly

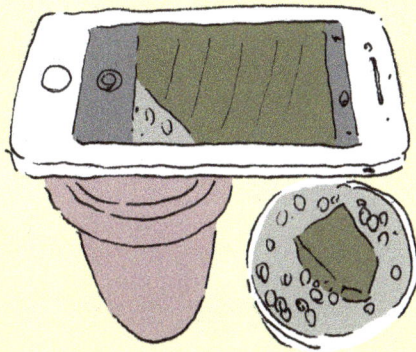

Shoot directly under a microscope with a smartphone.

The basic microstructures of wood

When the cross-plane of the hardwood specimen has been magnified 30X, we can see four kinds of wood structures , they are as follows:

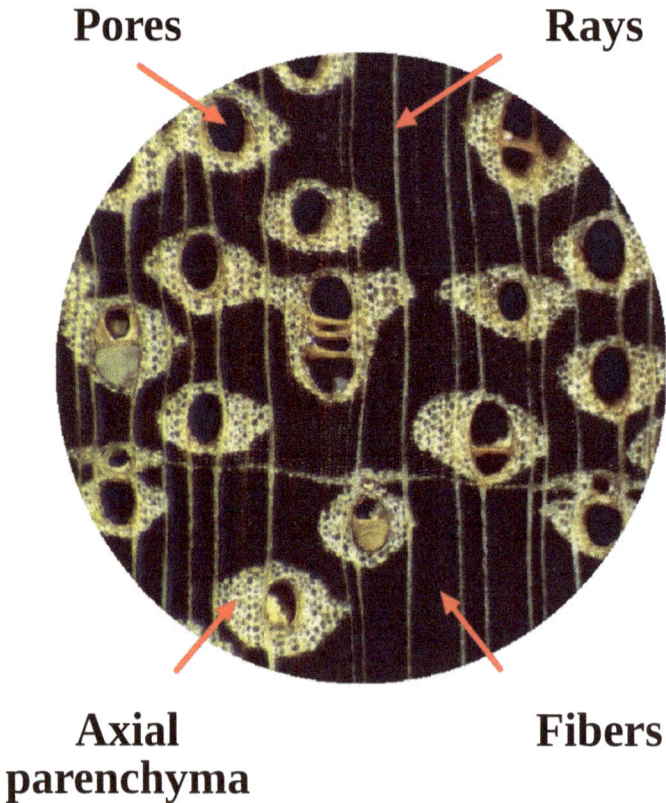

Pores **Rays**

Axial parenchyma **Fibers**

The basic microstructures of wood

Pores

Like some holes, wall is thick, colors are dark, shapes are different: round, oval, polygon, or irregular. Two or more pores can come in contact with one another and form multiple pores. Sometimes the inside of the pores have content.

Diameter 50-350 um

Rays

Vertical line of light color from the top of the image to the bottom. Some are wide and some are narrow. Some rays have content.

Ray wide 10-40 um, Few to 300 um

Axial parenchyma

Light colored, tiny cells, contact with each other most of the time to form different shapes: vasicentric, aliform, lozengealiform, winged-aliform, confluent, unilateral paratracheal, fine line, narrow band, wide band etc. Sometimes they diffuse among fibers that don't contact with each other or just two to several come together (diffuse-in-aggregate). Some have content.

Diameter 10-30 um

Fibers

Dark-colored background of the image consists of many tiny cells with thick walls.

Diameter 5-15 um

Direction of wood cross section image

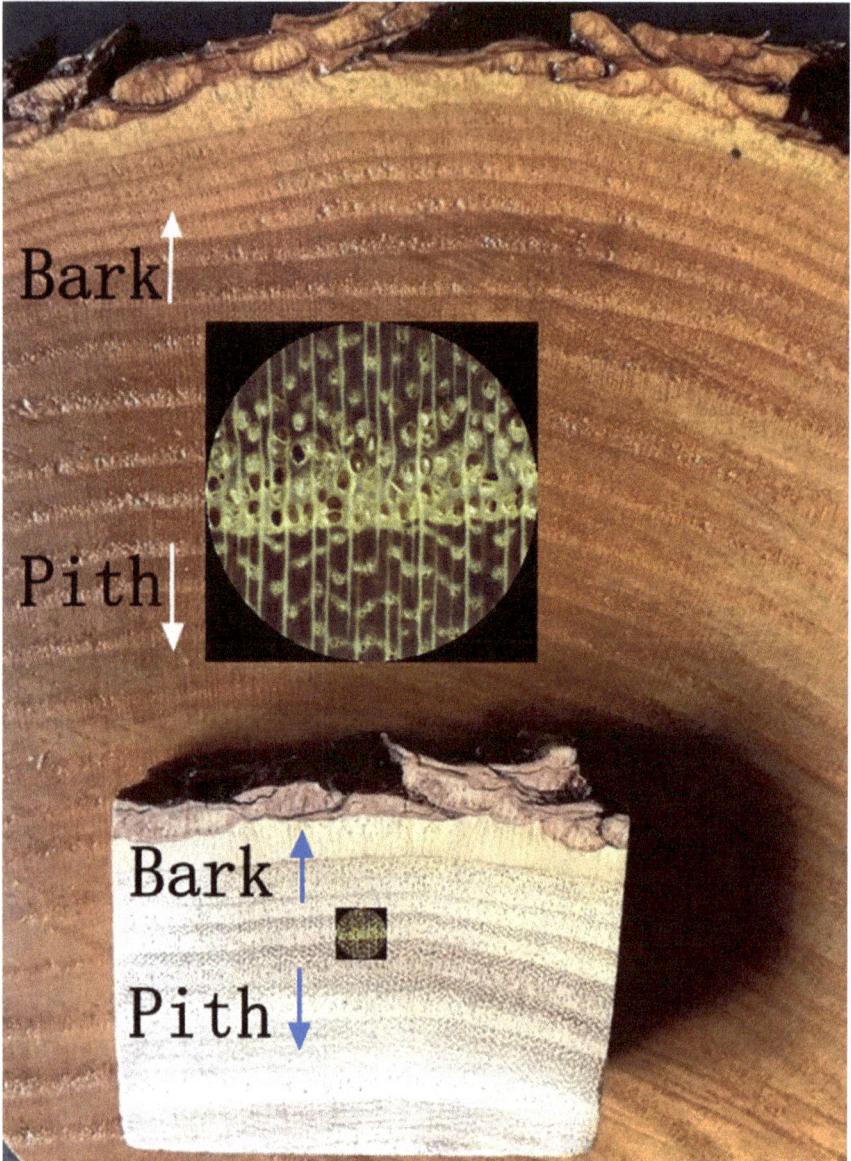

Image of wood specimen outside pointing to bark on the top.
Image of wood specimen inside pointing downwards to pith.

Direction of wood cross section image

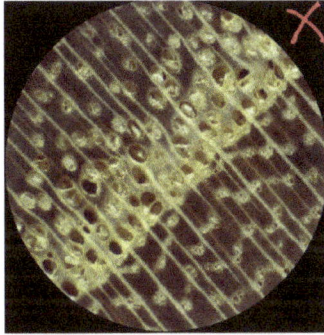

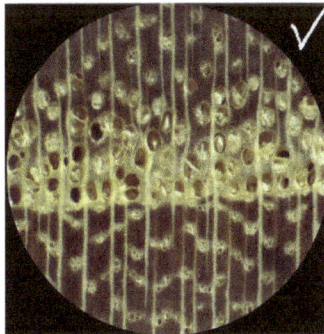

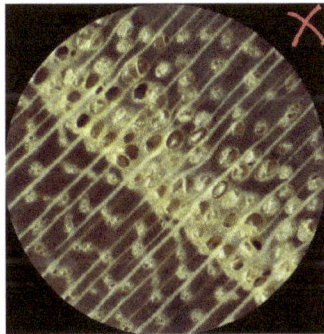

Zoom in to get 30 times view of the diameter

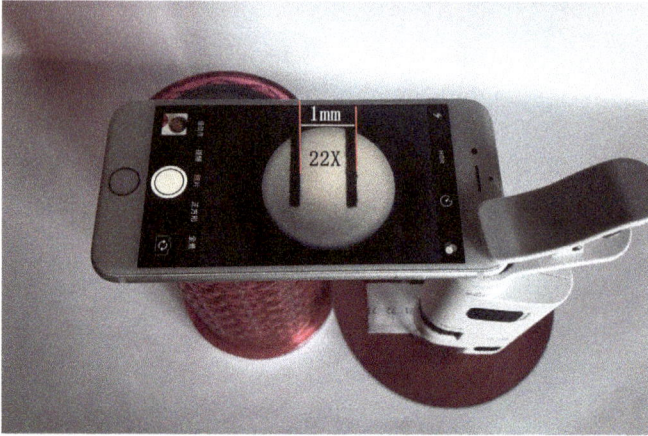

1. Use camera on ruler to measure zoom.

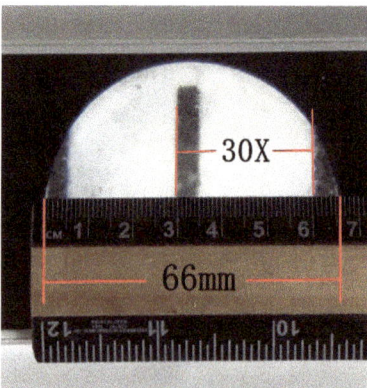

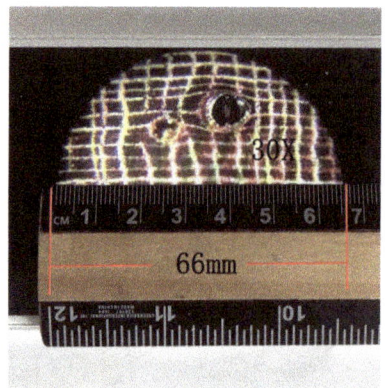

2. Use the zoom function on the phone to adjust the magnification to 30 times, and the diameter of the view is 66 millimeters.

3. A specimen with a view that is 66 millimeters in diameter is 30 times larger.

Cutting a square paper with a 66 millimeters diameter pore

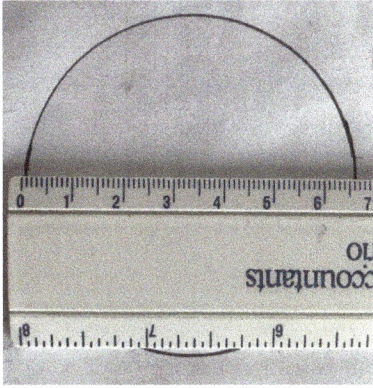

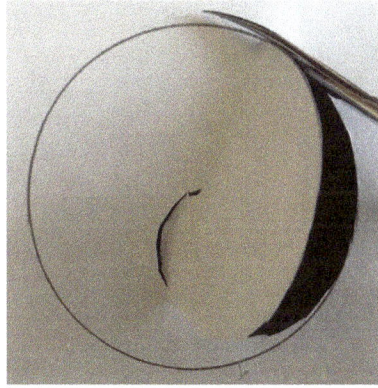

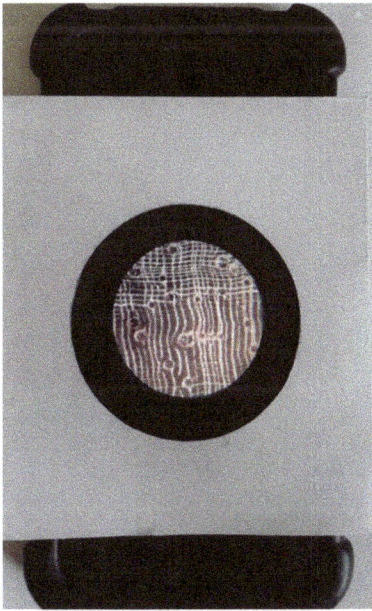

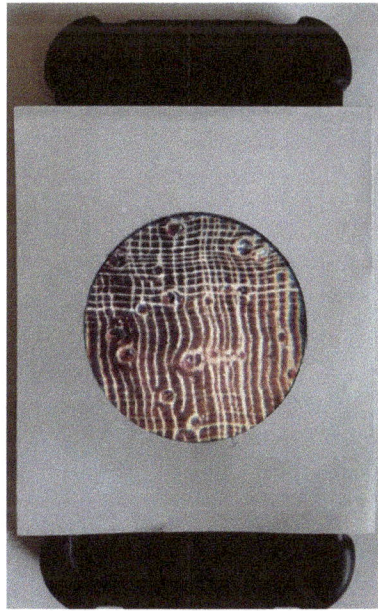

Act according to test results

Cut a 66 mm diameter hole on a piece of cardboard. When you are shooting a wood specimen, use the cardboard to cover it and adjust the image until it reaches the edge of the hole. This image has been magnified 30 times.

Photos in this Atlas

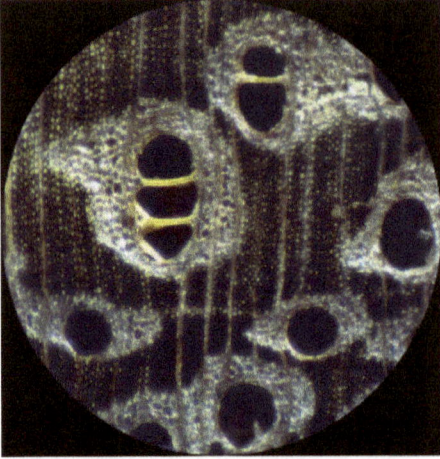

30X

Diameter: 2.0mm X30 = 60mm

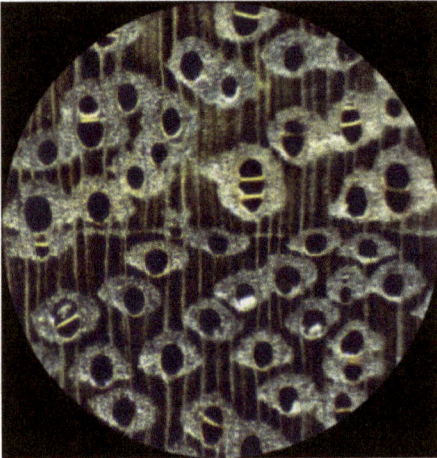

13X

Diameter: 4.61mm X13 = 60mm

Macro

Microscopic Characterization

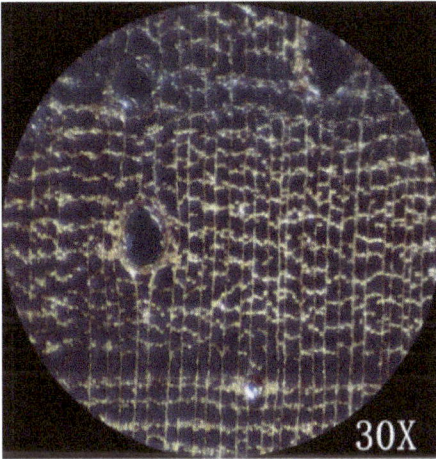

<= 5 pores per square millimetre

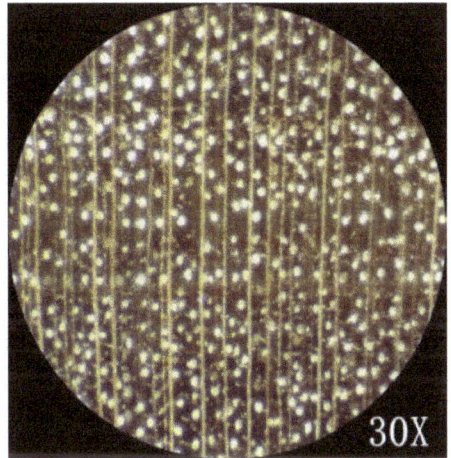

40 – 100 pores per square millimetre

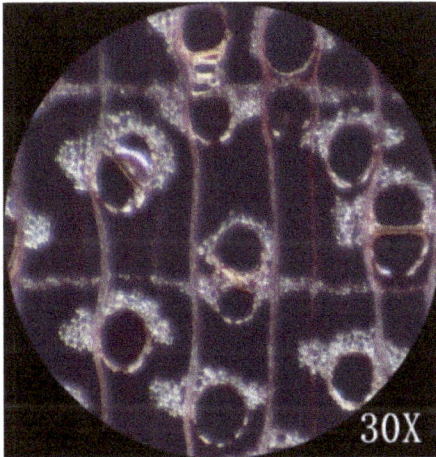

Rays per millimetre 4-12 / mm

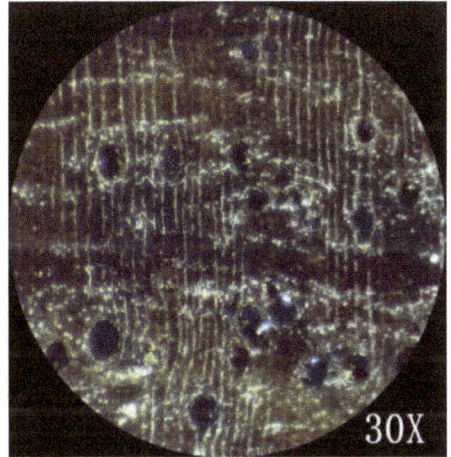

Rays per millimetre >= 12 /mm

Microscopic Characterization

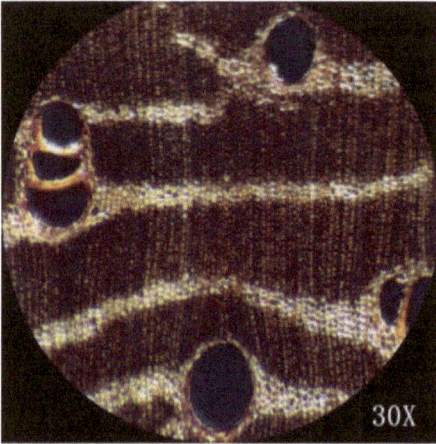

Diameter of pore
>= 200 μm

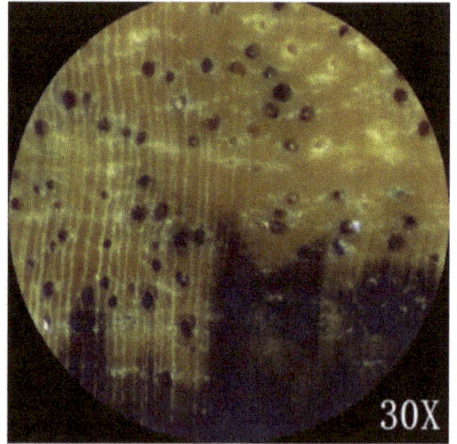

Diameter of pore
50 – 100 μm

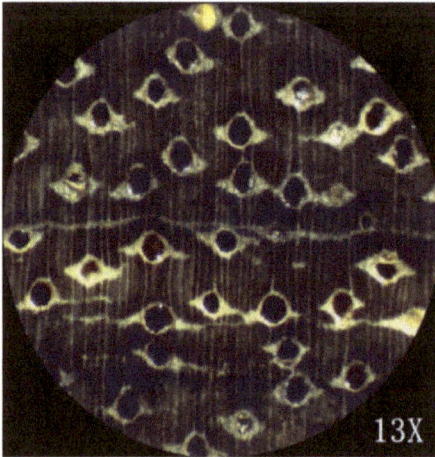

Axial parenchyma
aliform

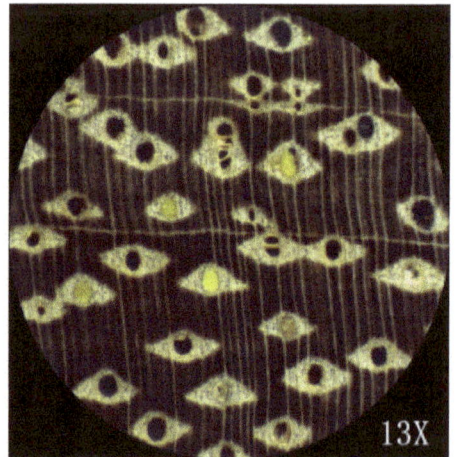

Axial parenchyma
lozenge-aliform

Microscopic Characterization

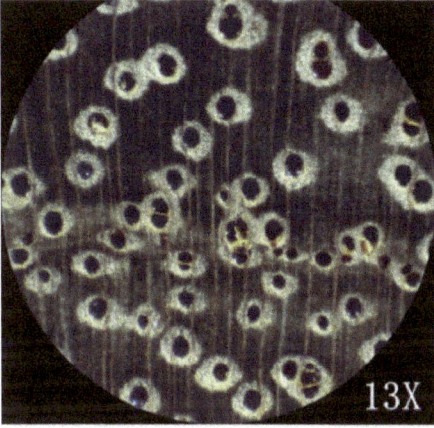

Axial parenchyma
vasicentric

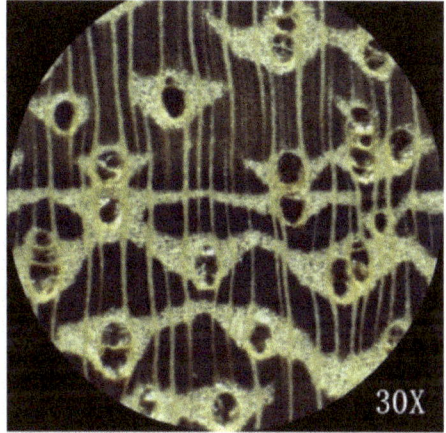

Axial parenchyma
confluent

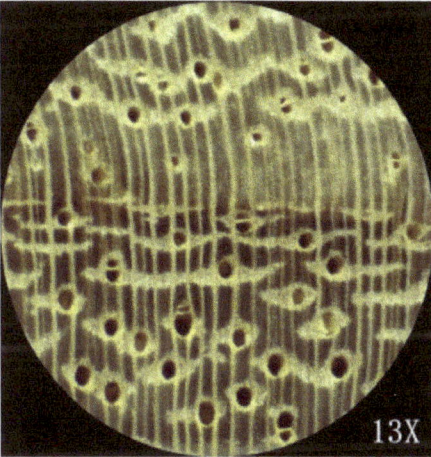

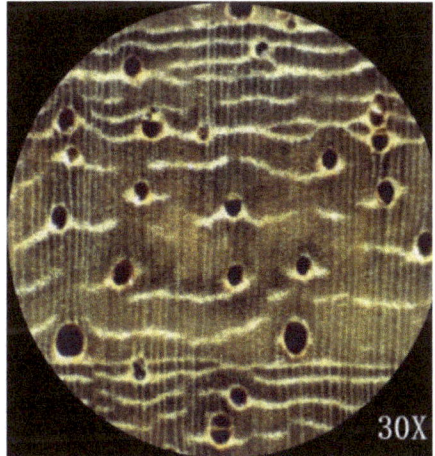

Axial parenchyma
confluent

Axial parenchyma
winged aliform

Microscopic Characterization

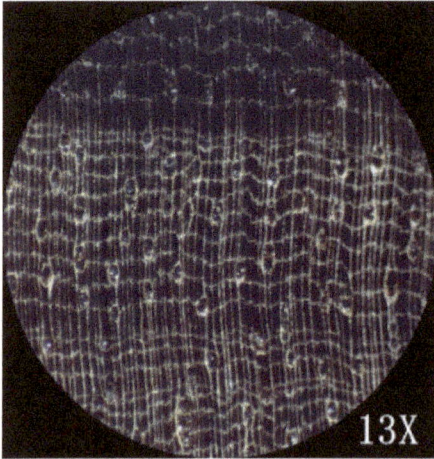

Axial parenchyma
Thin line

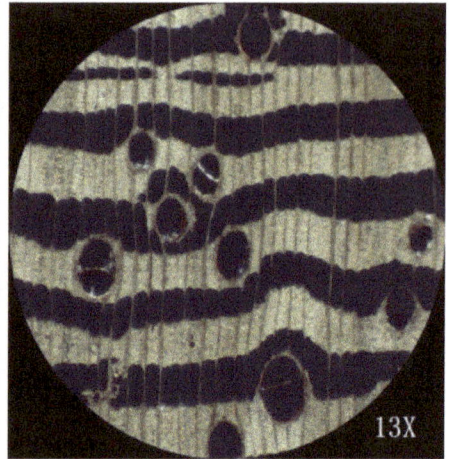

Axial parenchyma
broad band

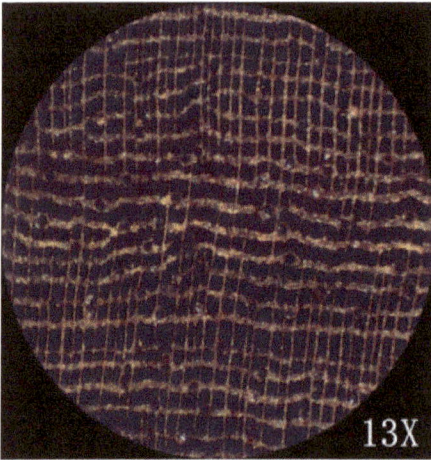

Axial parenchyma
narrow band

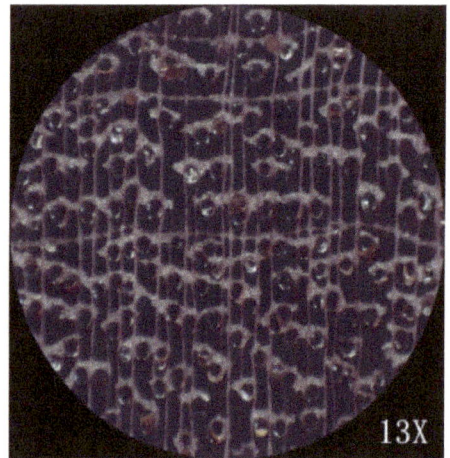

Axial parenchyma
unilateral paratracheal

Microscopic Characterization

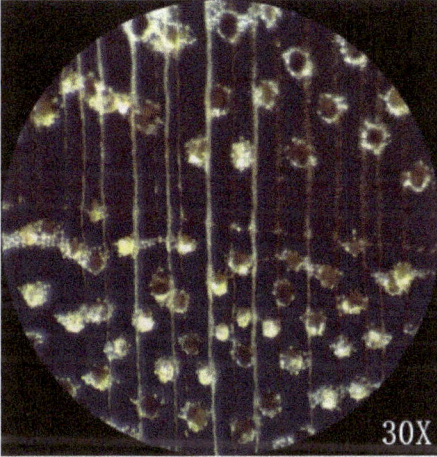

Axial parenchyma
Scanty paratracheal

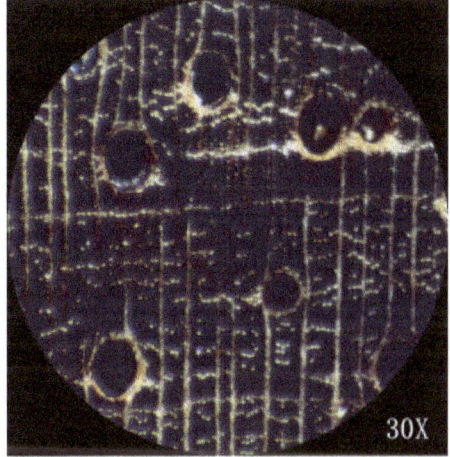

Axial parenchyma
diffuse-in-aggregates

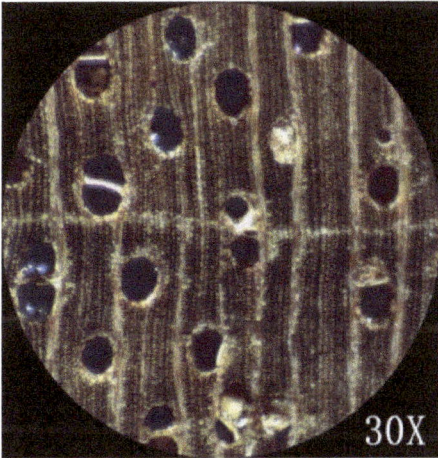

Growth ring
boundaries distinct

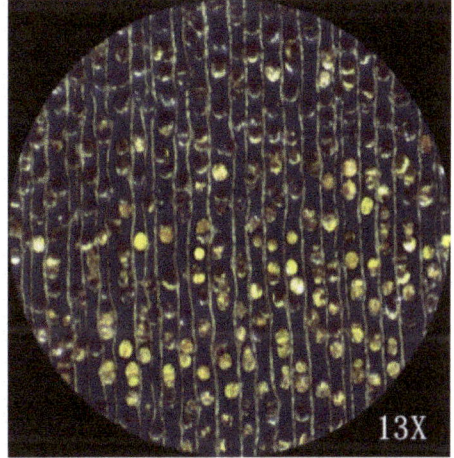

Growth ring boundaries
indistinct or absent

Microscopic Characterization

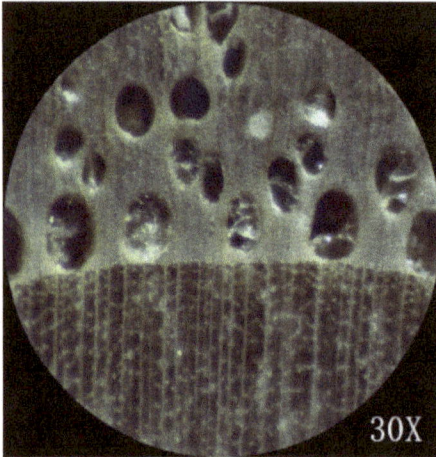

Growth ring
boundaries distinct

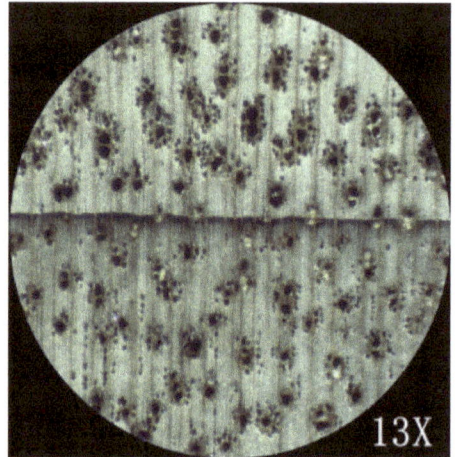

Growth ring
boundaries distinct

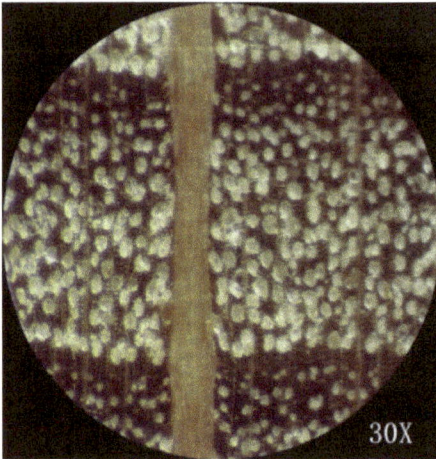

Rays of two
distinct sizes

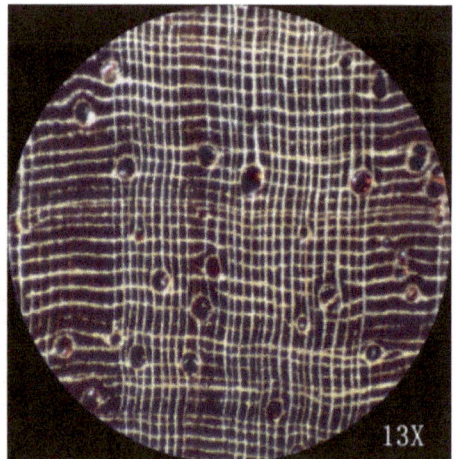

Axial parenchyma
reticulate

834 Photos

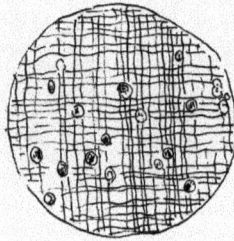

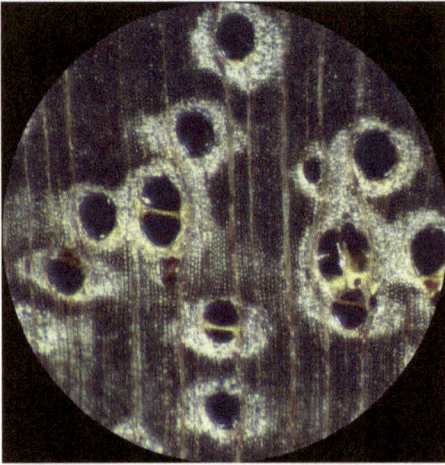

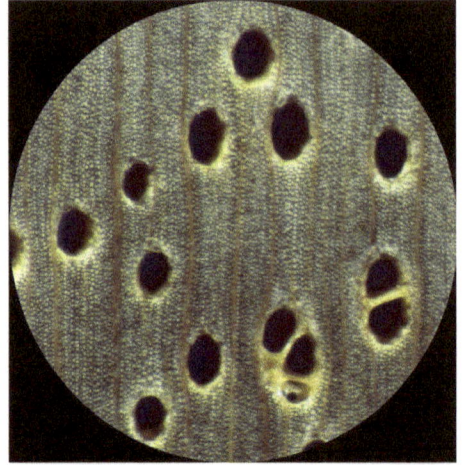

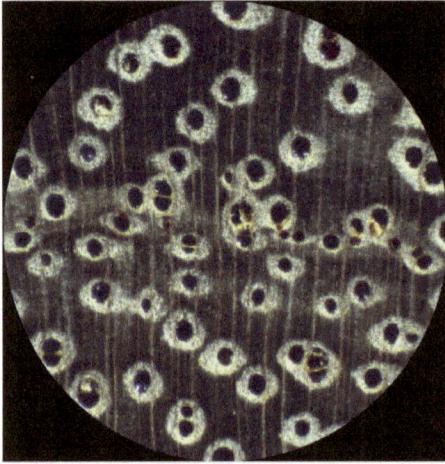

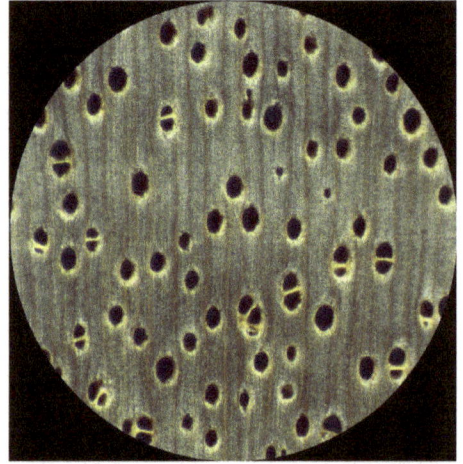

Acacia confusa
Formosa acacia

Acacia mangium
Brown salwood

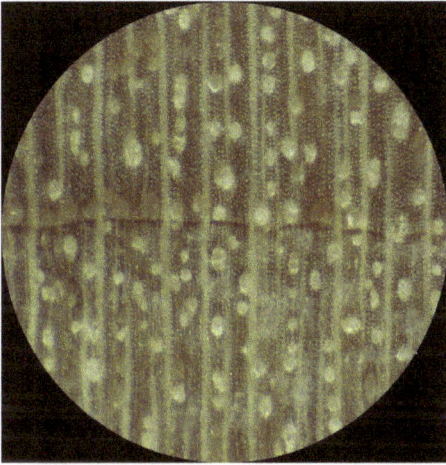

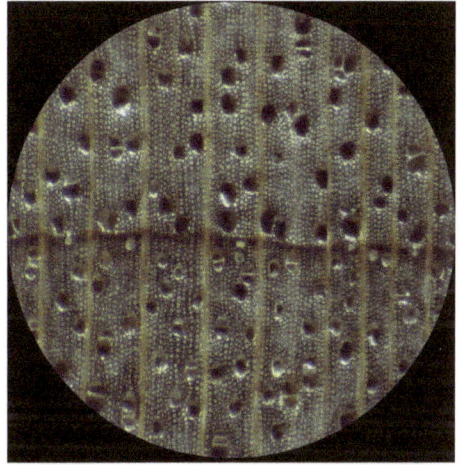

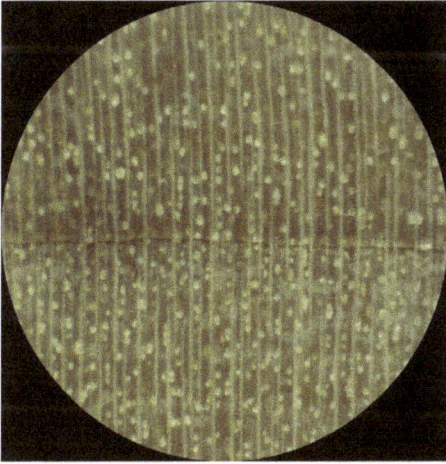

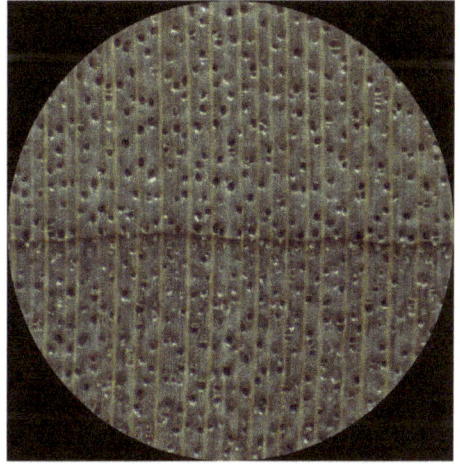

Acer negundo
Box elder

Acer saccharinum
Silver maple

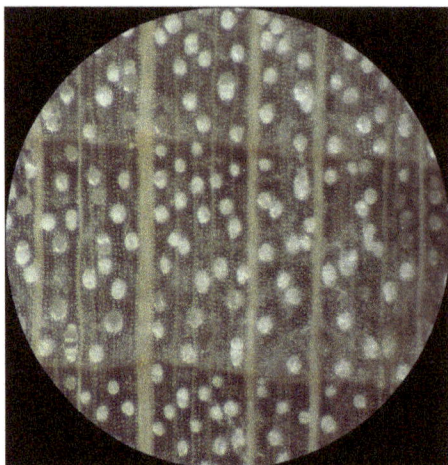

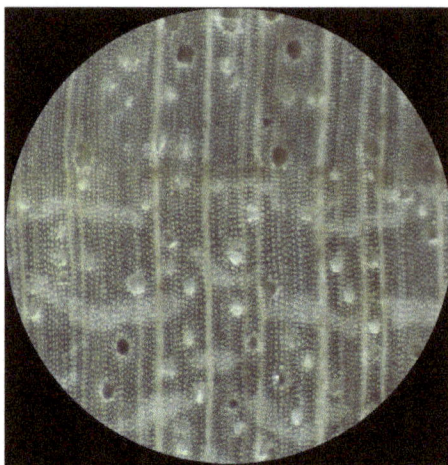

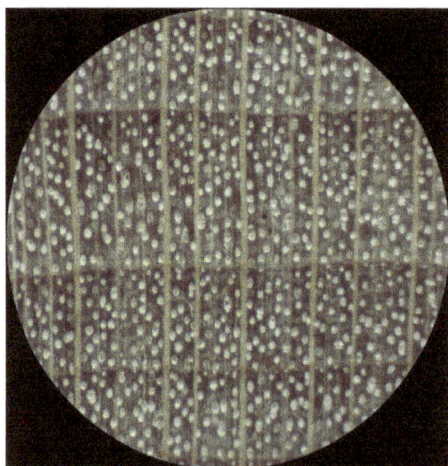

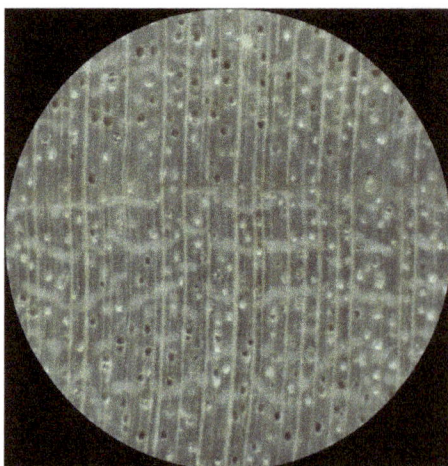

Acer saccharum
Sugar maple

Acer sinense
Chinese maple

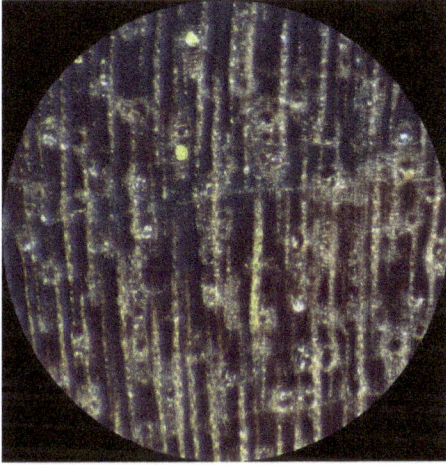

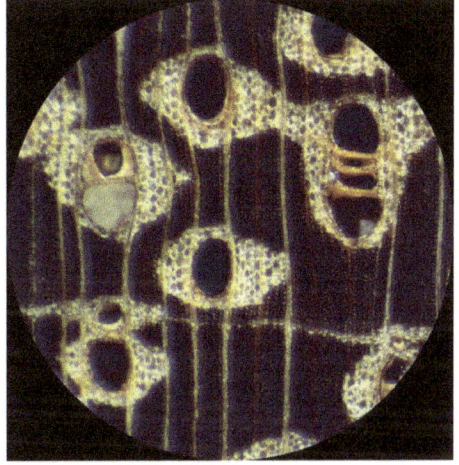

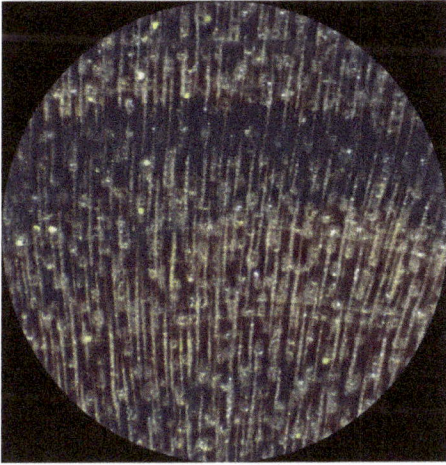

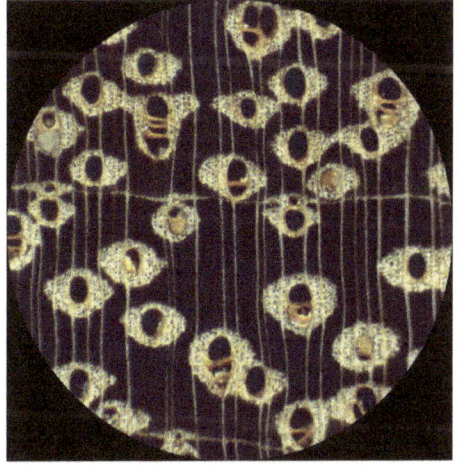

Aetoxylon sympetalum
Gaharu buaya

Afzelia bipindensis
Doussie

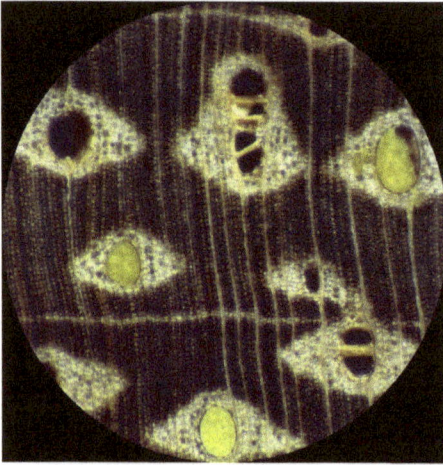

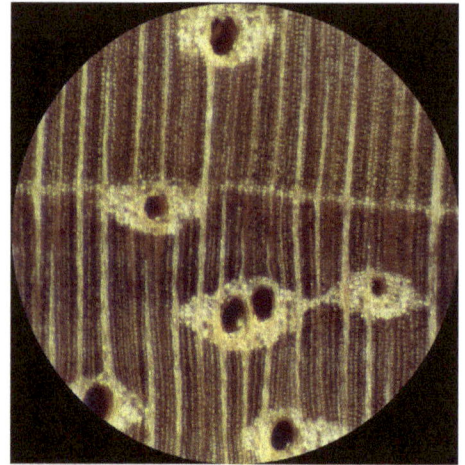

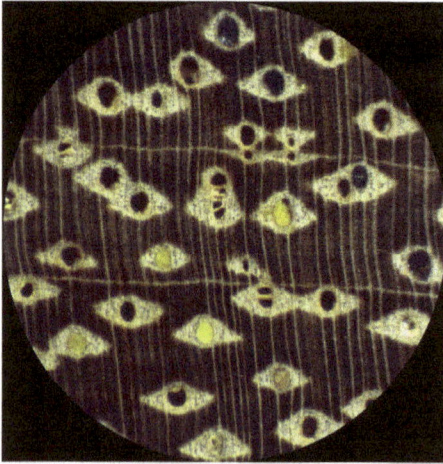

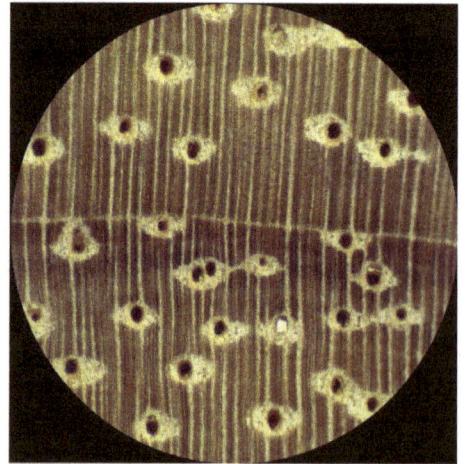

Afzelia quanzensis
E. African Afzelia

Afzelia xylocarpa
Makharmorng

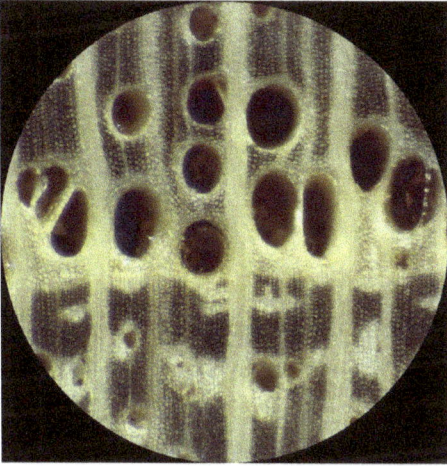

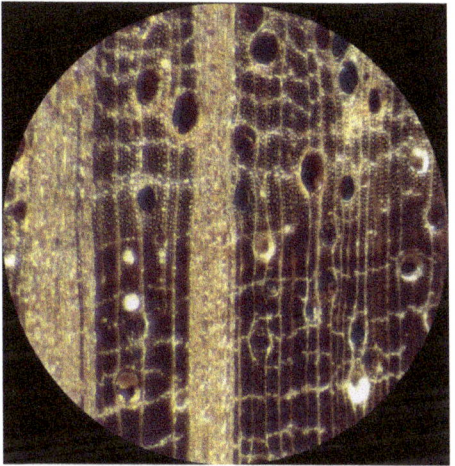

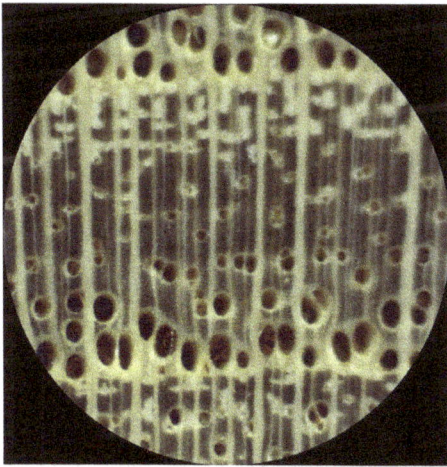

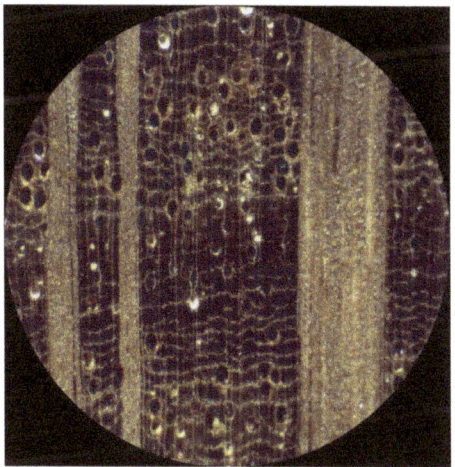

Ailanthus altissima
Tree of heaven

Allocasuarina luehmanni
Australian buloke

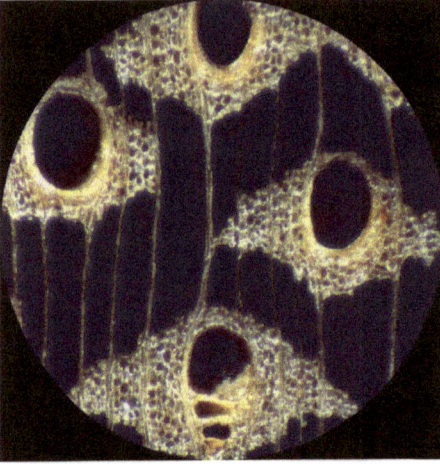
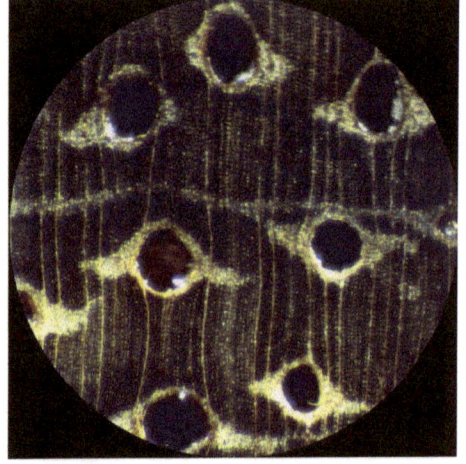
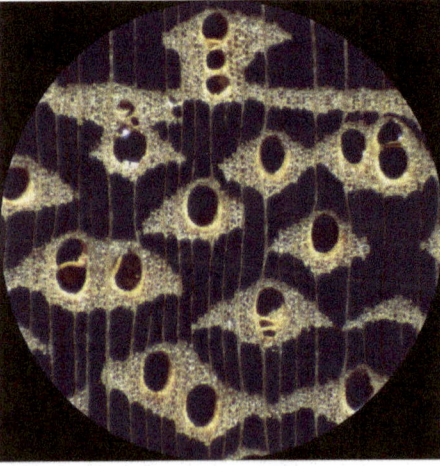
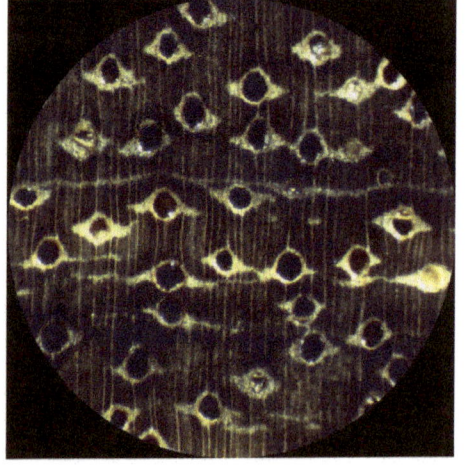

Andira surinamensis
Angelim

Aphanocalyx heitzii
Andoung

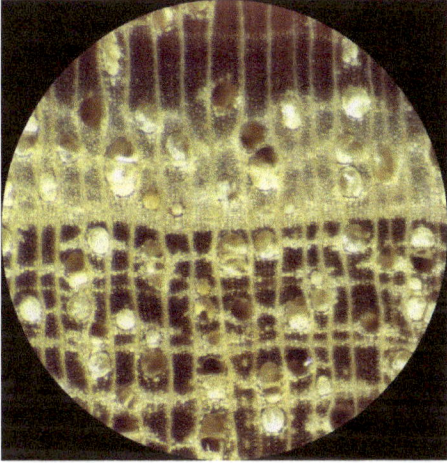

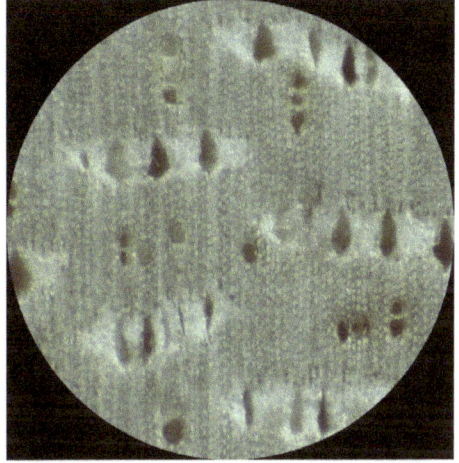

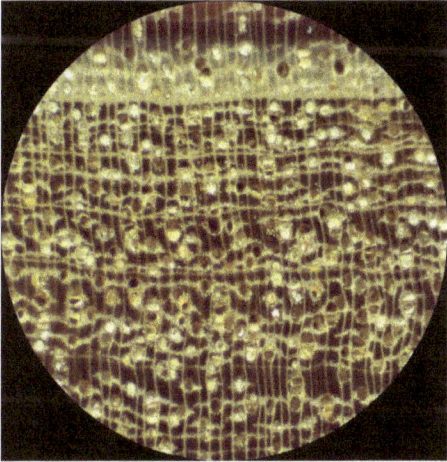

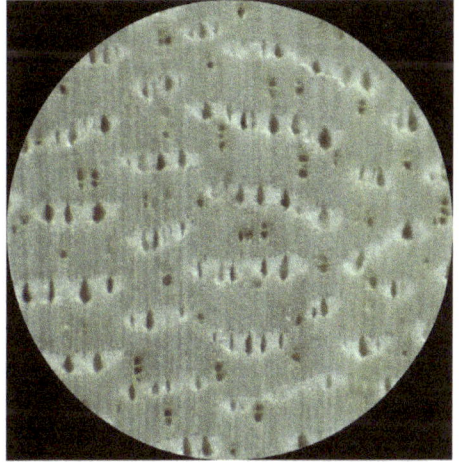

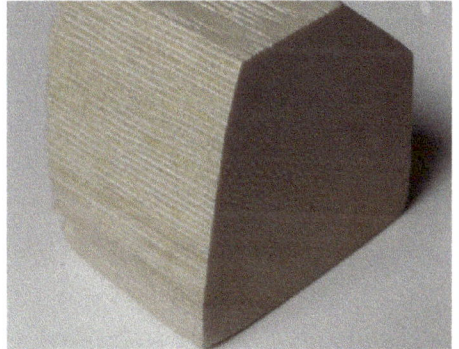

Apuleia leiocarpa
Garapa

Aquilaria sinensis
Agar wood

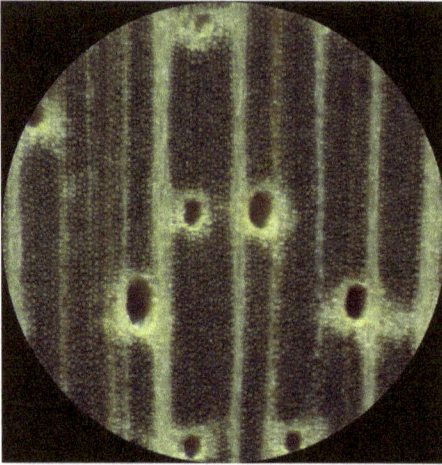
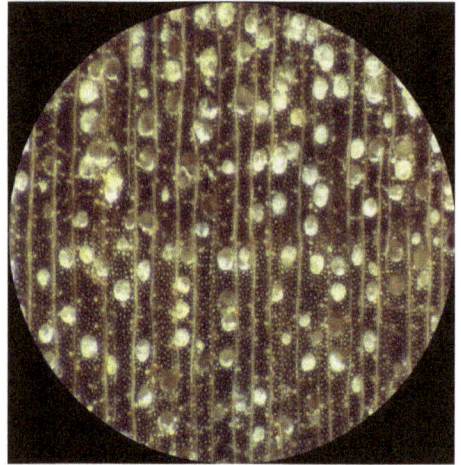
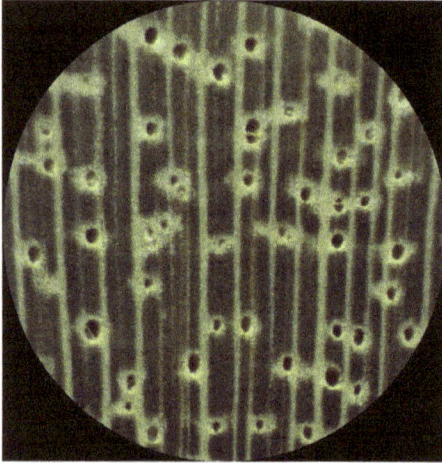
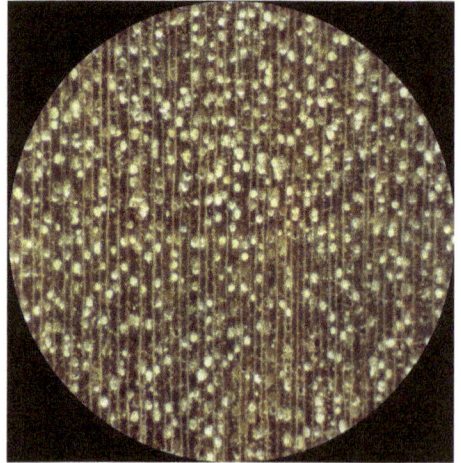

Artocarpus dadah
Keledang

Aspidosperma polyneuron
Ibira romi

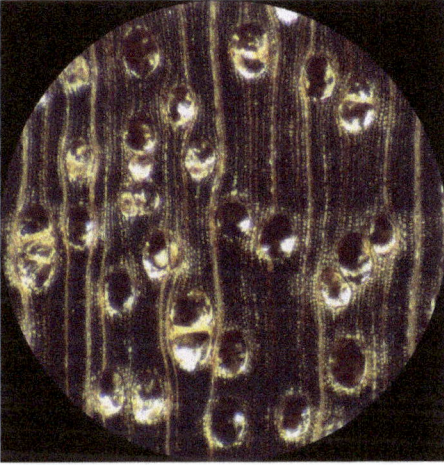

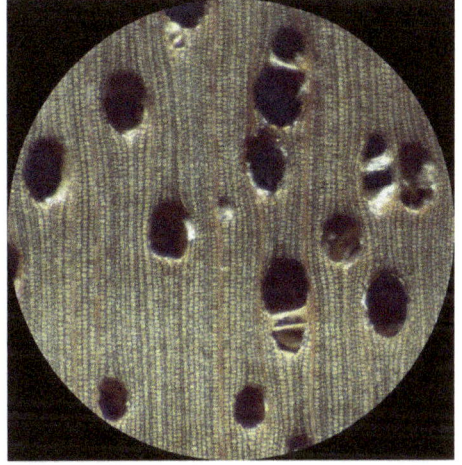

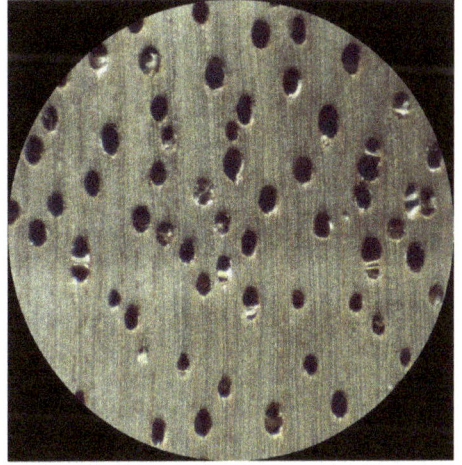

Astronium
     fraxinifolium
Goncalo alves

Aucoumea klaineana
Angouma

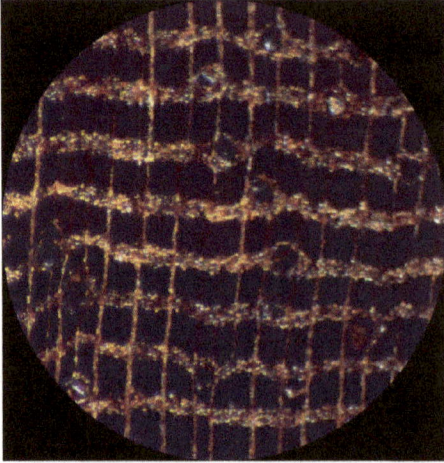

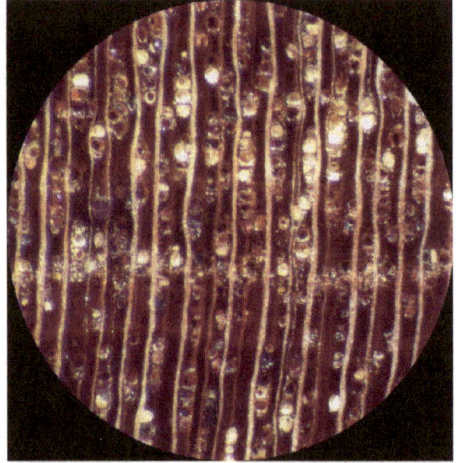

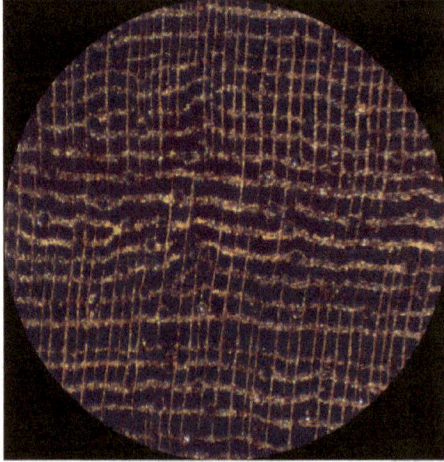

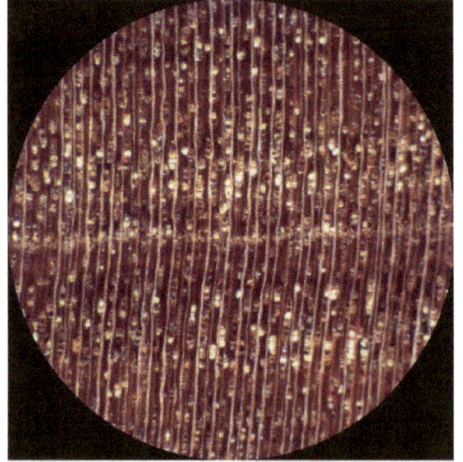

Baphia nitida
Camwood

Berchemia zeyheri
Pink ivory

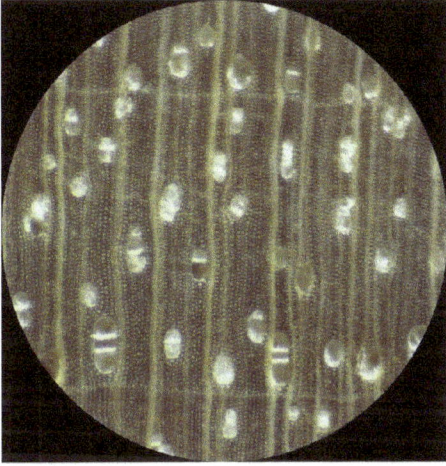

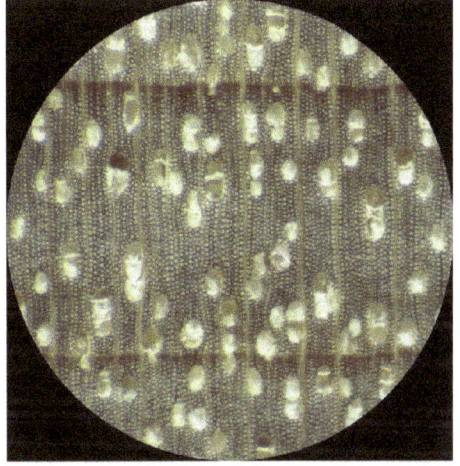

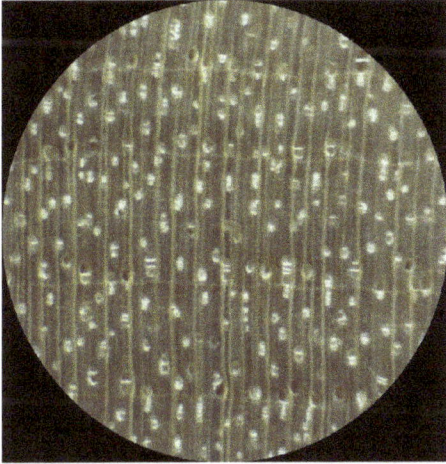

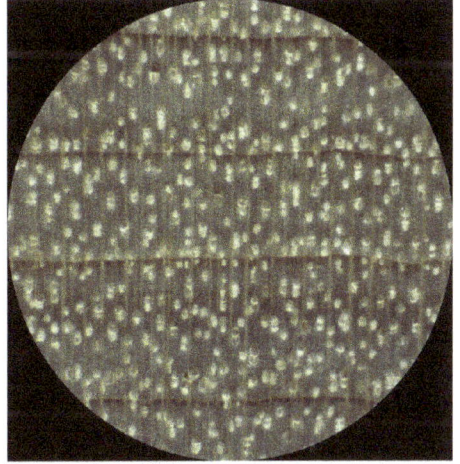

Betula chinensis
Jian hua

Betula papyrifera
Paper birch

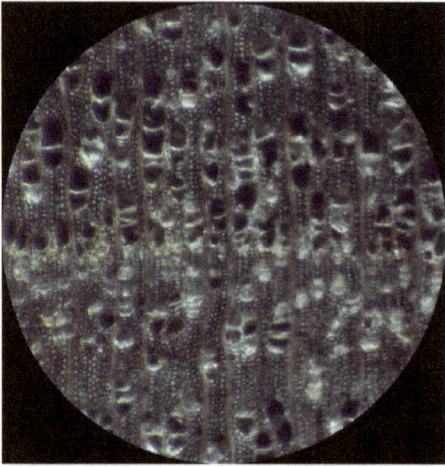

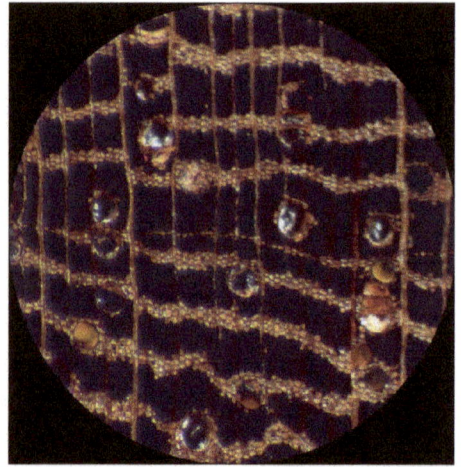

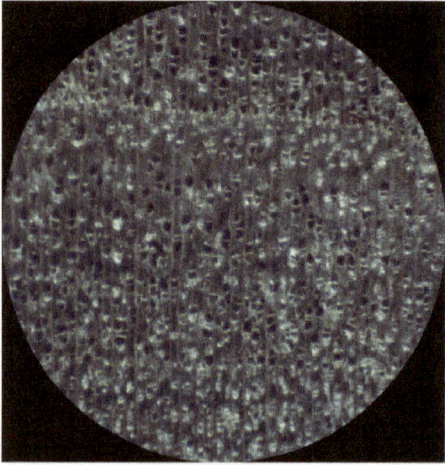

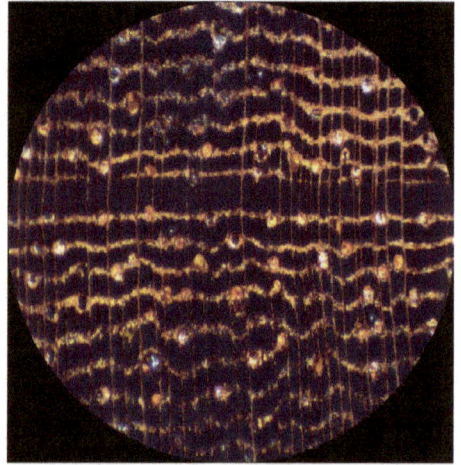

Bischofia polycarpa
Chong yang mu

Bobgunnia fistuloides
Pau Rosa

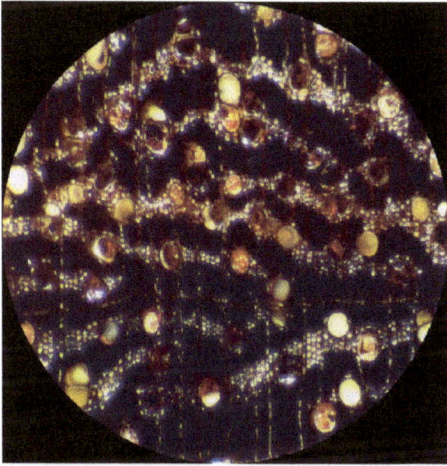

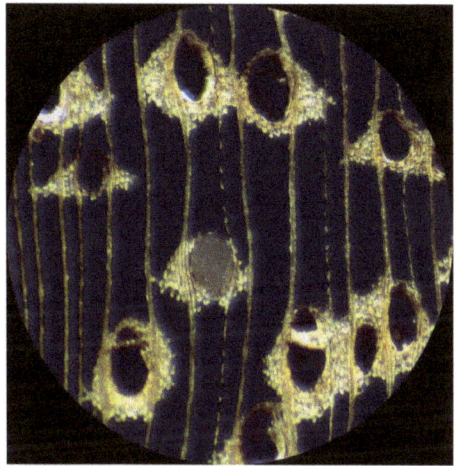

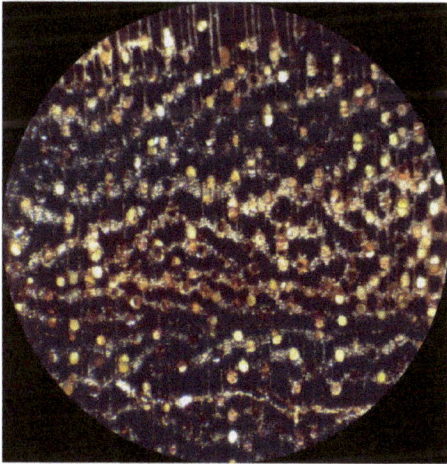

Bobgunnia
madagascariensis
Pao rosa

Bowdichia nitida
Sucupira

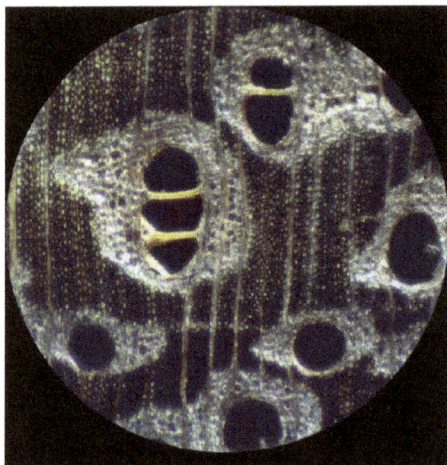

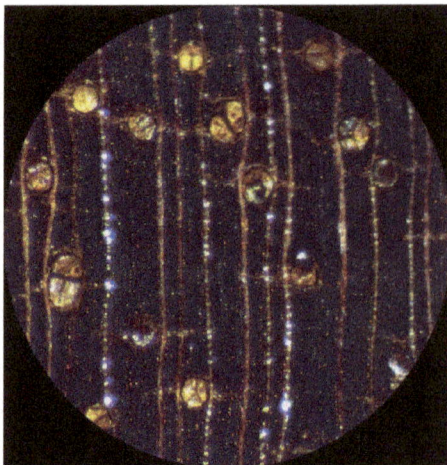

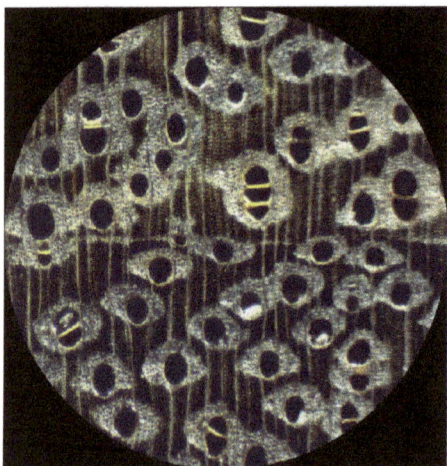

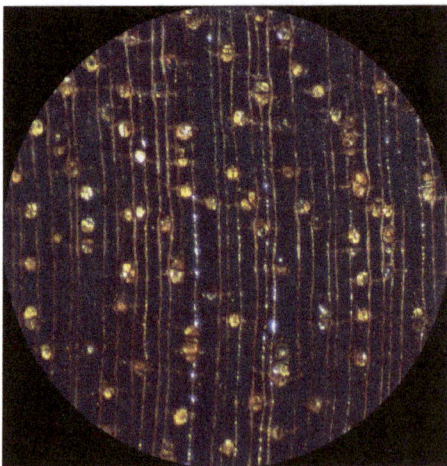

Bowdichia virgilioides
Sucupira

Brosimum guianense
Snakewood

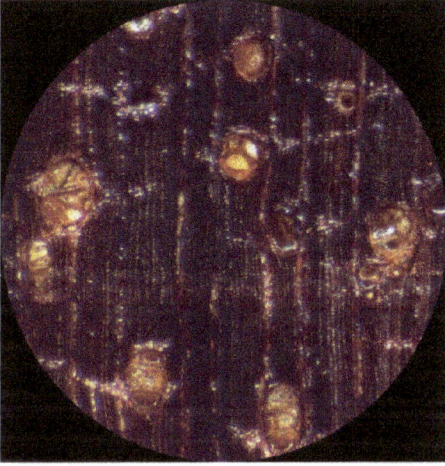

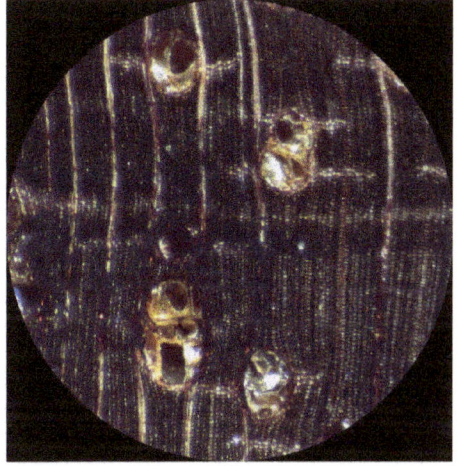

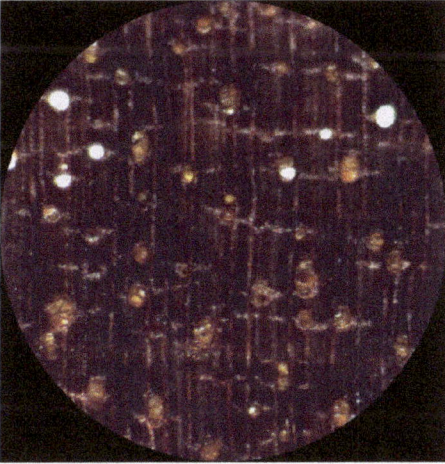

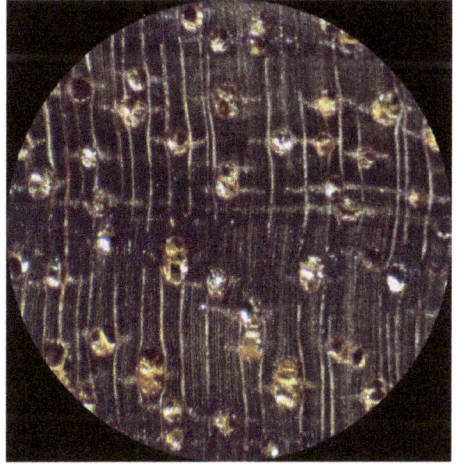

Brosimum rubescens
Satine rubane

Brosimum utile
Cow tree

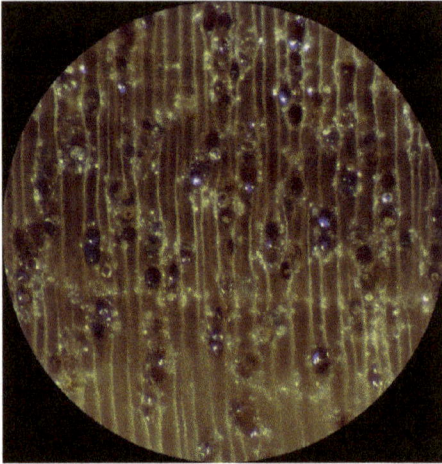

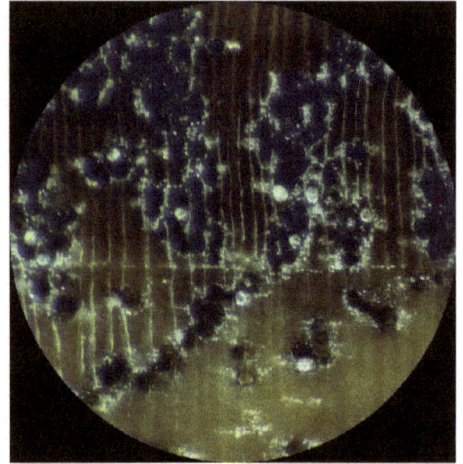

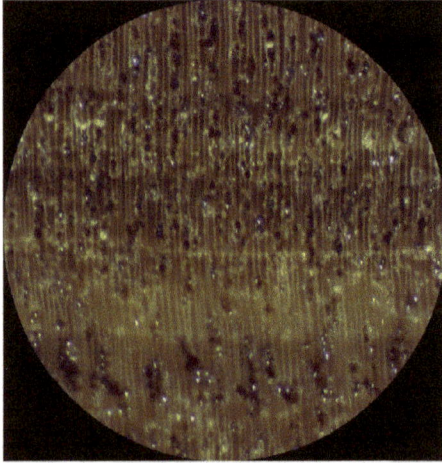

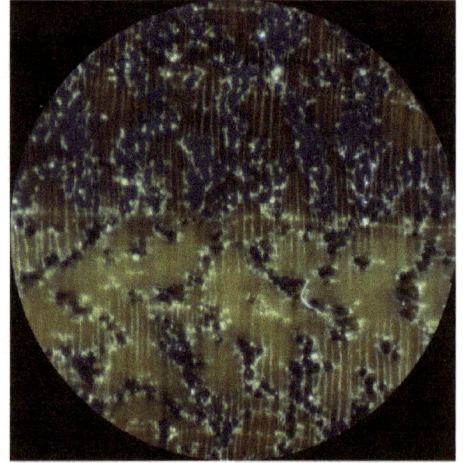

Bulnesia arborea
Verawood

Bulnesia sarmientoi
Gaicwood

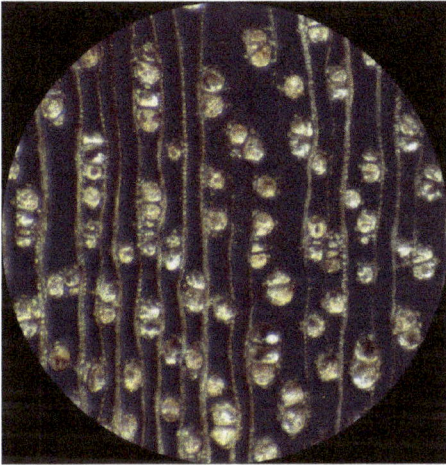

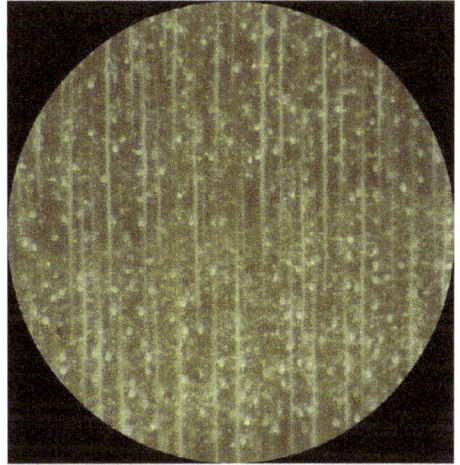

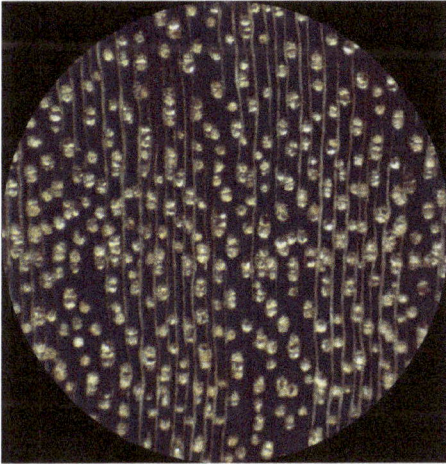

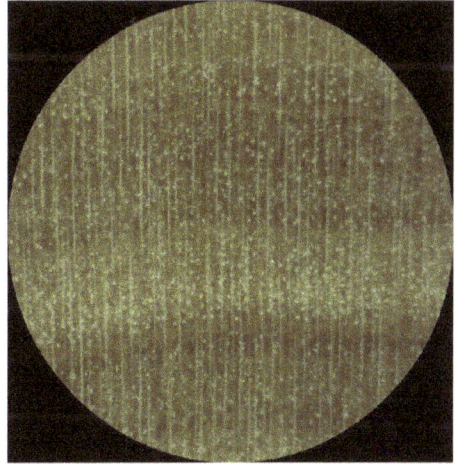

Burretiodendron hsienmu
Nghien tree

Buxus microphylla
Boxwood

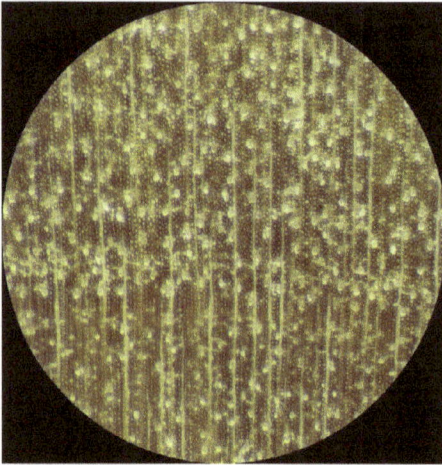

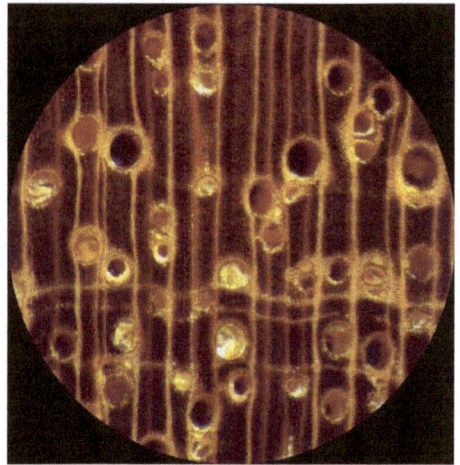

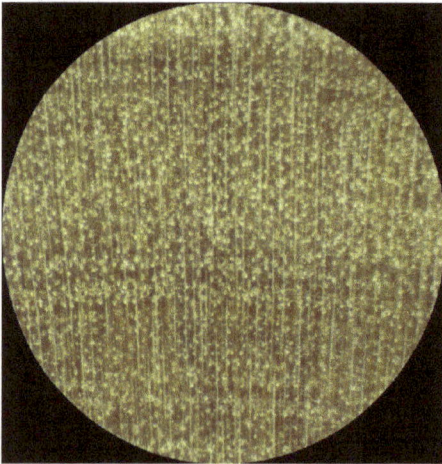

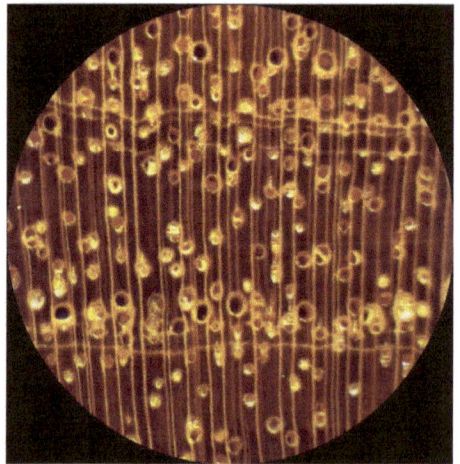

Buxus sinica
Boxwood

Caesalpinia sappan
Caesalipinia

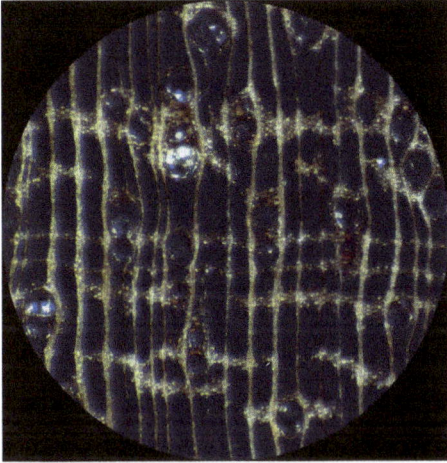

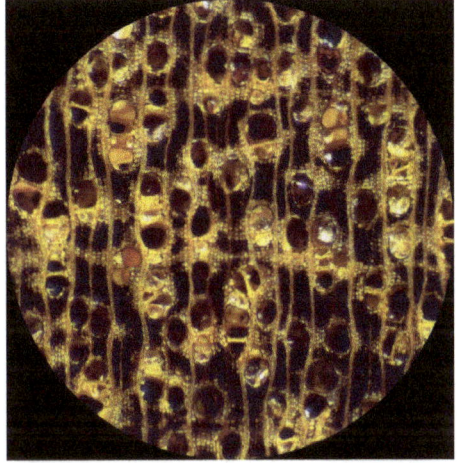

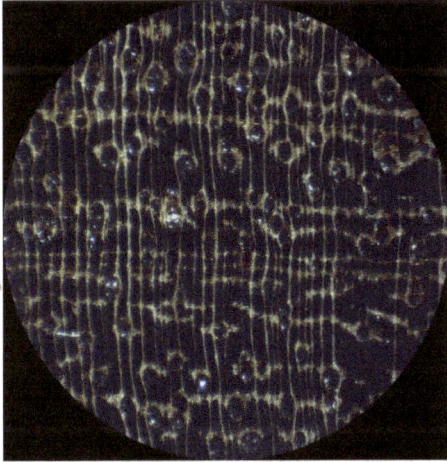

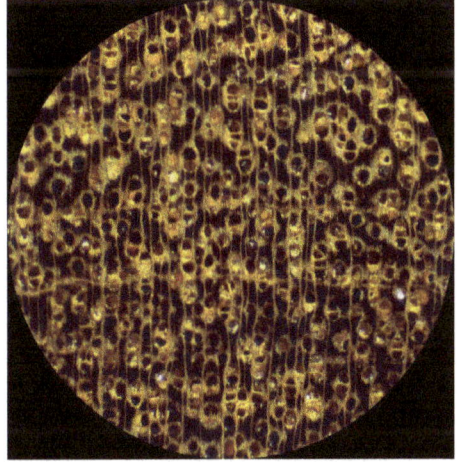

Caesalpinia ebano
Ebano

Caesalpinia echinata
Pau Brasil

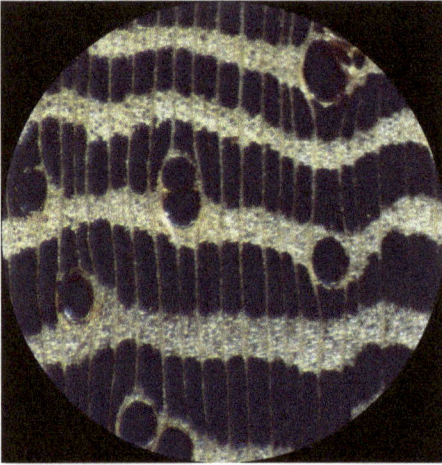

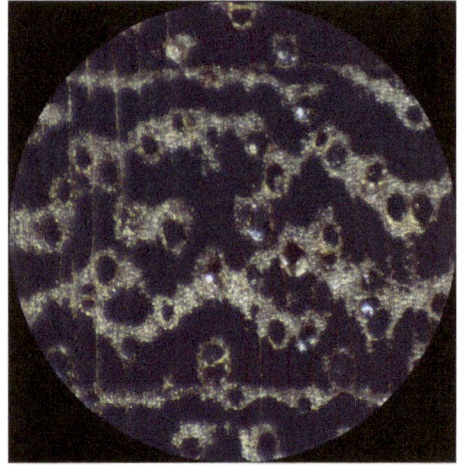

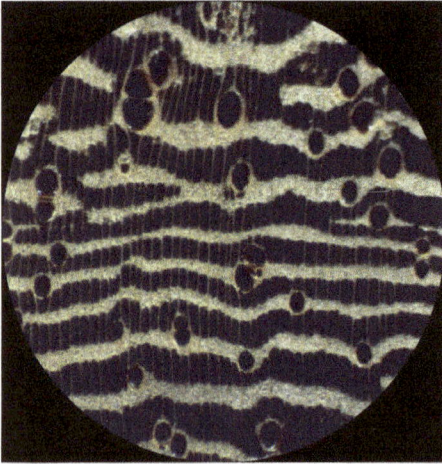

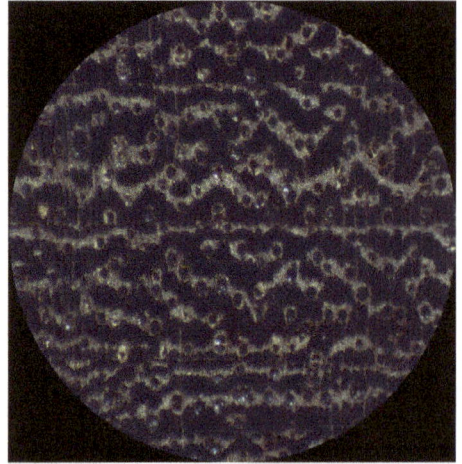

Caesalpinia granadillo
Brown ebony

Caesalpinia paraguariensis
Guayacan

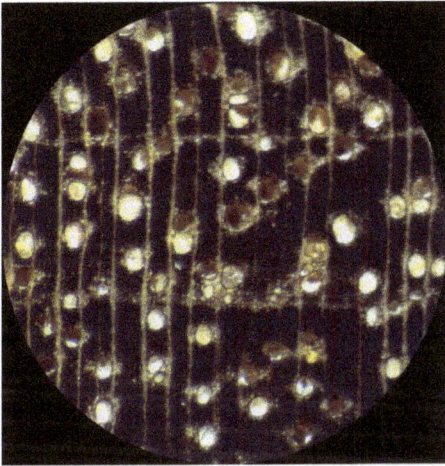

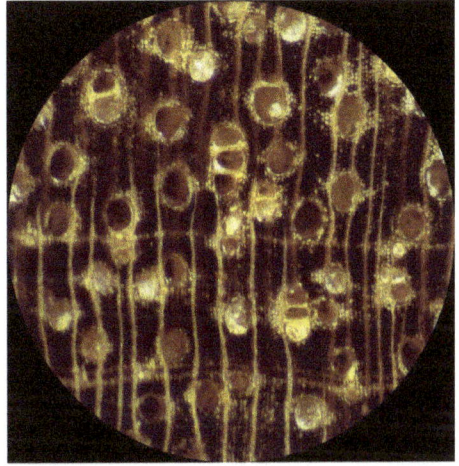

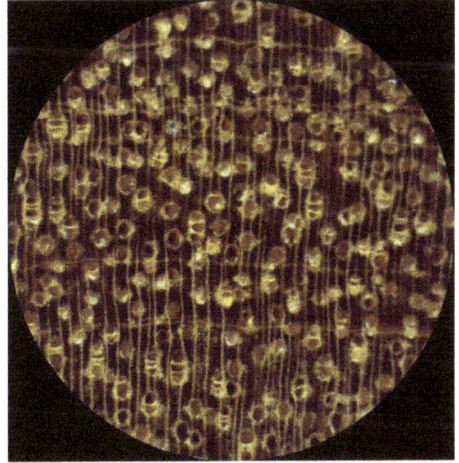

Caesalpinia platyloba
Chacteviga

Caesalpinia violacea
Brasiletto

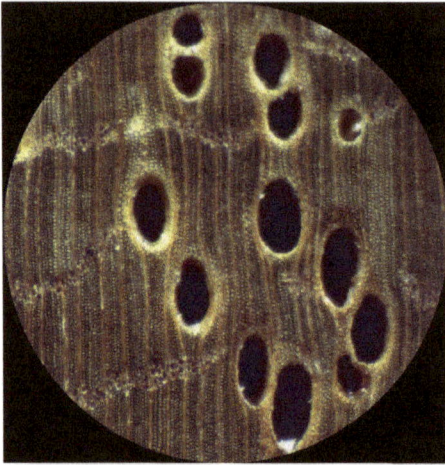

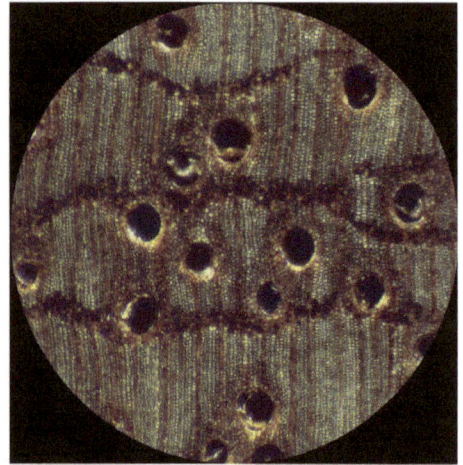

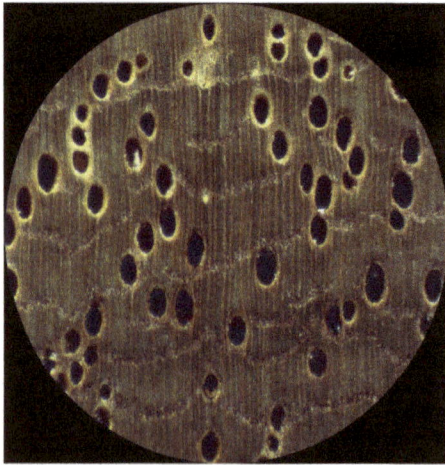

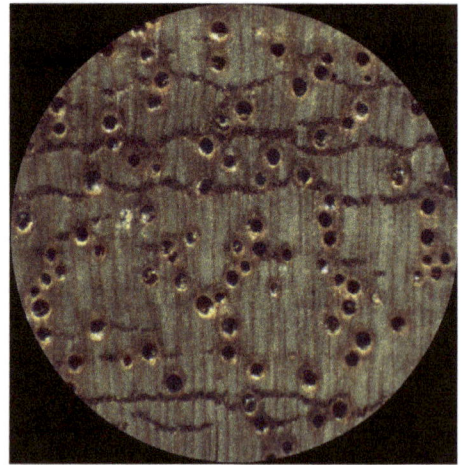

Calophyllum
    brasiliense
Santa maria

Calophyllum
    inophyllum
Beach calopgyllum

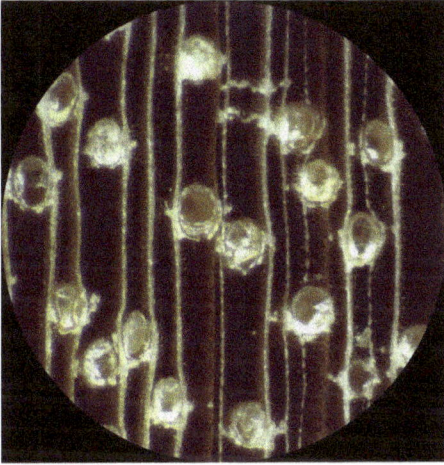

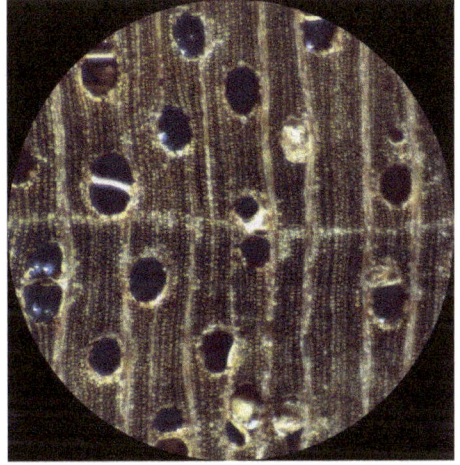

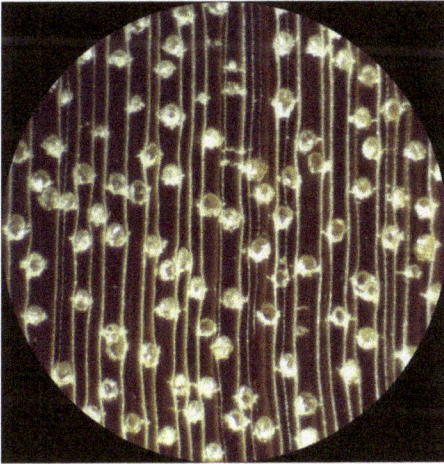

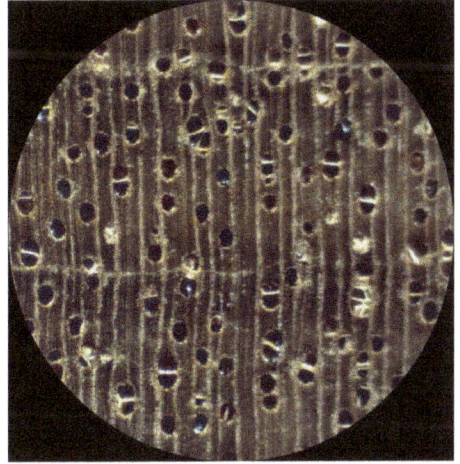

Cantleya corniculata
Dedaru

Carapa guianensis
Crabwood

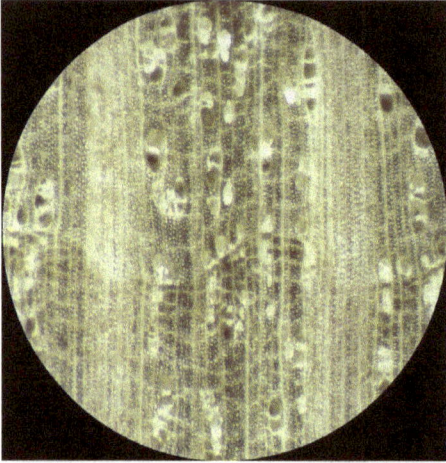

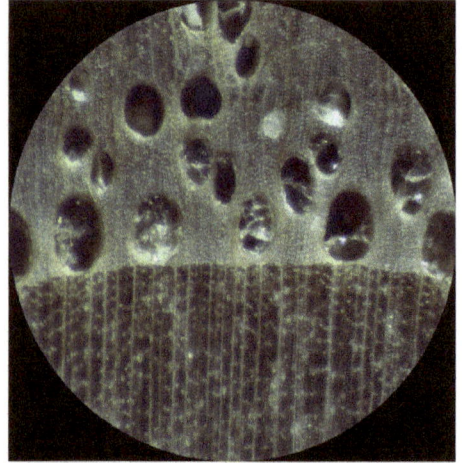

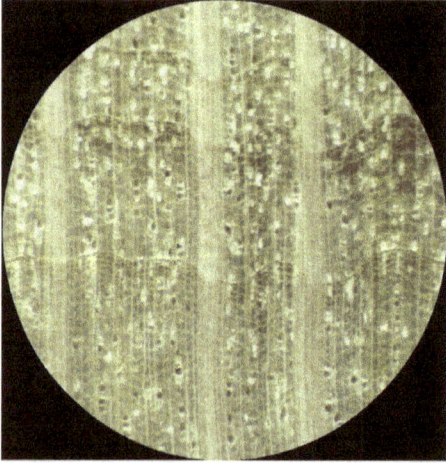

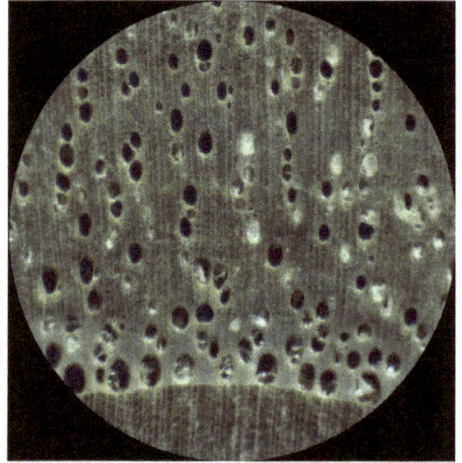

Carpinus caroliniana
Hornbeam

Castanea mollissima
Chinese chestnut

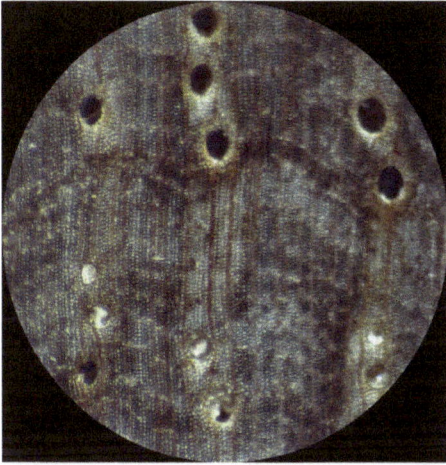

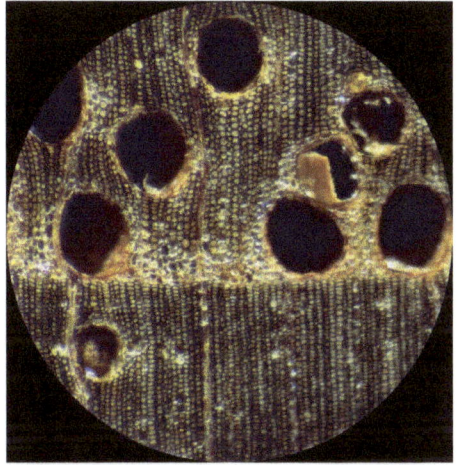

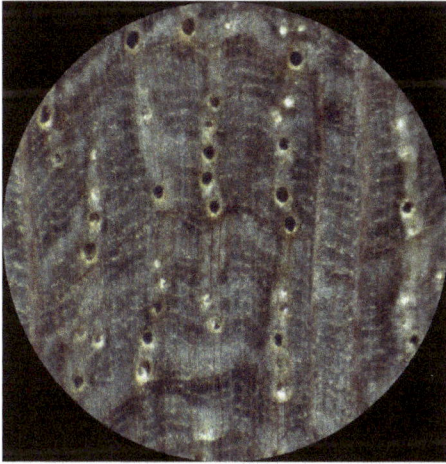

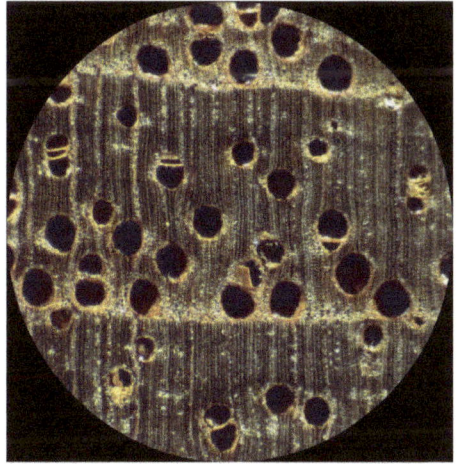

Cstanopsis hystrix
Hong zhui

Cedrela odorata
Acajou rouge

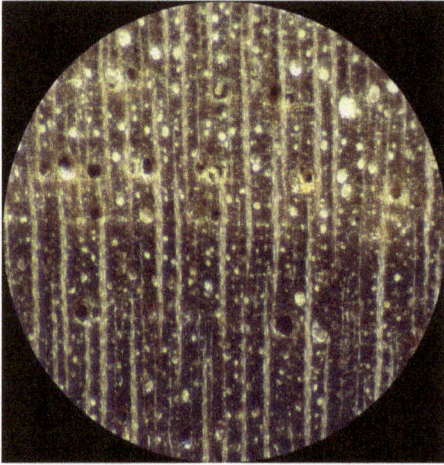

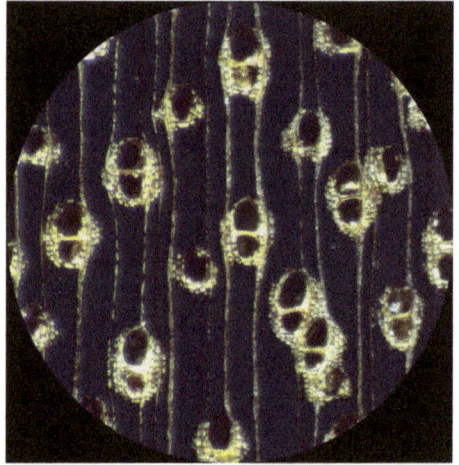

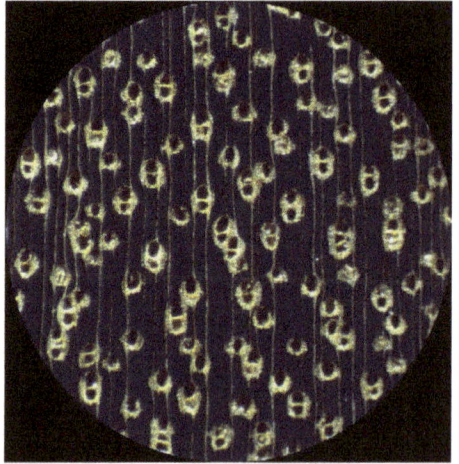

Cercocarpus ledifolius
Mountain mahogany

Chlorocardium rodiei
Greenheart

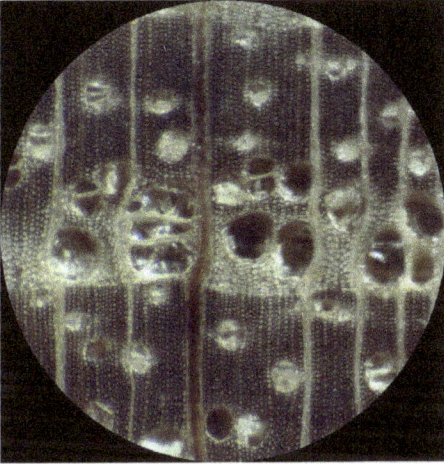

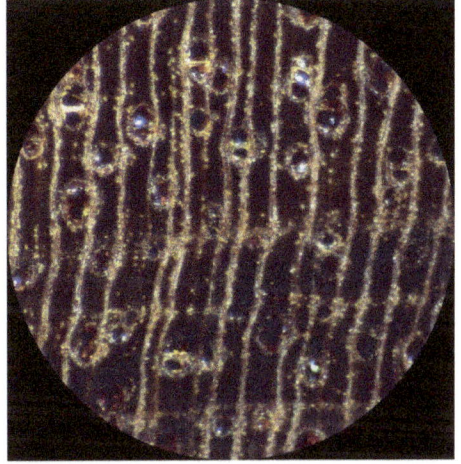

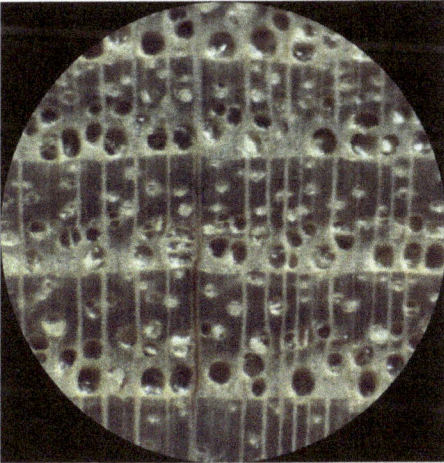

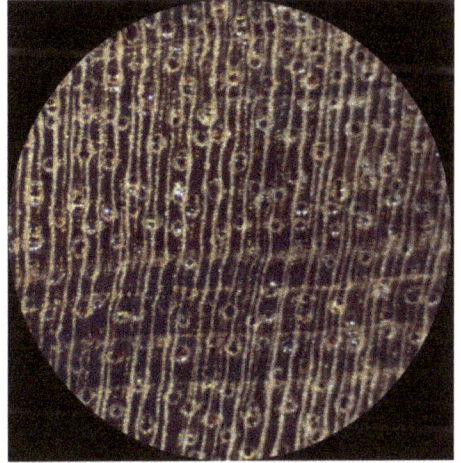

Choerospondias
        axillaris
Lapsi

Colophospermum mopane
Mopani

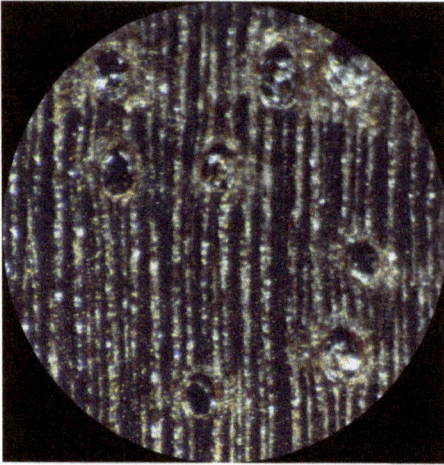

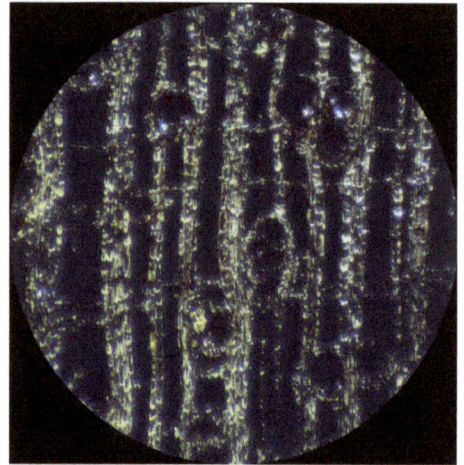

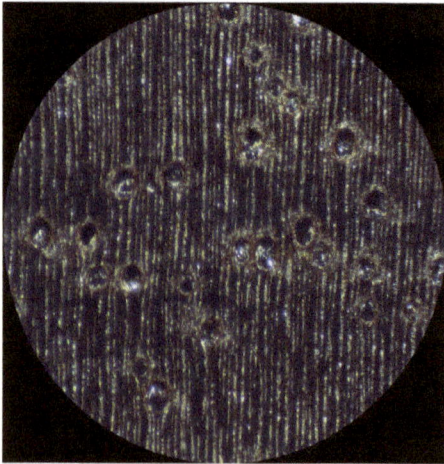

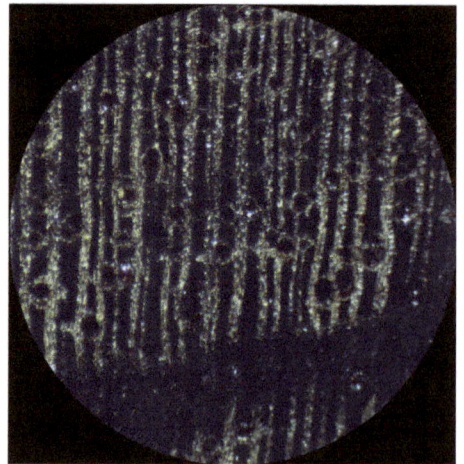

Combretum imberbe
Leadwood

Cordia dodecandra
Ziricote

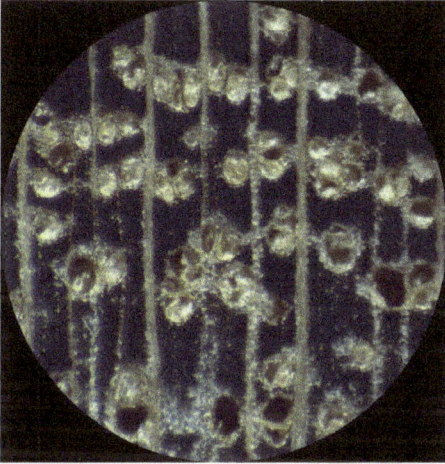

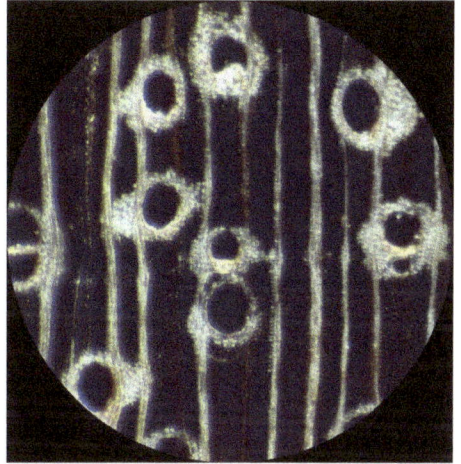

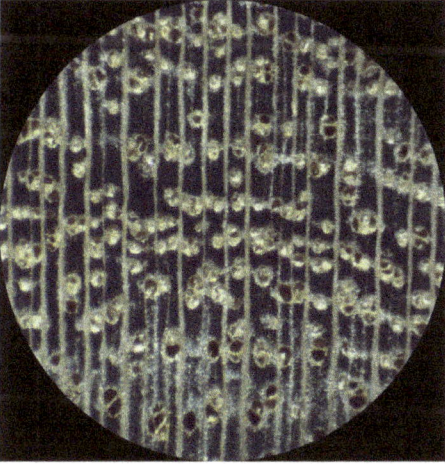

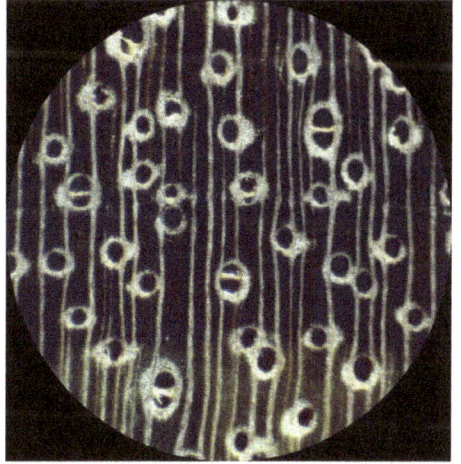

Cordia trichotoma
Peterebi

Cylicodiscus gabunensis
Adoum

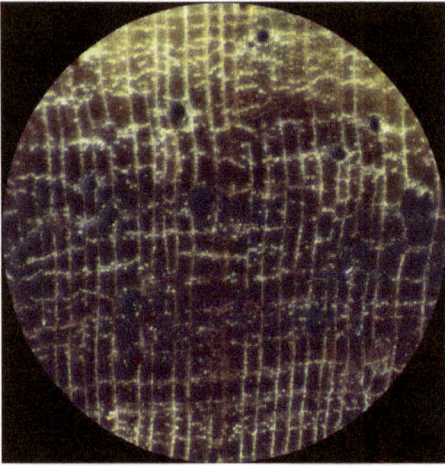

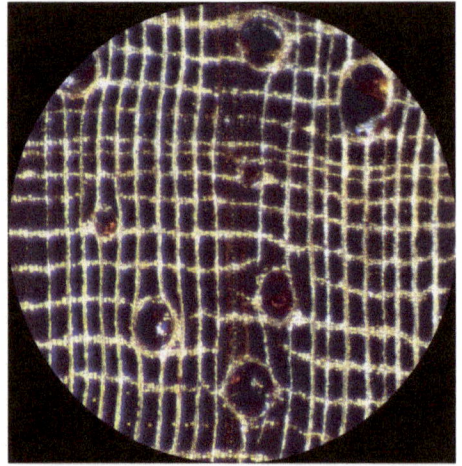

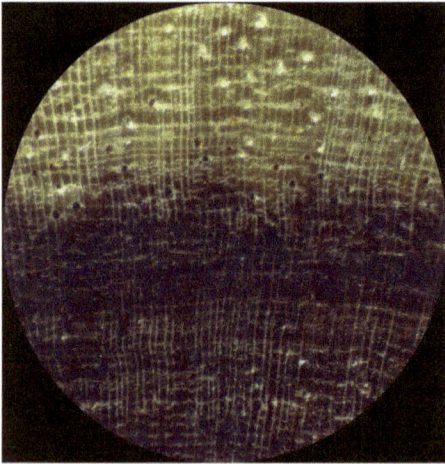

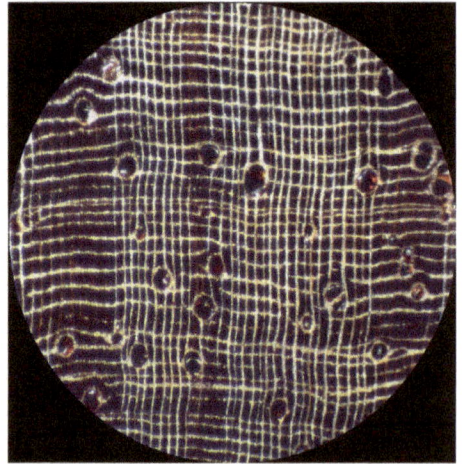

Dalbergia annamensis
Trac Day

Dalbergia bariensis
Neangnuon

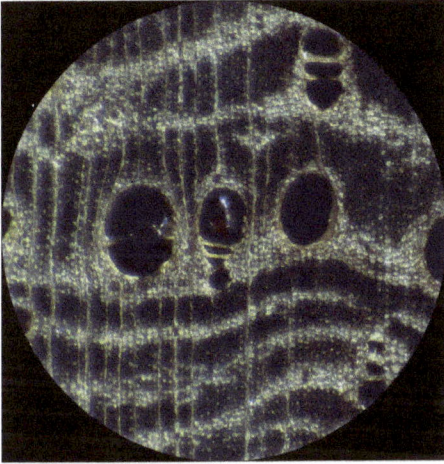

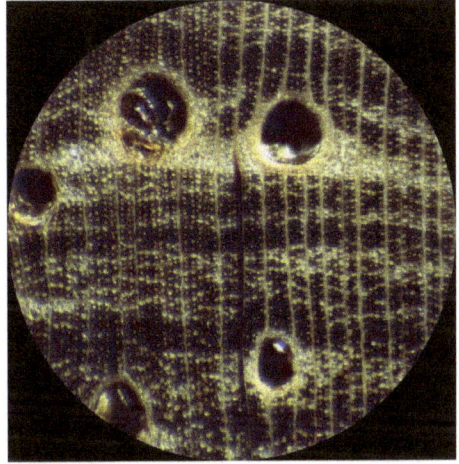

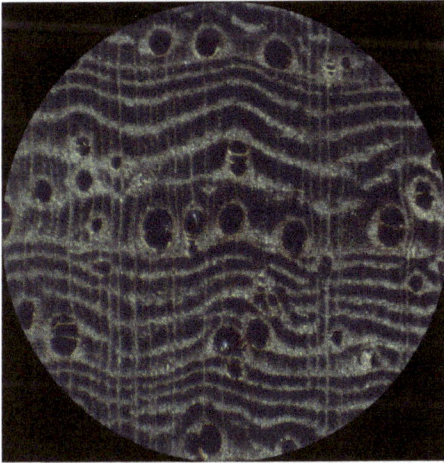

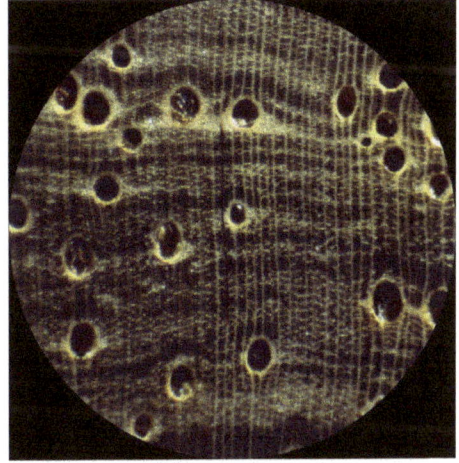

Dalbergia baronii
Madagascar Rosewood

Dalbergia brownei
Browns Indian-rosewood

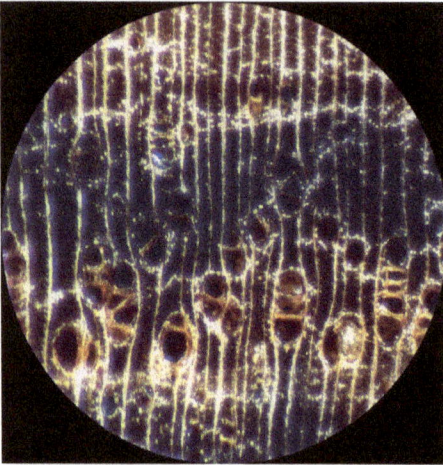

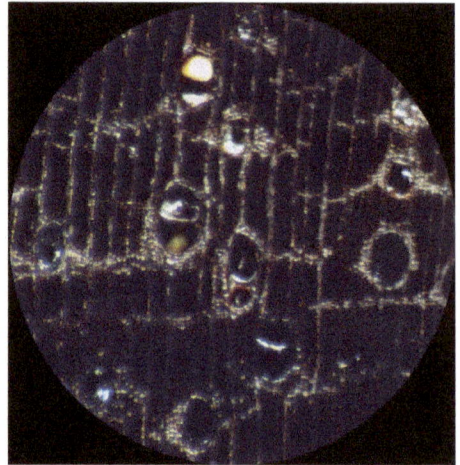

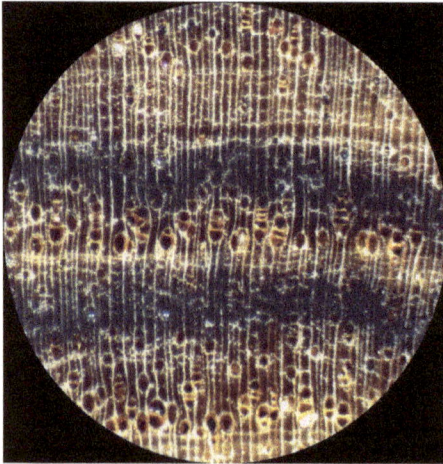

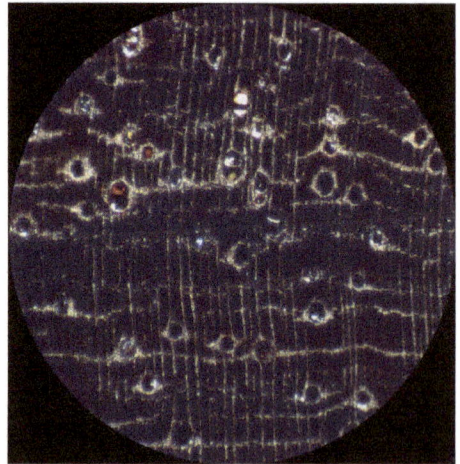

Dalbergia cearensis
Kingwood

Dalbergia cochinchinensis
Siamese Rosewood

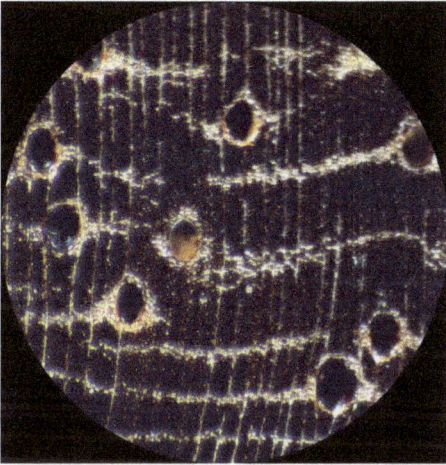

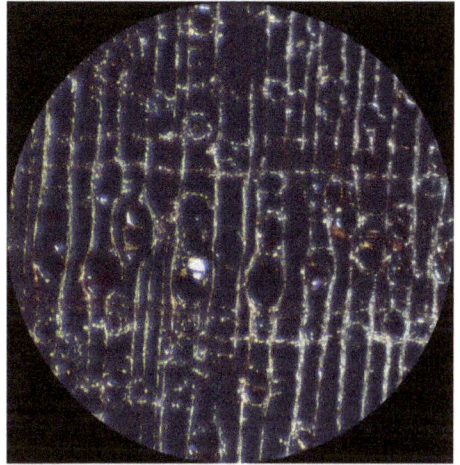

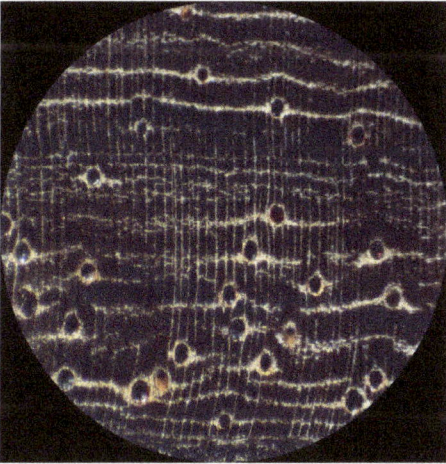

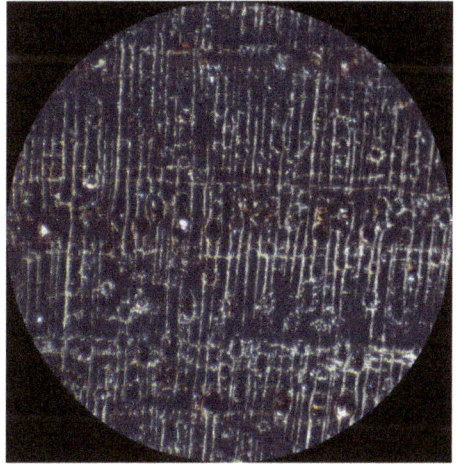

*Dalbergia
    cochinchinensis*
Siamese Rosewood

*Dalbergia
    congestiflora*
Camotillo rosewood

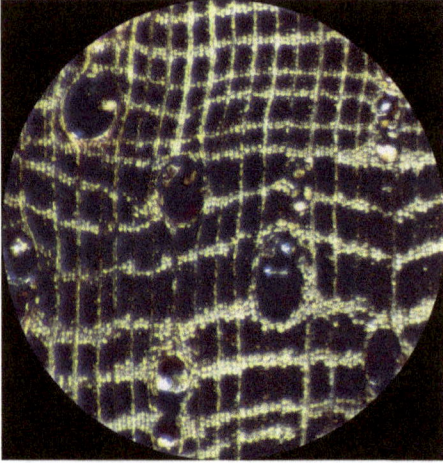

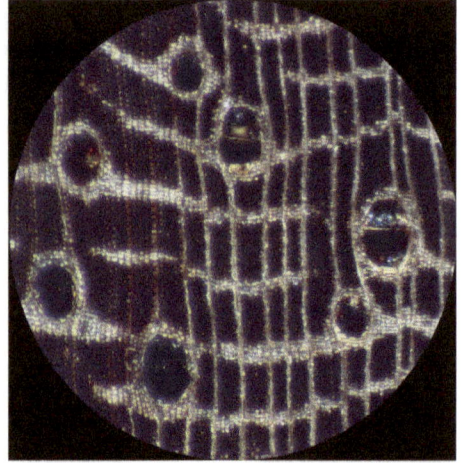

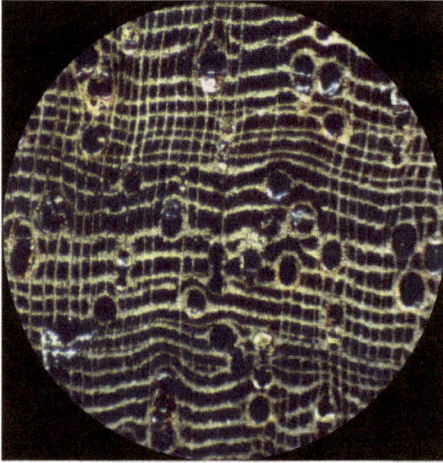

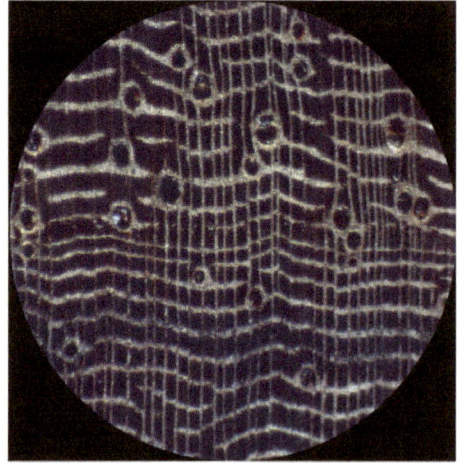

Dalbergia cultrata
Burma Blackwood

Dalbergia cultrata
Burma Blackwood

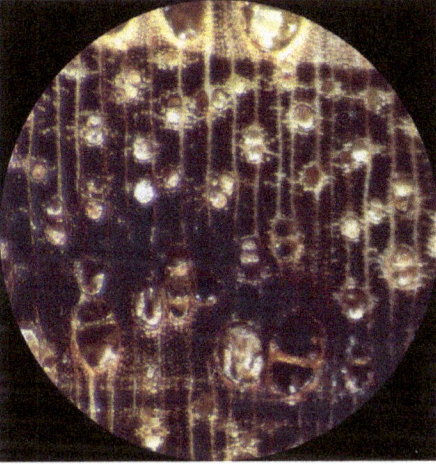

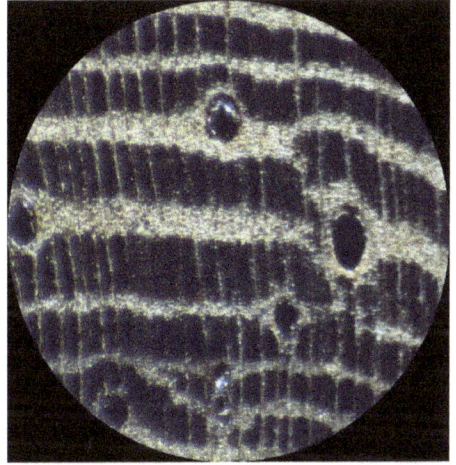

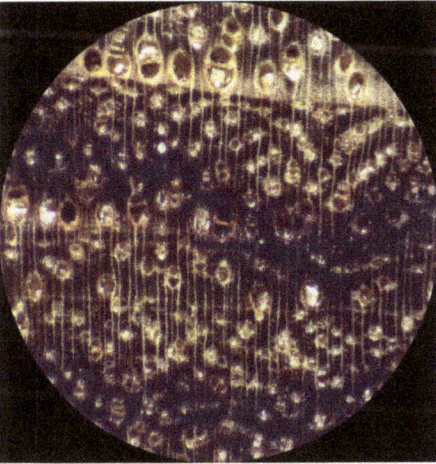

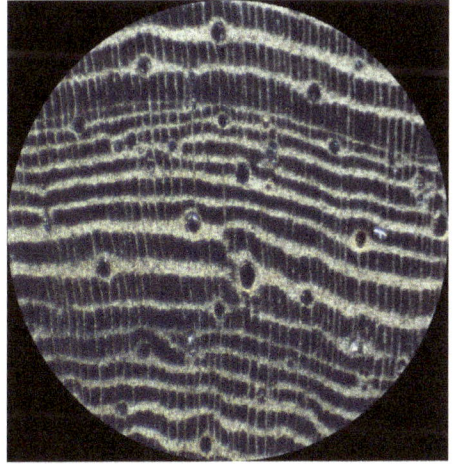

Dalbergia frutescens
Brazilian tullipwood

Dalbergia fusca
Black Rosewood

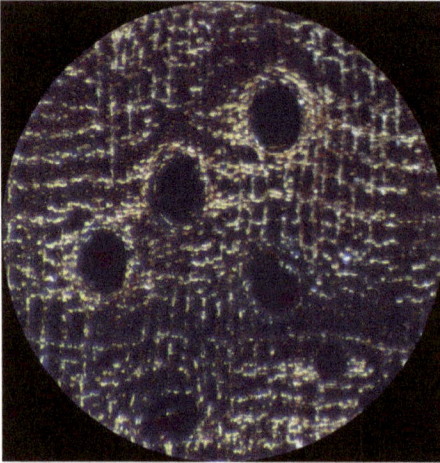

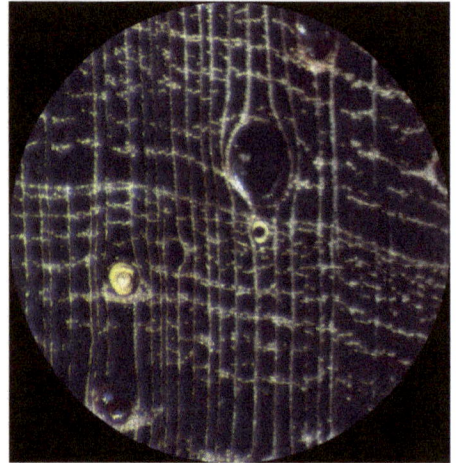

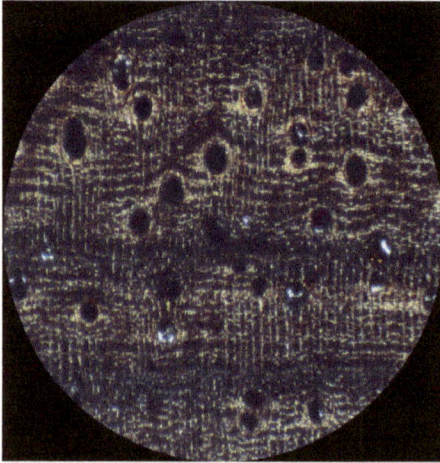

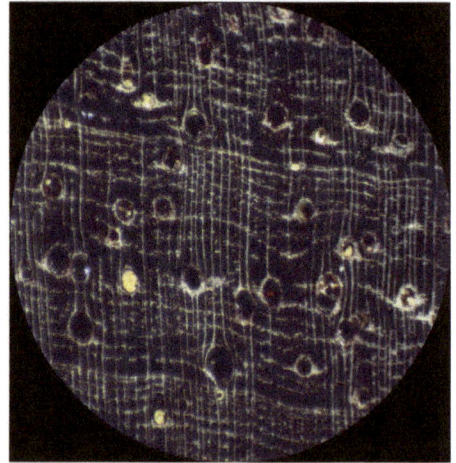

Dalbergia granadillo
Granadillo Cocobolo

Dalbergia greveana
Madagascar Rosewood

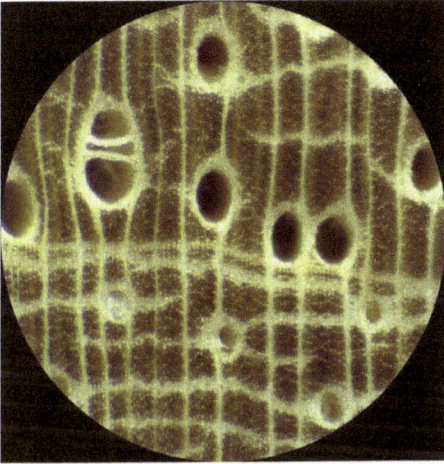

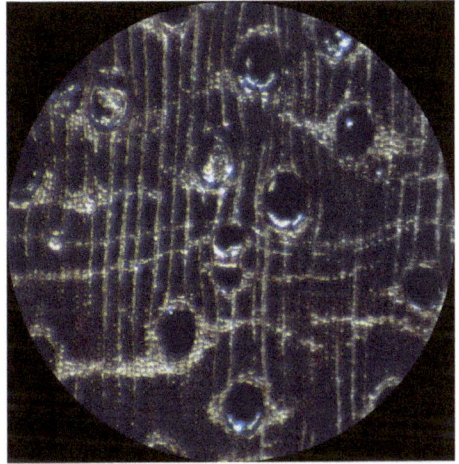

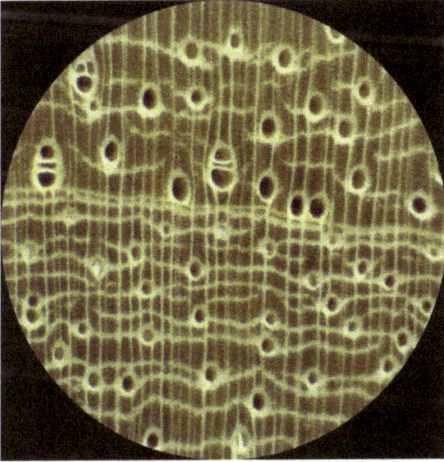

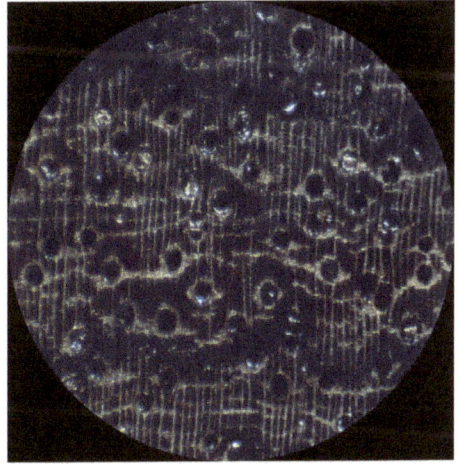

Dalbergia hubeana
Hubei Rosewood

Dalbergia latifolia
East Indian Rosewood

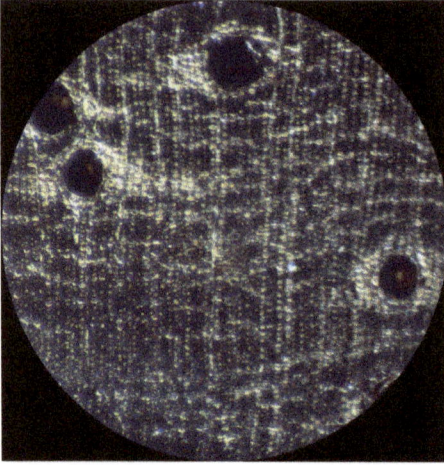

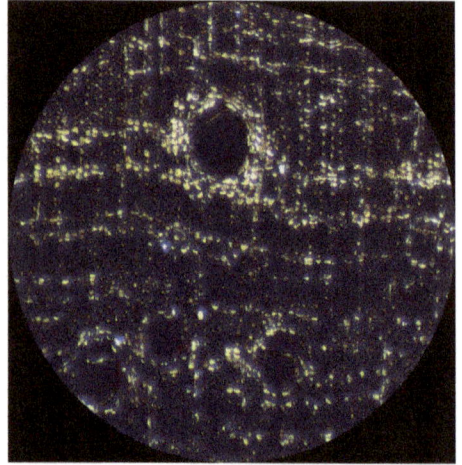

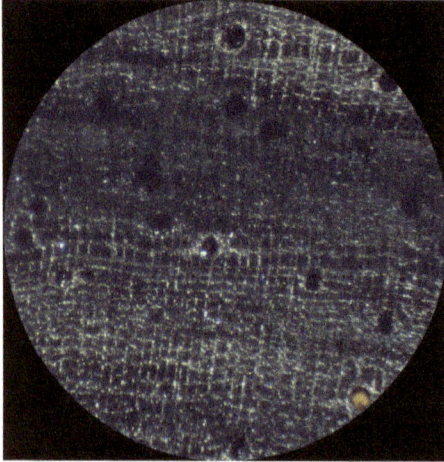

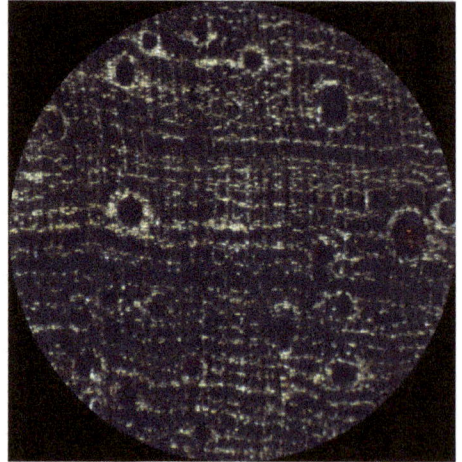

Dalbergia louvelii
Madagascar rosewood

Dalbergia maritima
Bois de Rose

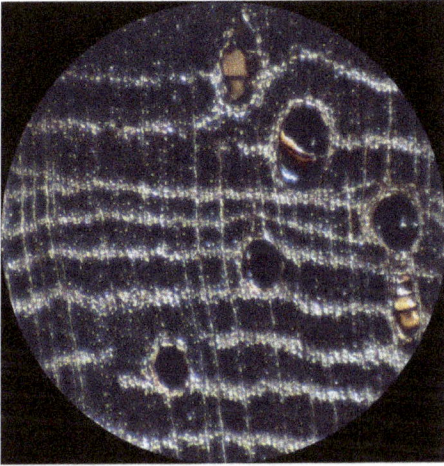

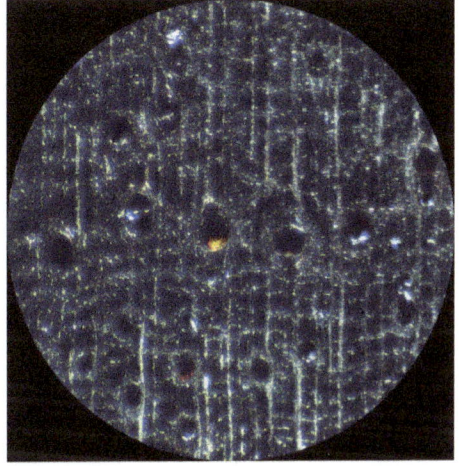

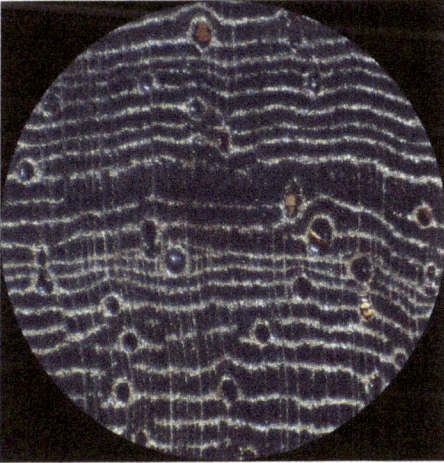

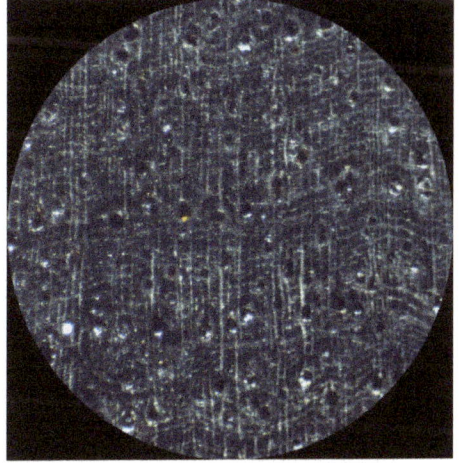

Dalbergia matami
Violetwood

Dalbergia melanoxylon
East African Black wood

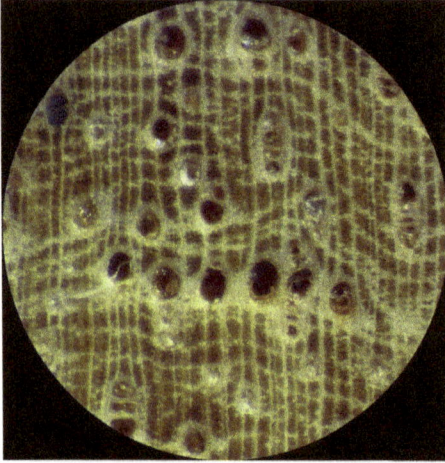

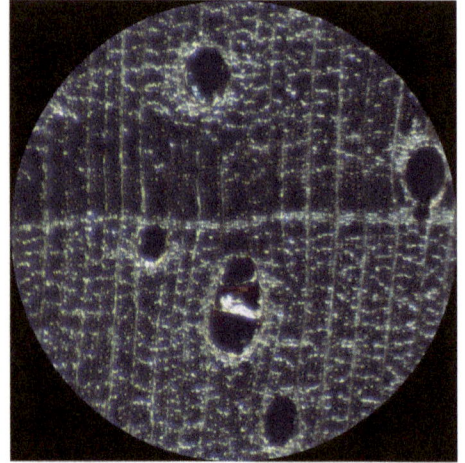

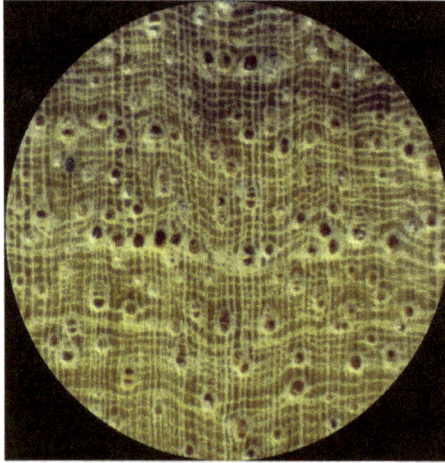

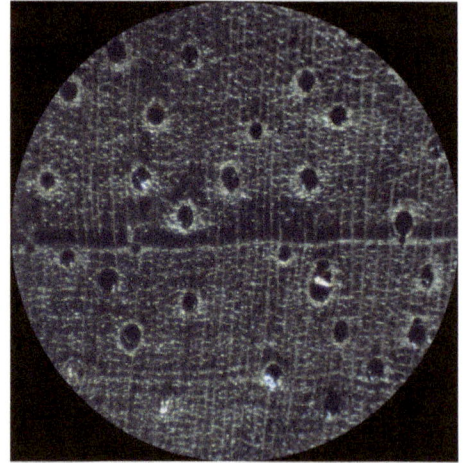

Dalbergia melanoxylon
East African Black wood

Dalbergia nigra
Brazilian rosewood

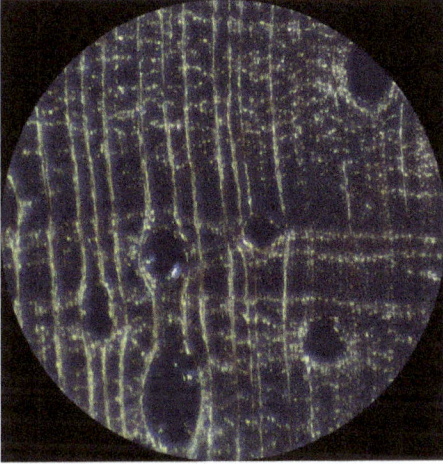

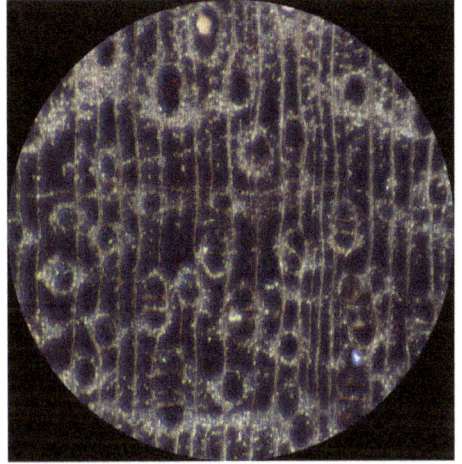

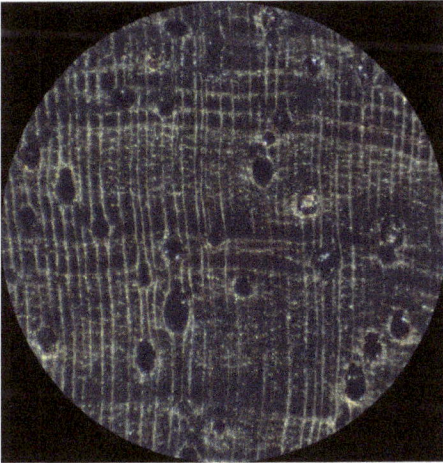

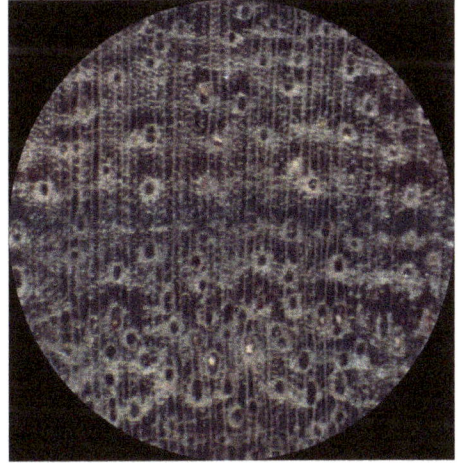

Dalbergia nigra
Brazilian rosewood

Dalbergia nitidula
Glossy flat-bean

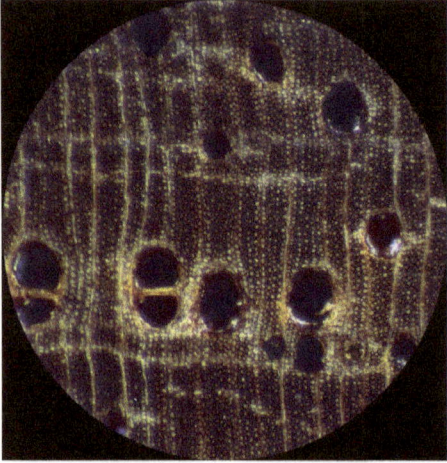

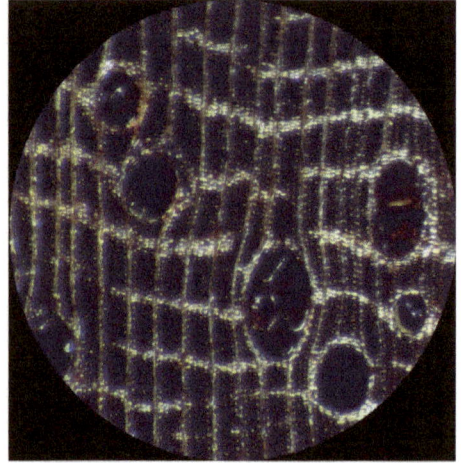

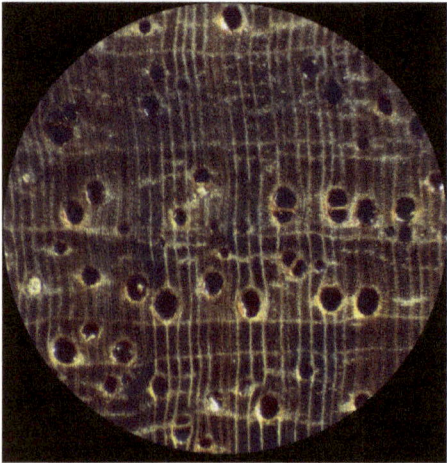

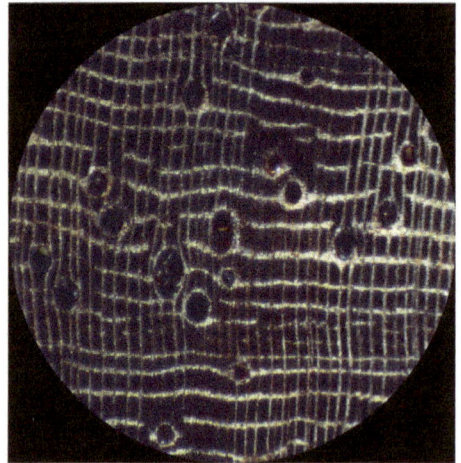

Dalbergia odorifera
Scented wood

Dalbergia oliveri
Burma Tulipwood

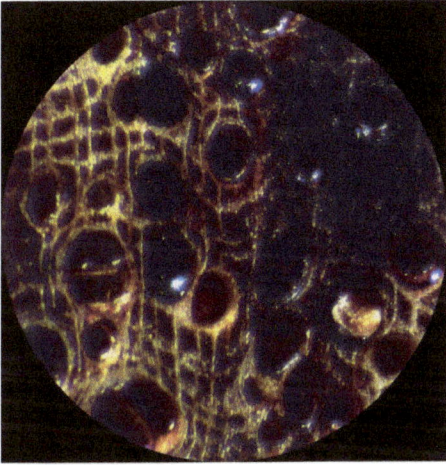

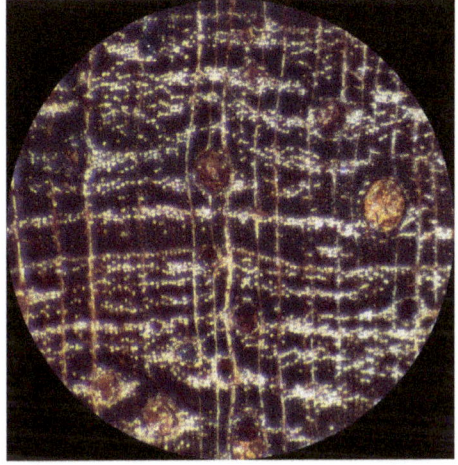

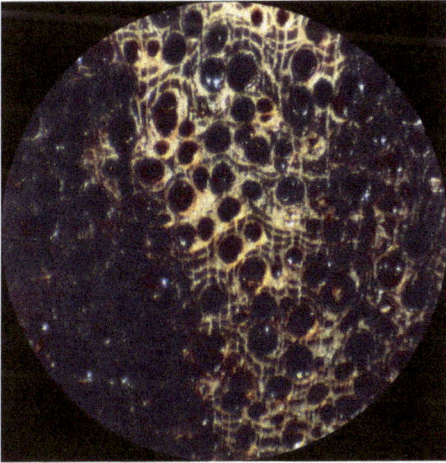

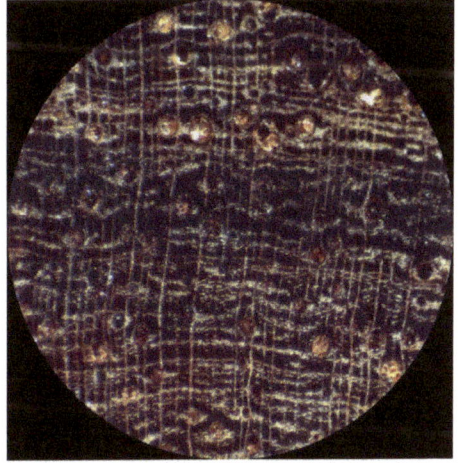

Dalbergia parviflora
Akar Laka

Dalbergia
purpurascens
Palisander

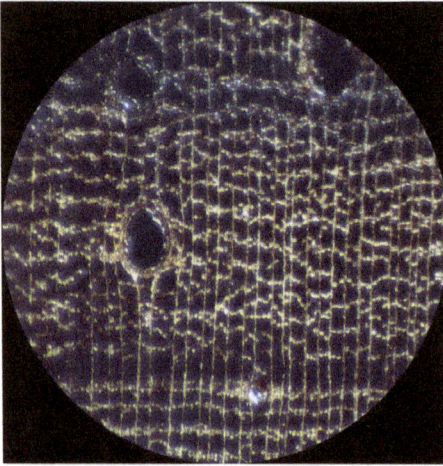

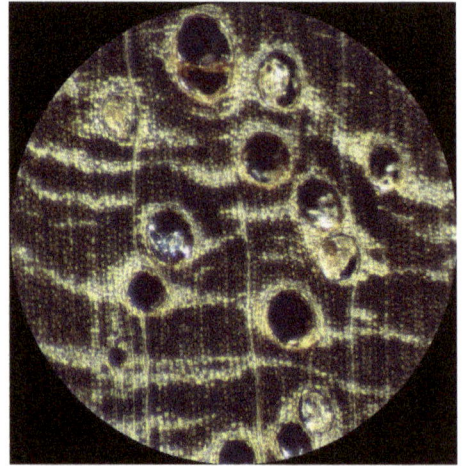

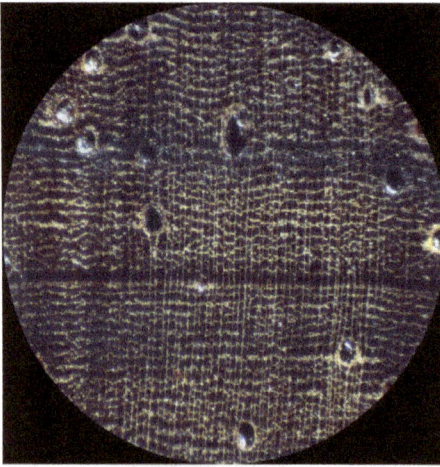

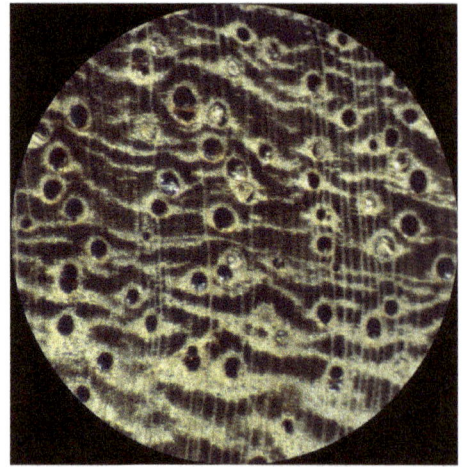

Dalbergia retusa
Cocobolo

Dalbergia sissoo
Sissoo

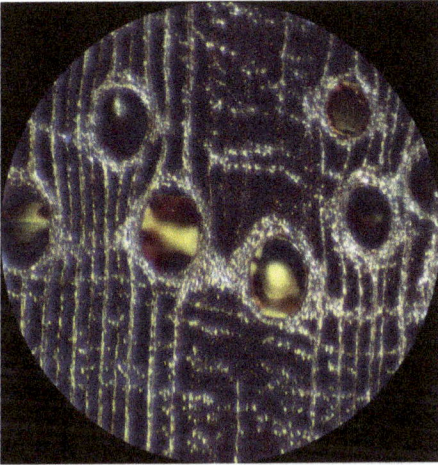

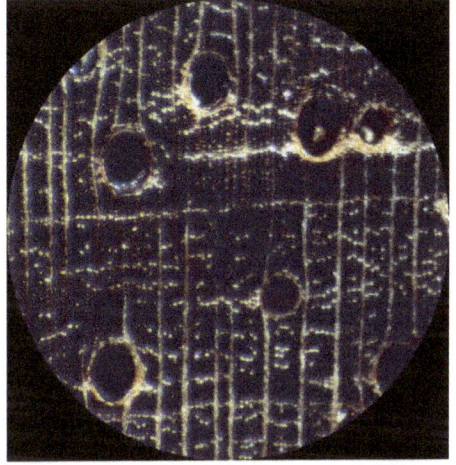

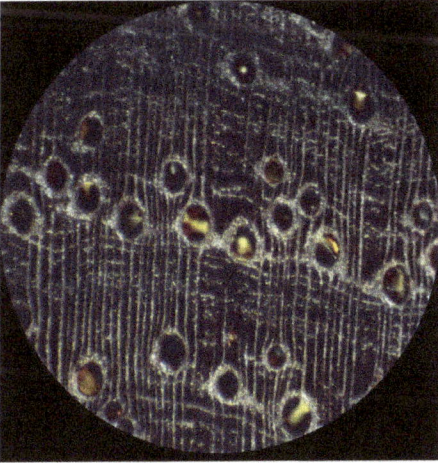

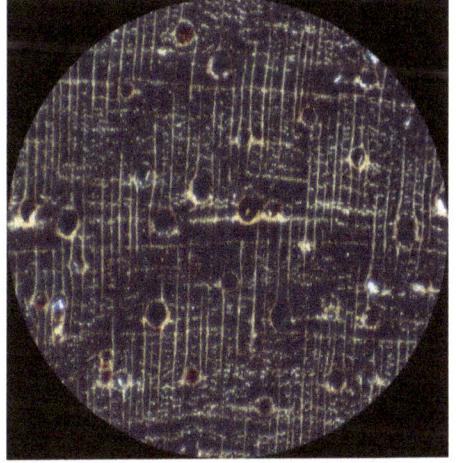

Dalbergia spruceana
Amazon rosewood

Dalbergia stevensonii
Honduras Rosewood

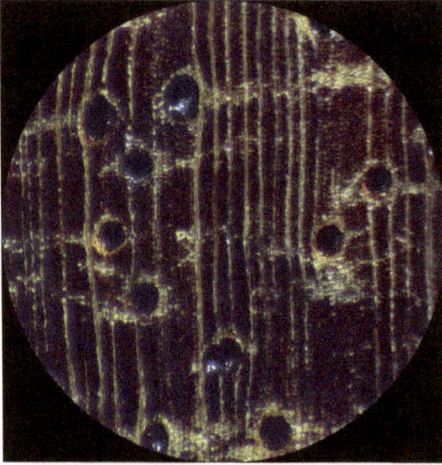

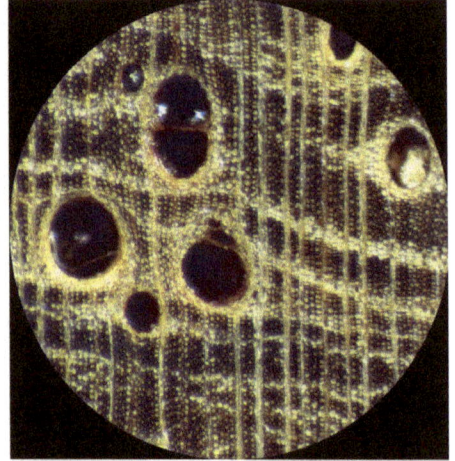

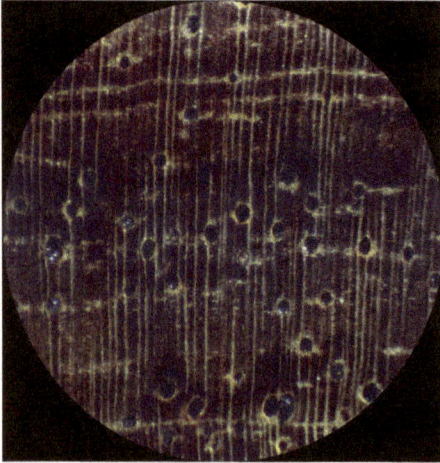

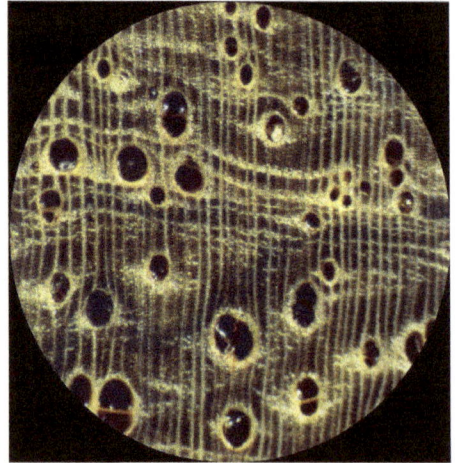

Dalbergia tonkinensis
Sua

Dalbergia tucurensis
Guatemalan Rosewood

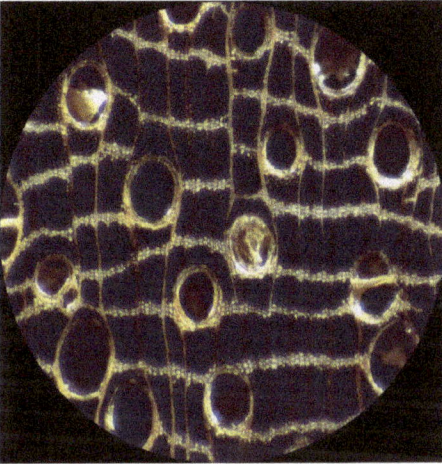

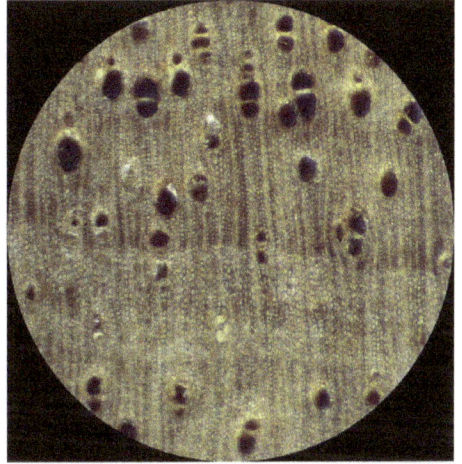

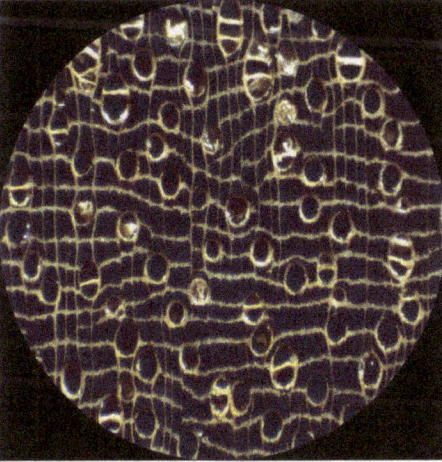

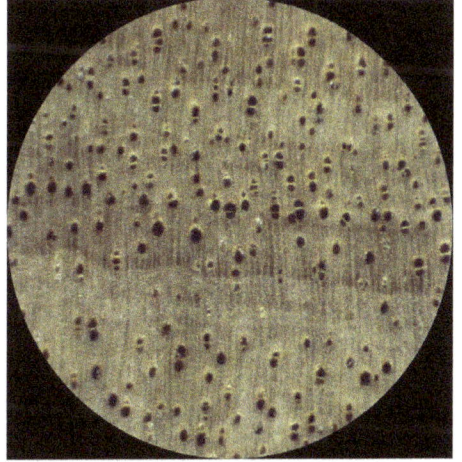

Dialium platysepalum
Keranji

Dimocarpus longan
Longan

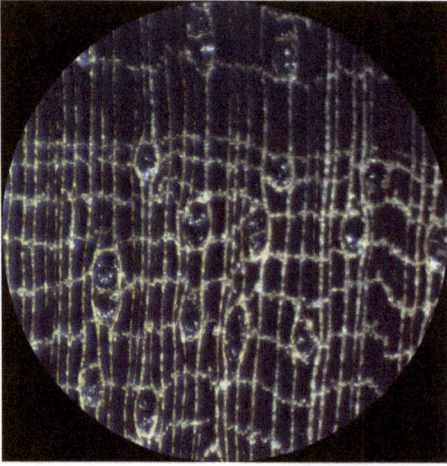

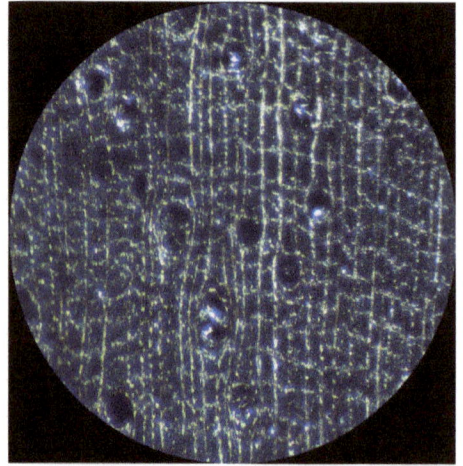

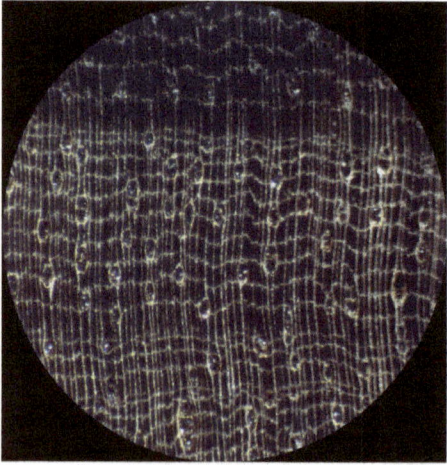

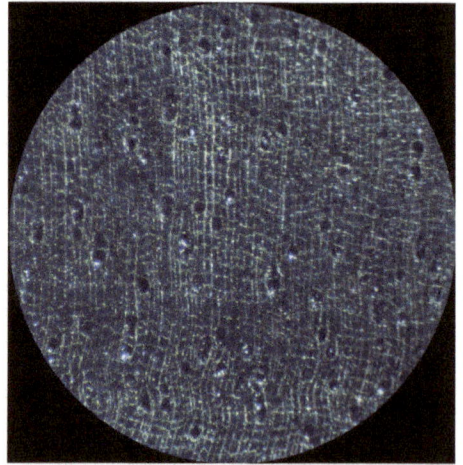

Diospyros celebica
Macassar ebony

Diospyros crassiflora
Gaboon ebony

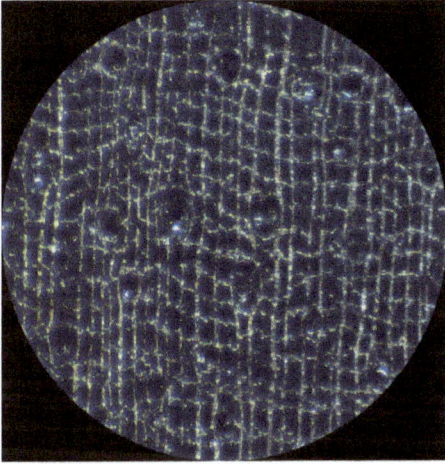

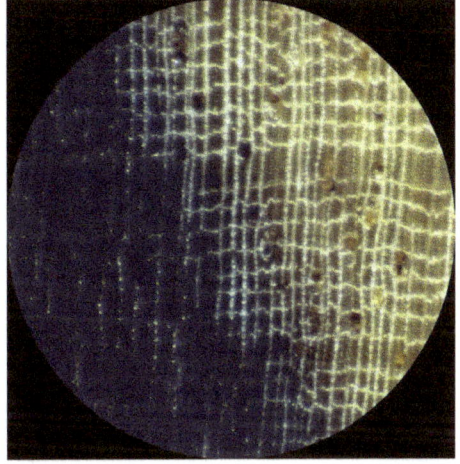

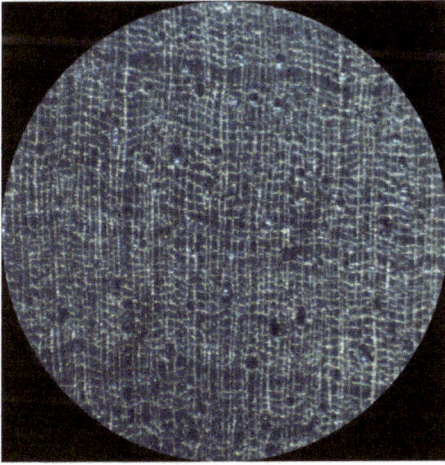

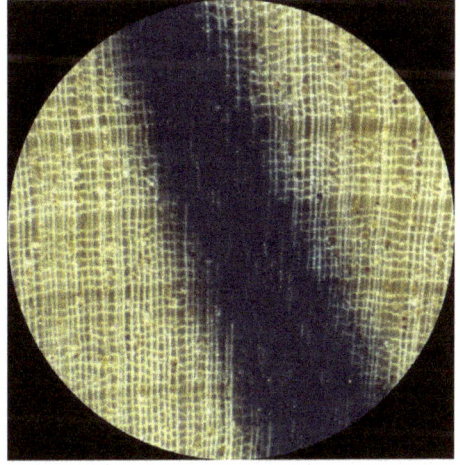

Diospyros ebenum
Ceylon ebony

Diospyros malabarica
Black and white ebony

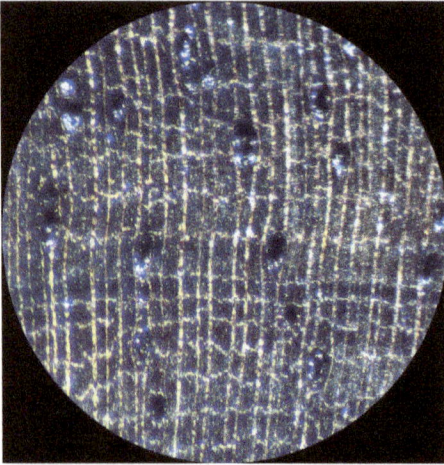

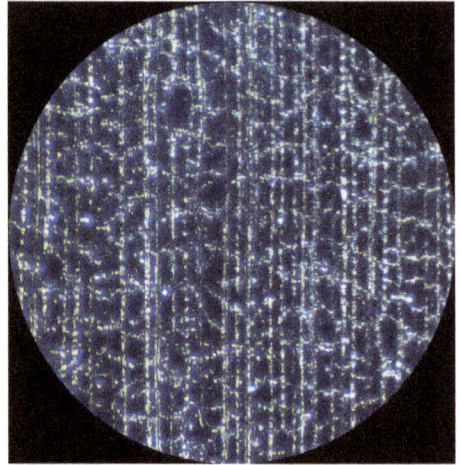

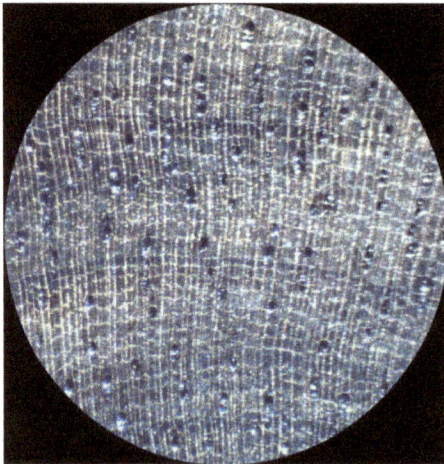

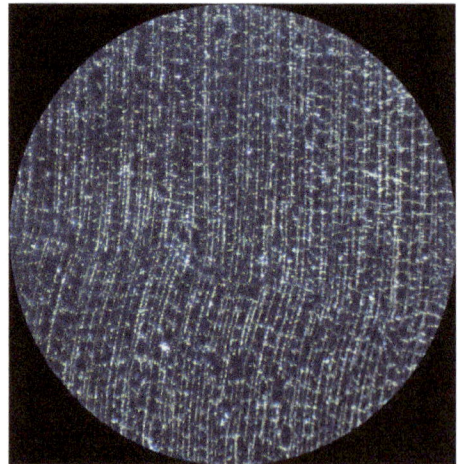

Diospyros mun

Vietnamese ebony

Diospyros philippinensis

Mabolo

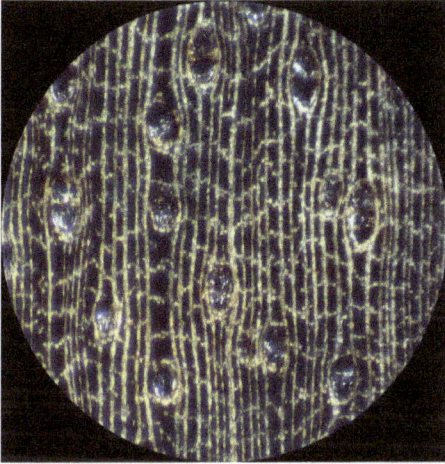

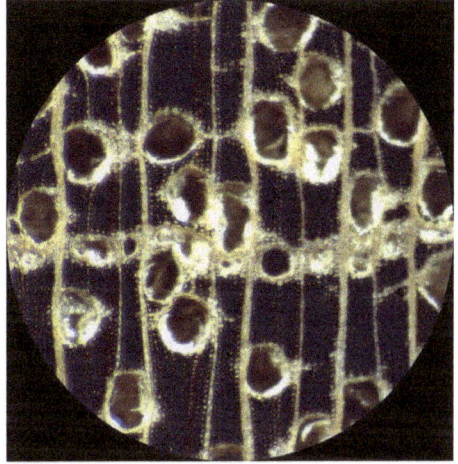

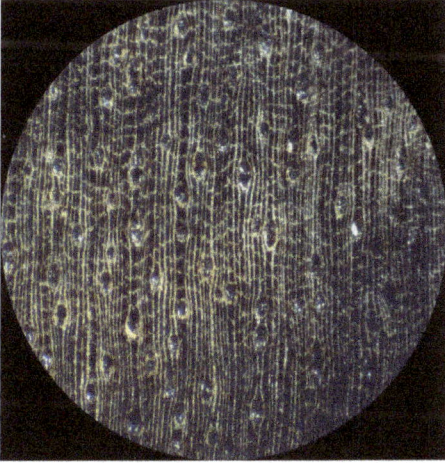

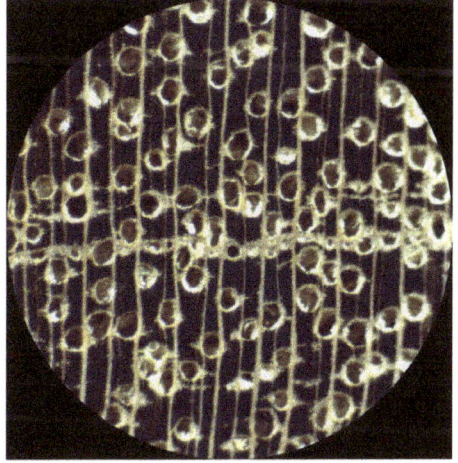

Diospyros pilosanthera
Bolong-eta

Dipterocarpus confertus
Keruing

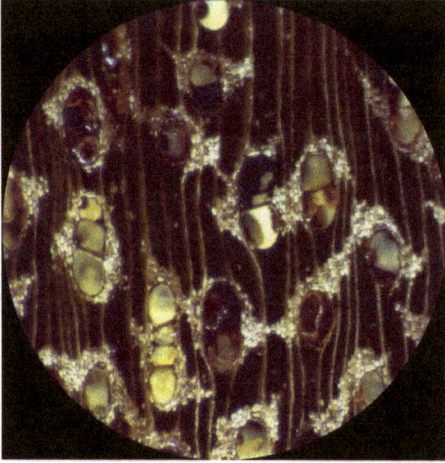

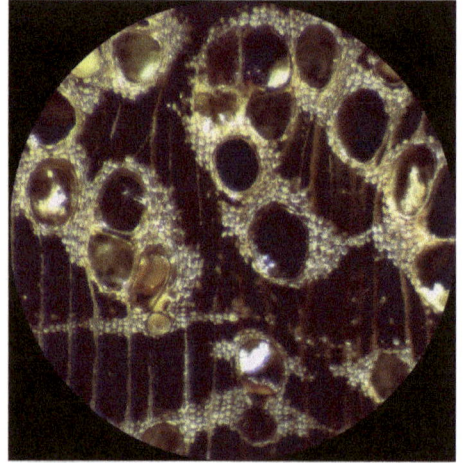

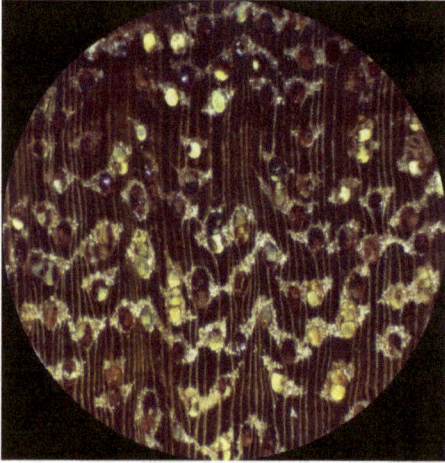

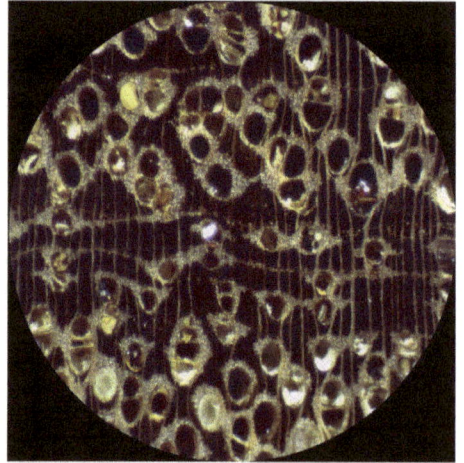

Dipteryx odorata
Cumaru

Dipteryx oleifera
Almendro

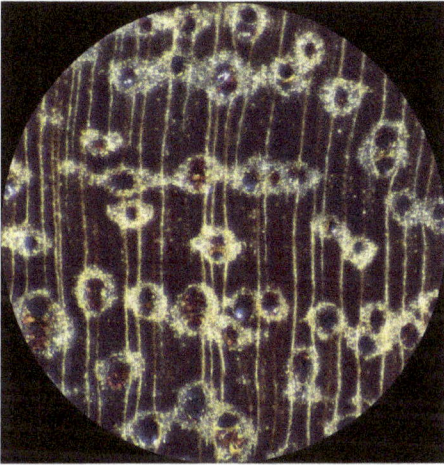

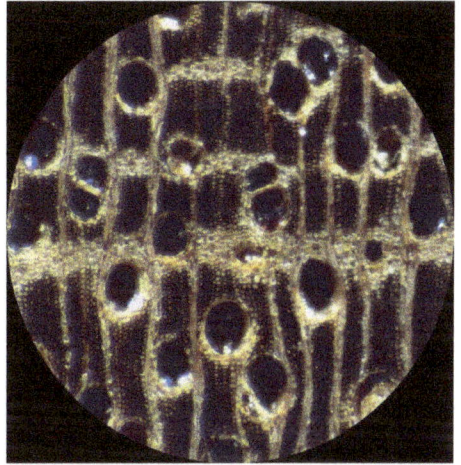

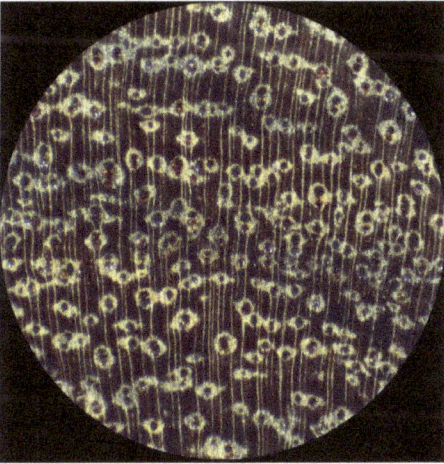

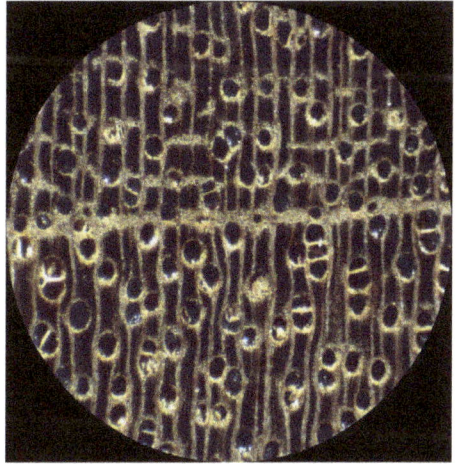

Ebenopsis ebano
Texas ebony

*Entandrophragma
cylindricum*
Sapele

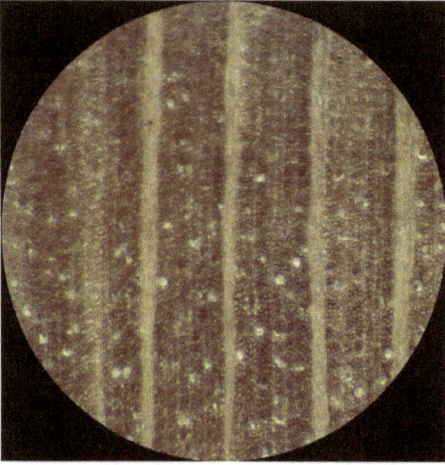

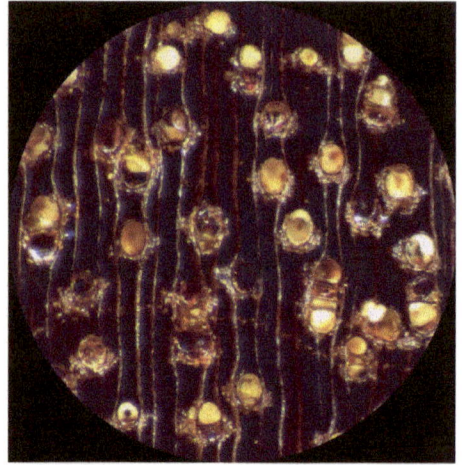

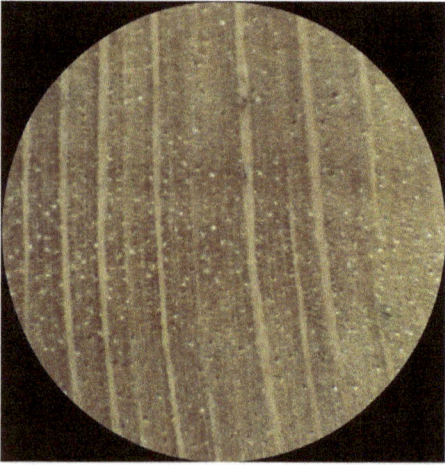

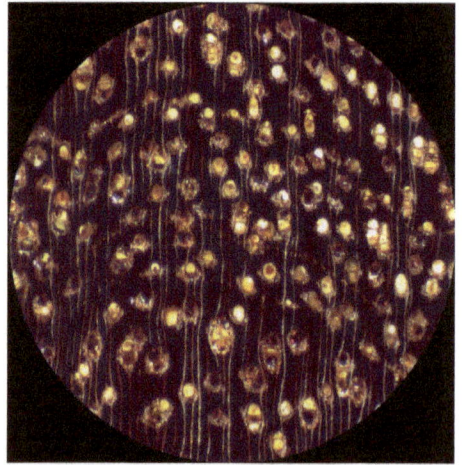

Erica arborea
Tree heath

Erythrophleum chlorostachys
Cooktown ironwood

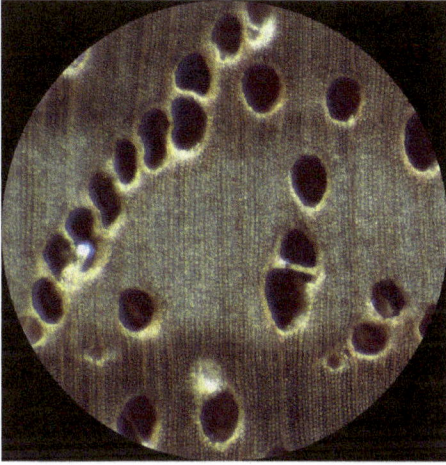

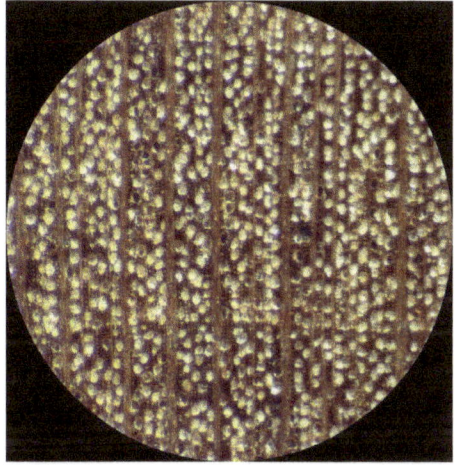

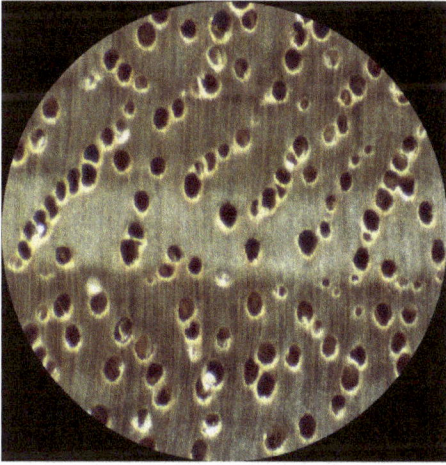

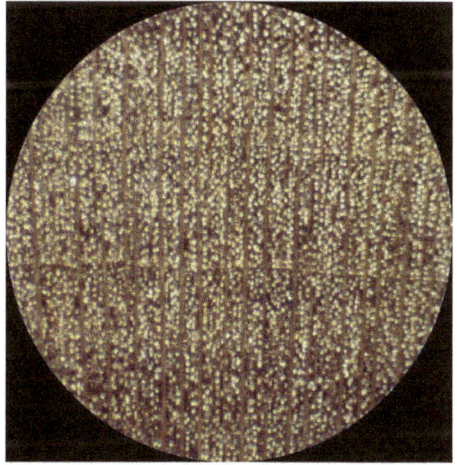

Eucalyptus grandis
Flooded Gum

Euryodendron excelsum
Zhu xue mu

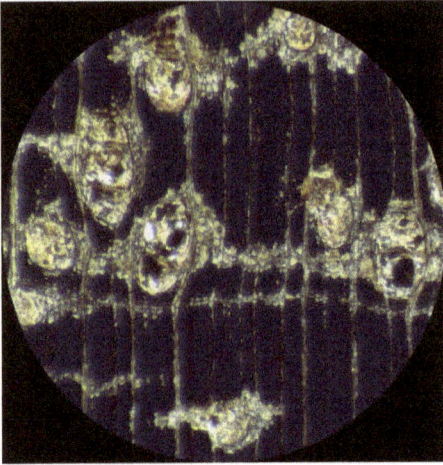

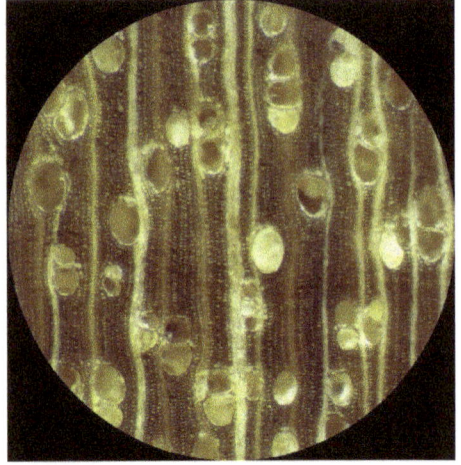

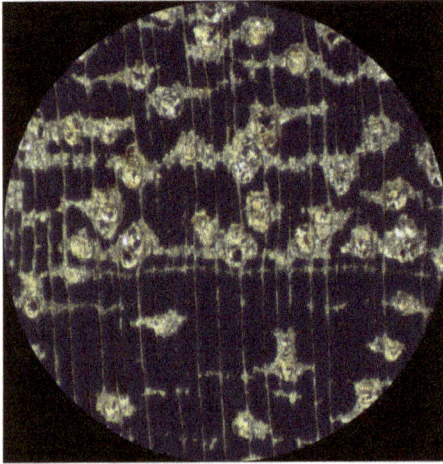

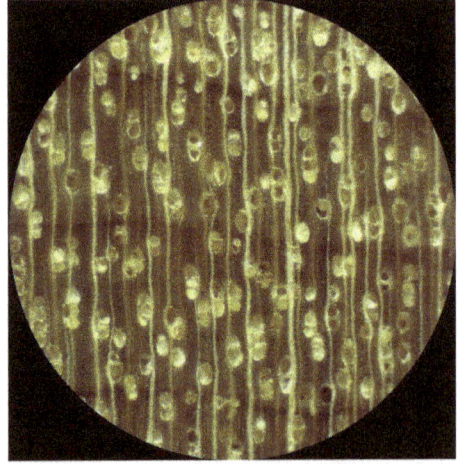

Eusideroxylon zwageri
Belian

*Euxylonphora
paraensis*
Yellow heart

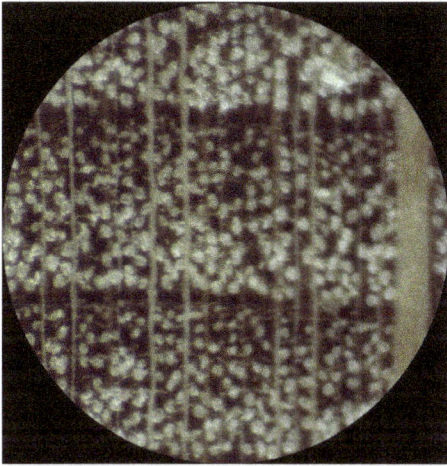

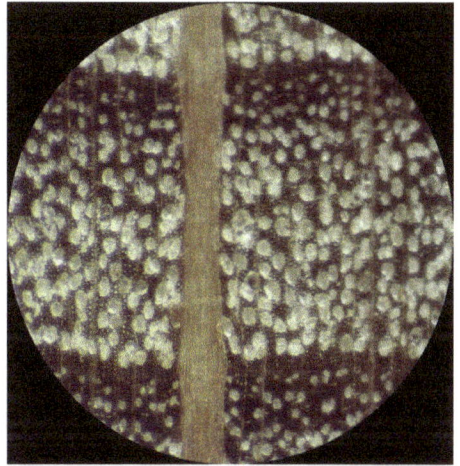

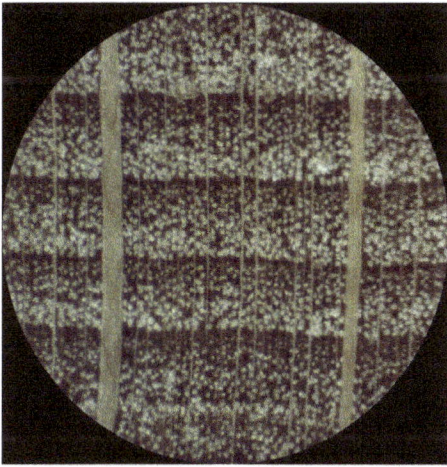

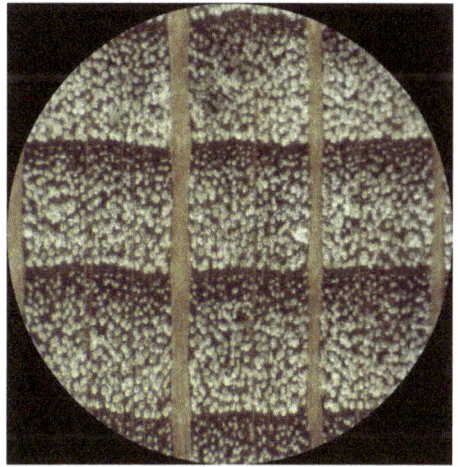

Fagus longipetiolata
Shui qing gang

Fagus sylvatica
European Beech

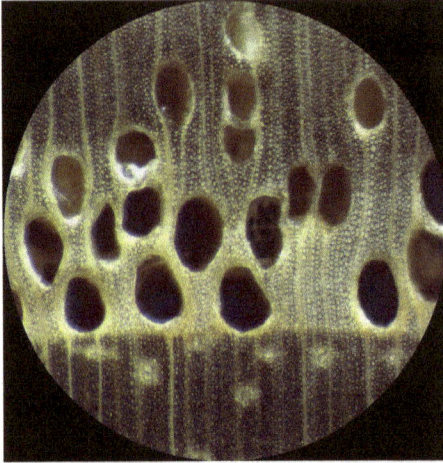

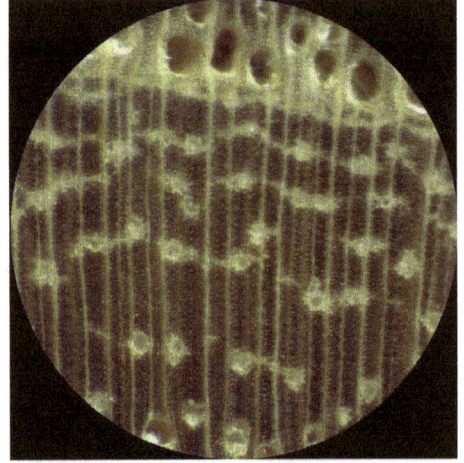

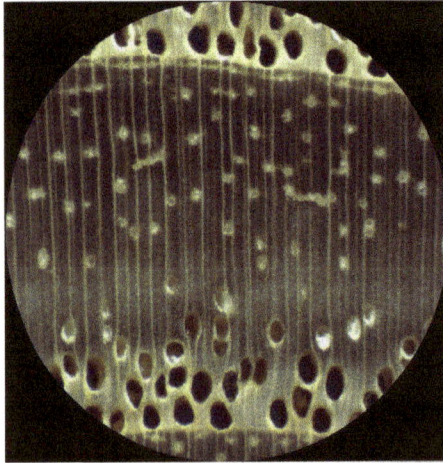

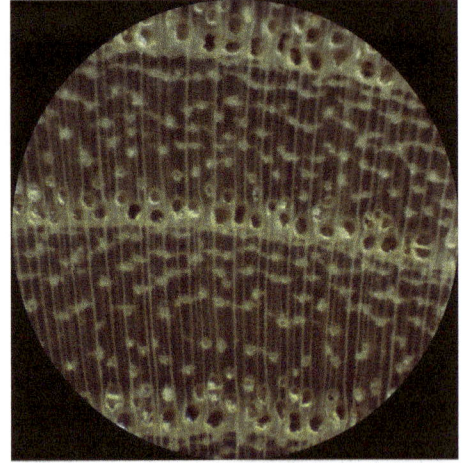

Fraxinus americana
White Ash

Fraxinus chinensis
Chinese Ash

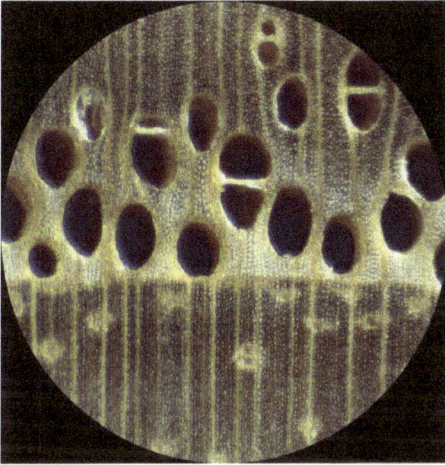

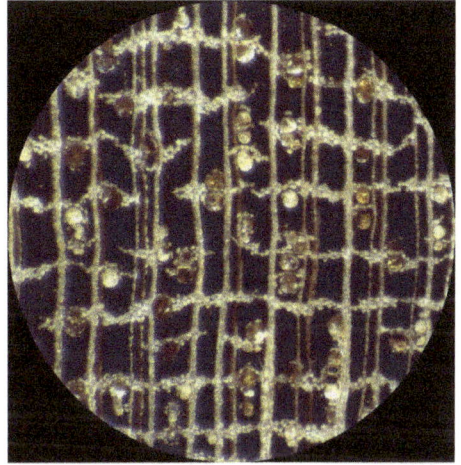

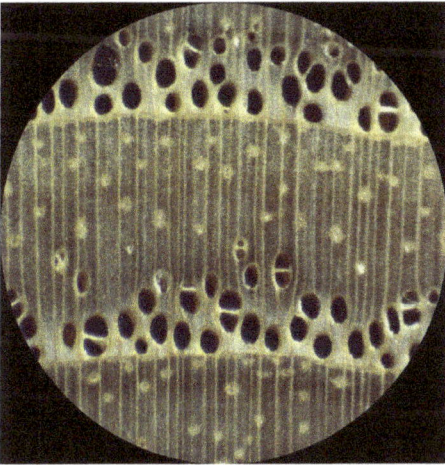

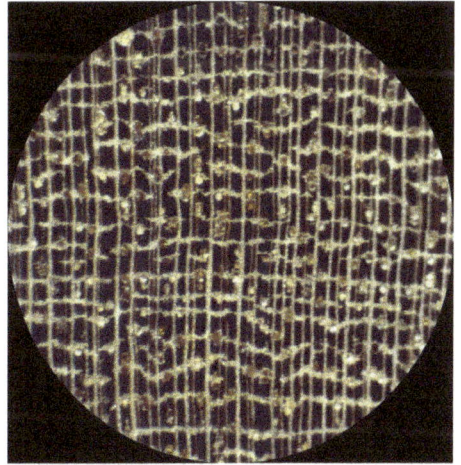

Fraxinus mandshurica
Manchurican Ash

Garcinia paucinervis
Jin Si Li

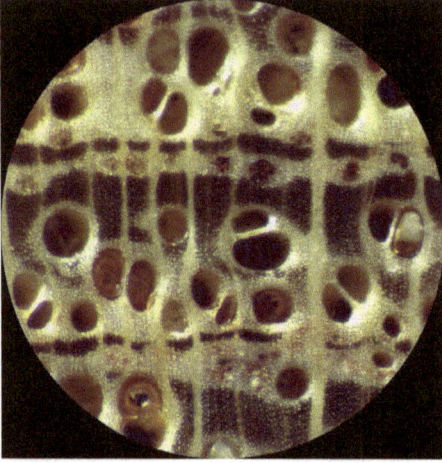

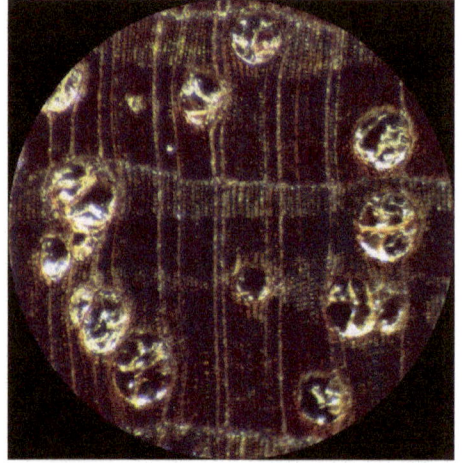

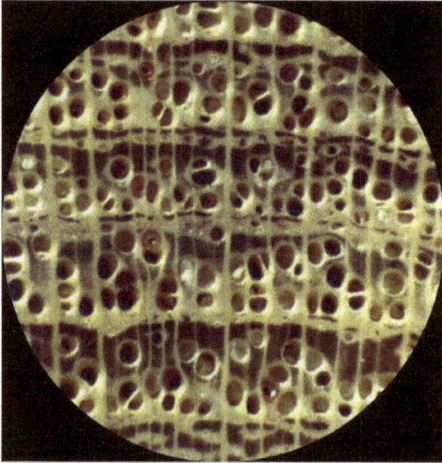

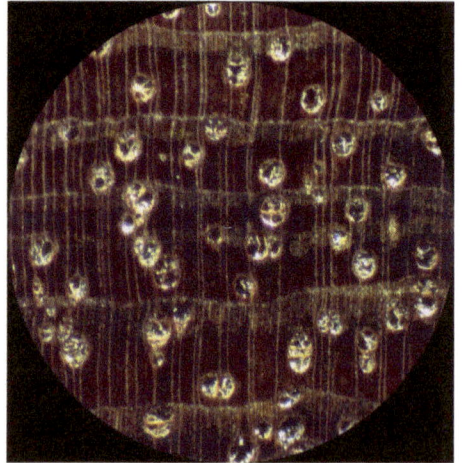

Gleditsia triacanthos
Honeylocust

Gluta renghas
Rengas

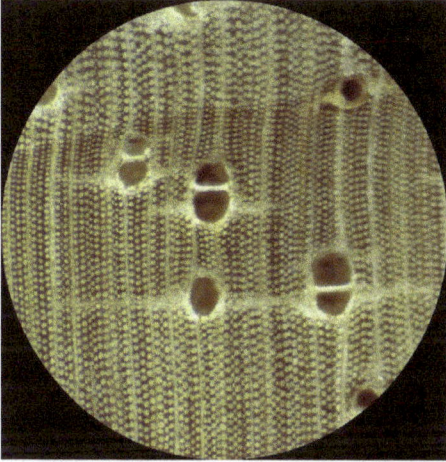

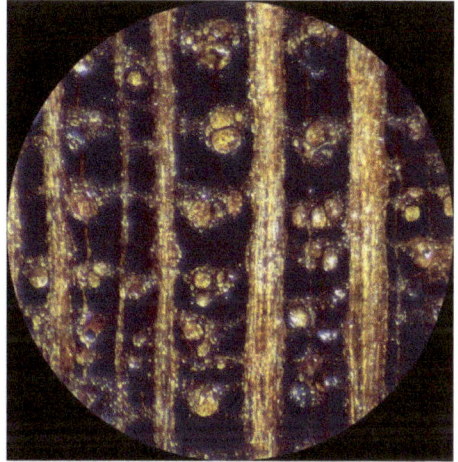

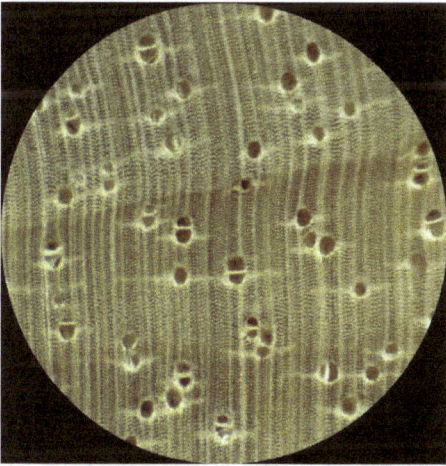

Gonystylus bancanus
Ramin

Grevillea striata
Beefwood

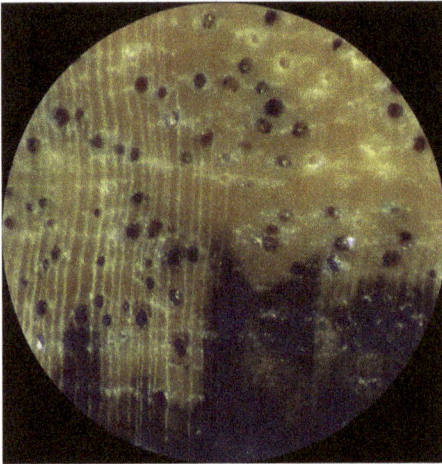

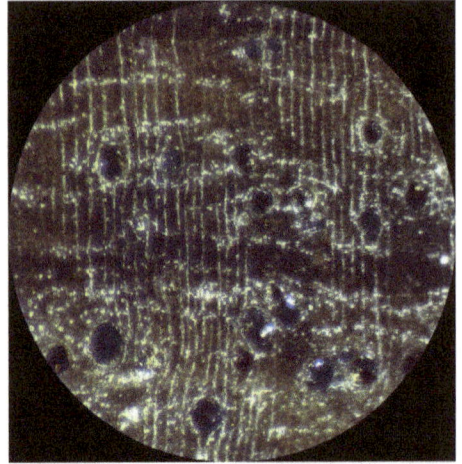

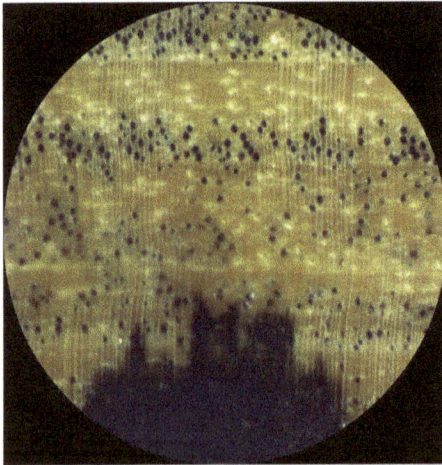

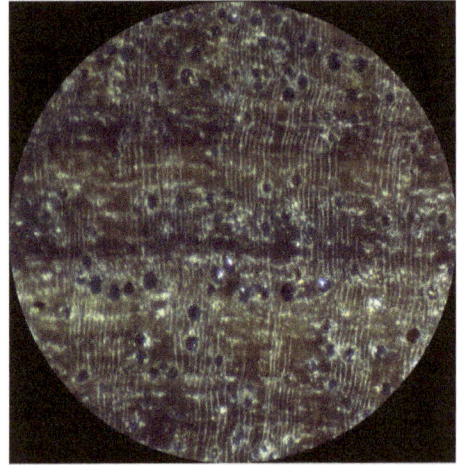

Guaiacum coulteri
Lignum Vitae

Guaiacum officinale
Lignum Vitae

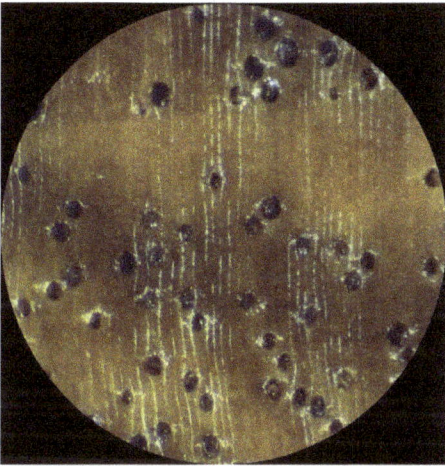

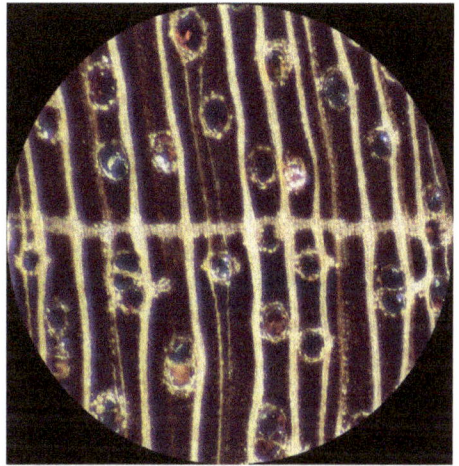

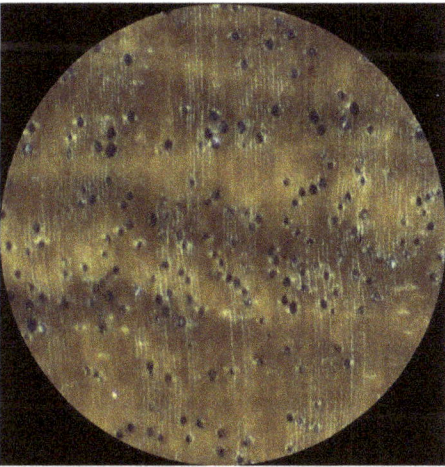

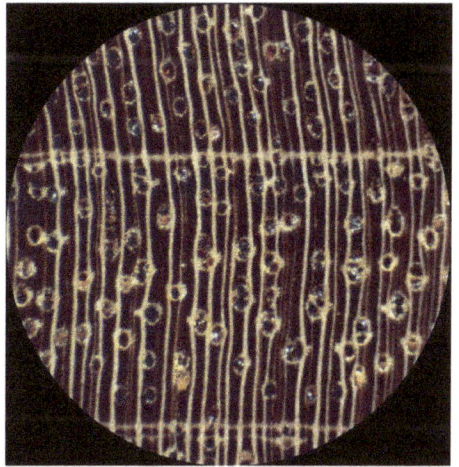

Guaiacum sanctum
Lignum Vitae

Guibourtia chodatiana
Curunai

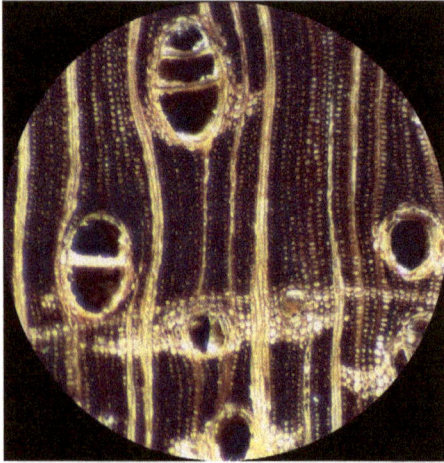

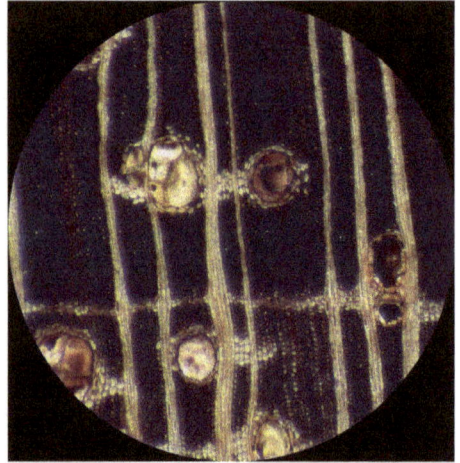

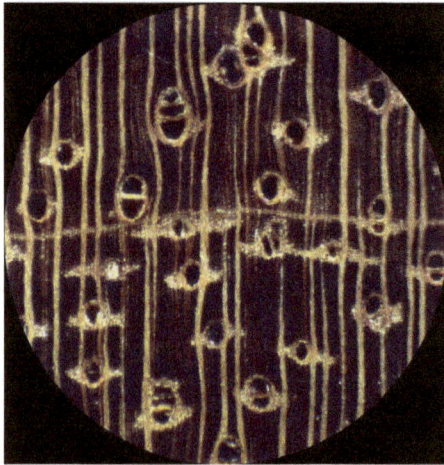

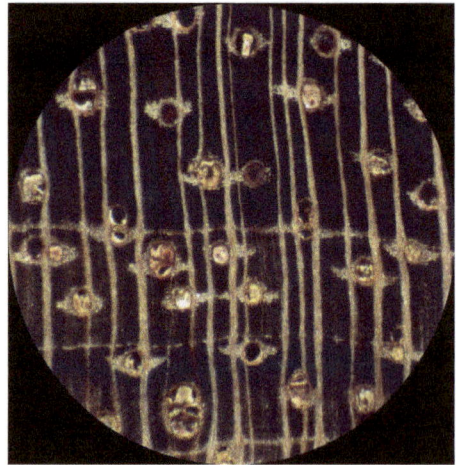

Guibourtia demeusei
Gabon Kevazingo

Guibourtia ehie
Ovangkol

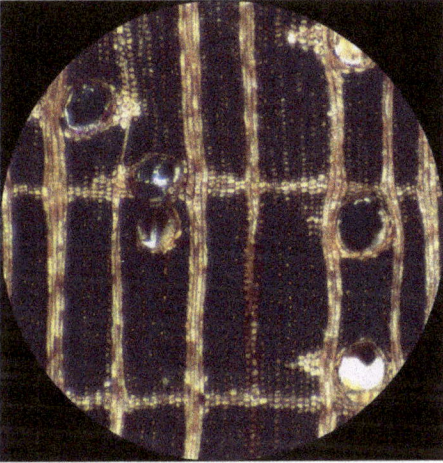

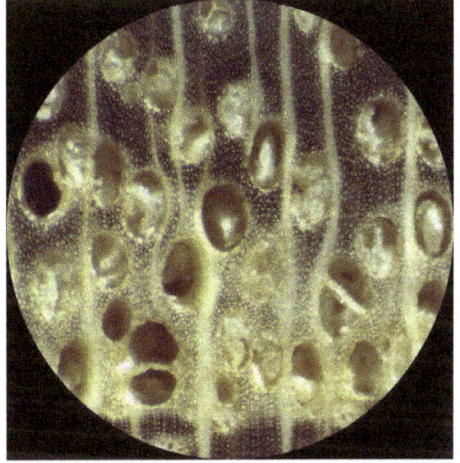

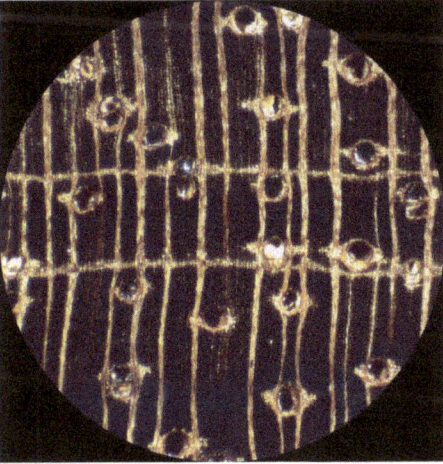

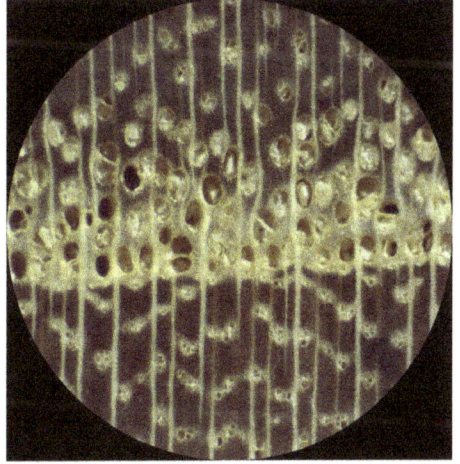

Guibourtia tessmanii
Bubinga

Gymnocladus dioica
Kentucky Coffee Tree

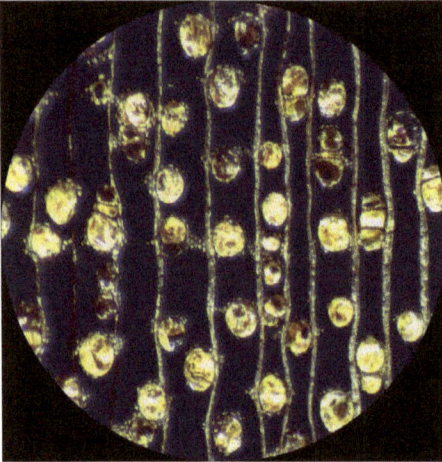

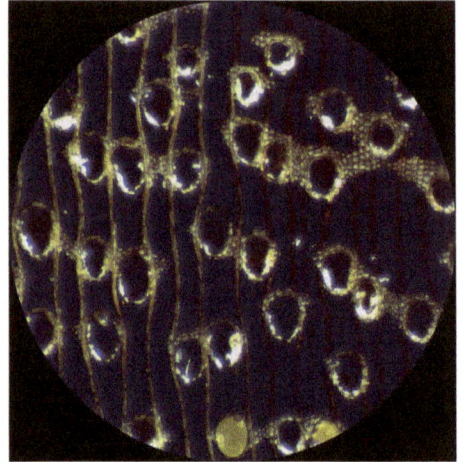

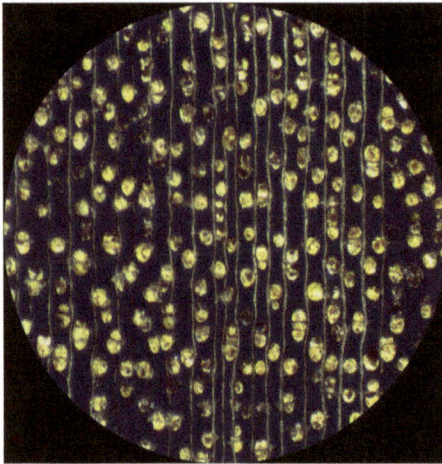

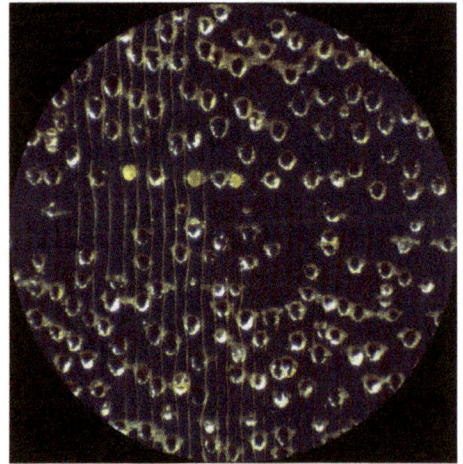

Handroanthus billbergii
Ipe

Handroanthus capitatus
Trumpet Tree

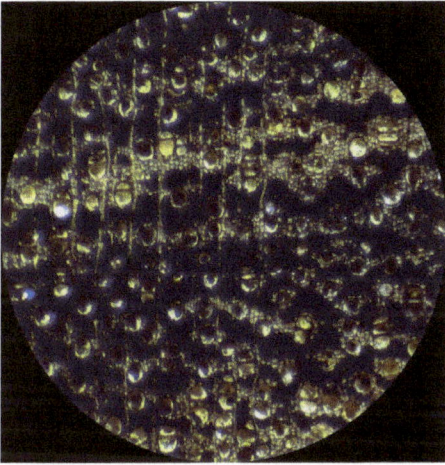

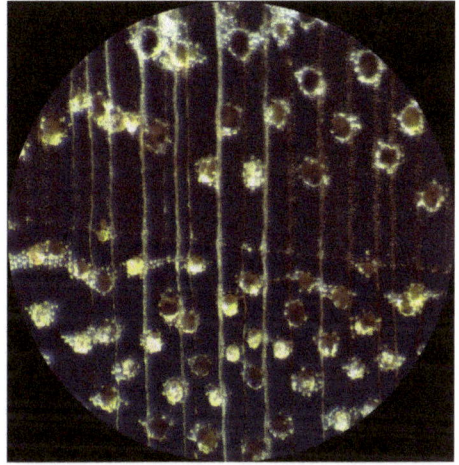

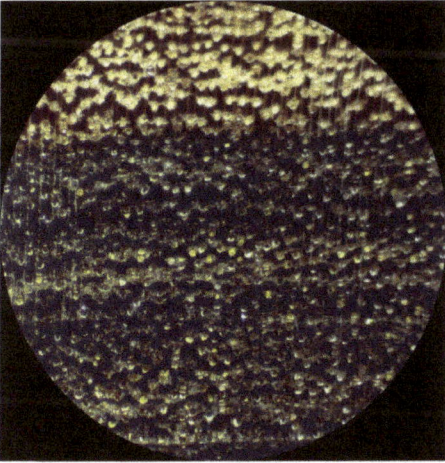

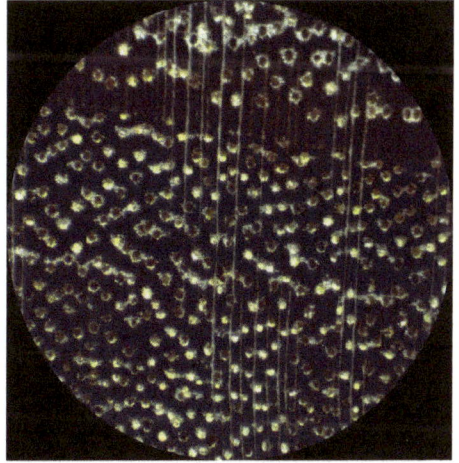

Handroanthus chrysanthus
Roble Amarillo

Handroanthus heptaphyllus
Lapacho Negro

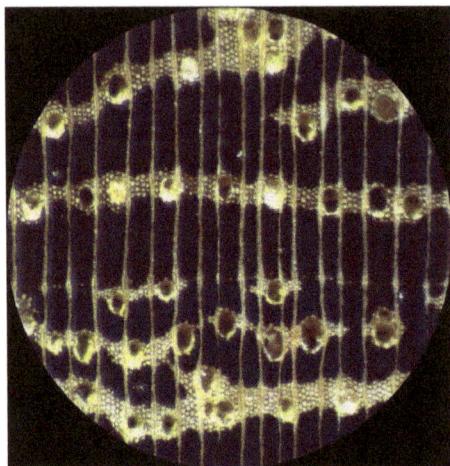

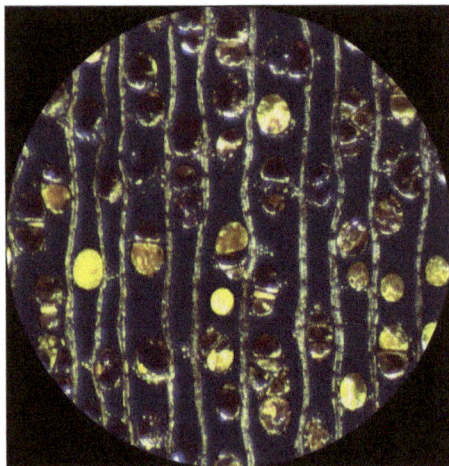

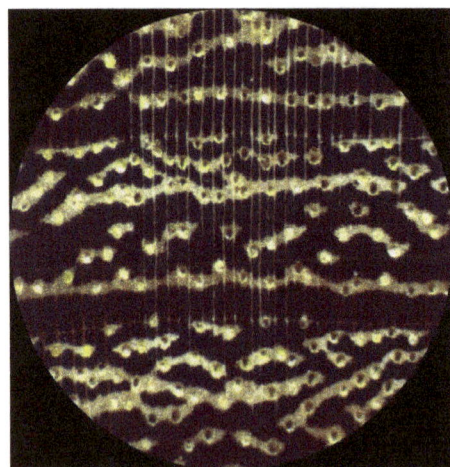

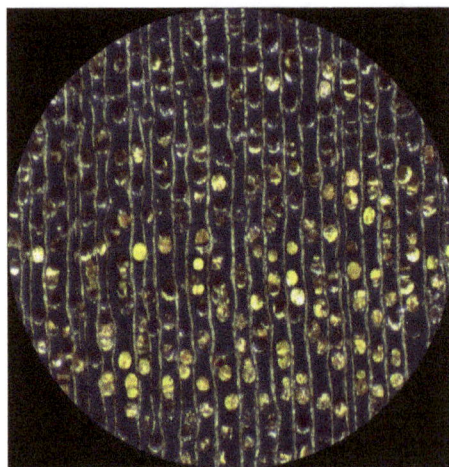

*Handroanthus
    impetiginosus*
Pink Ipe

*Handroanthus
    serratifolius*
Bethabara

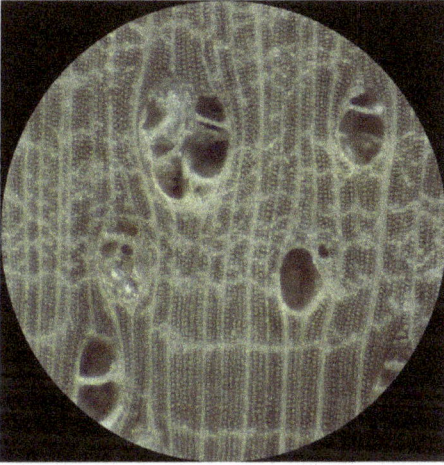

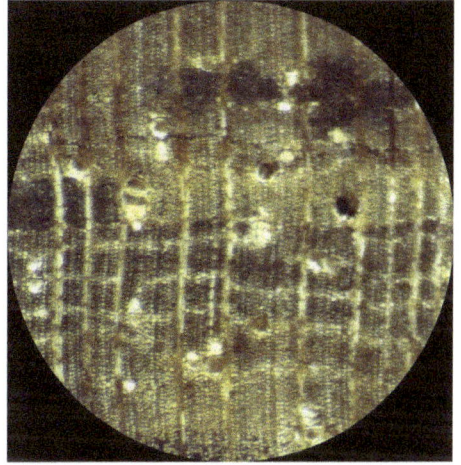

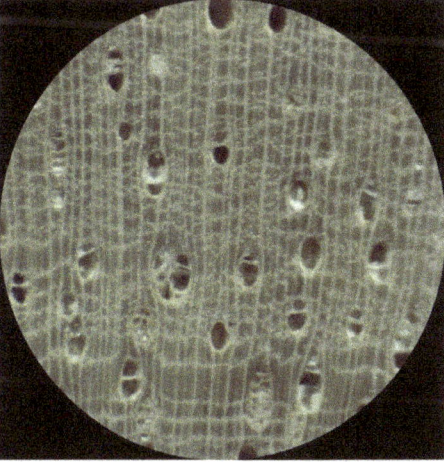

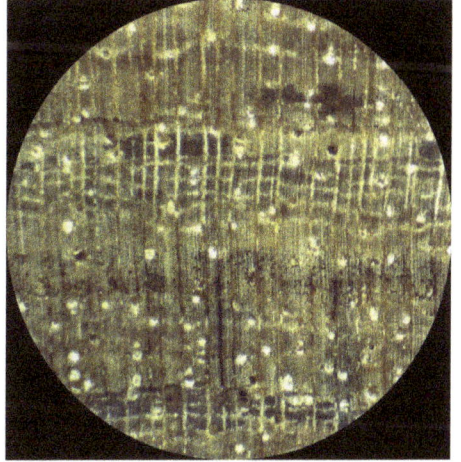

Hevea brasiliensis
Rubbertree

Hopea reticulata
Tie ling

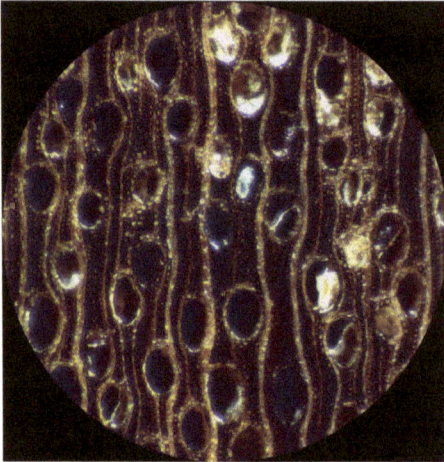

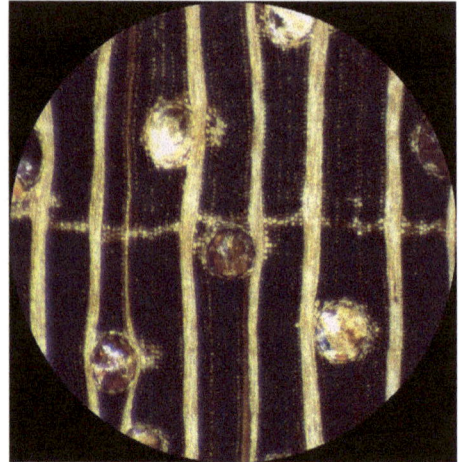

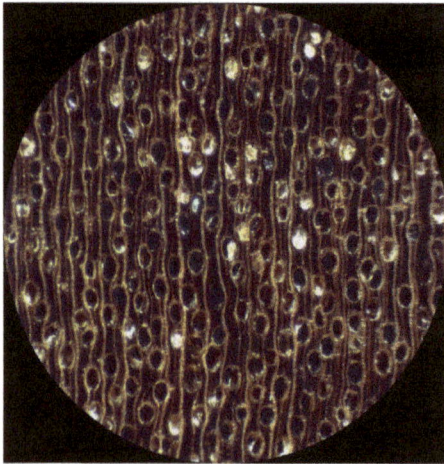

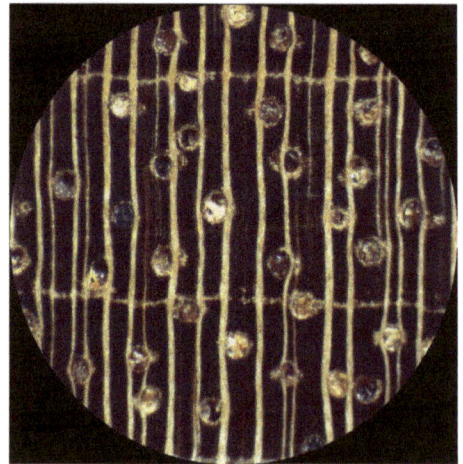

Humiria balsamifera
Oloroso

Hymenaea courbaril
Jatoba

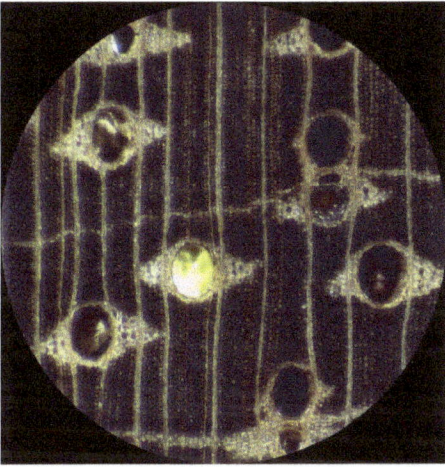

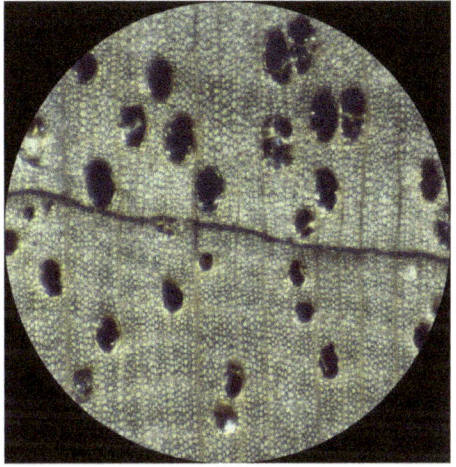

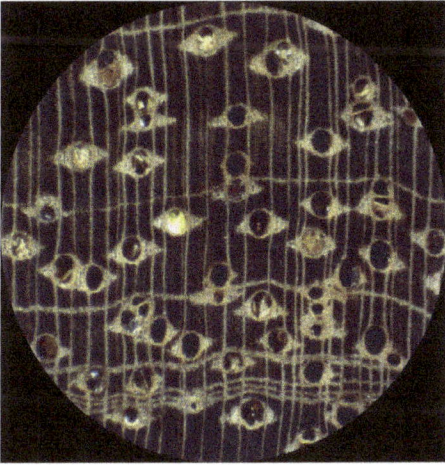

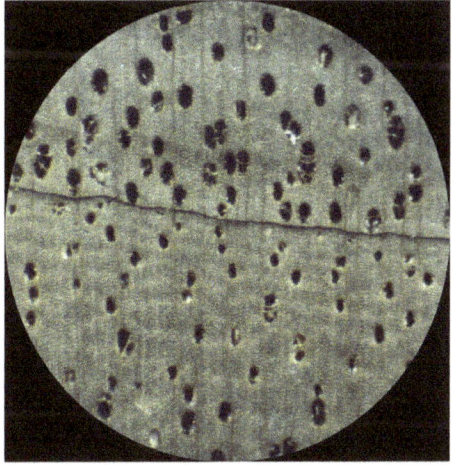

Intsia bijuga
Borneo Teak

Juglans cinerea
Butternut

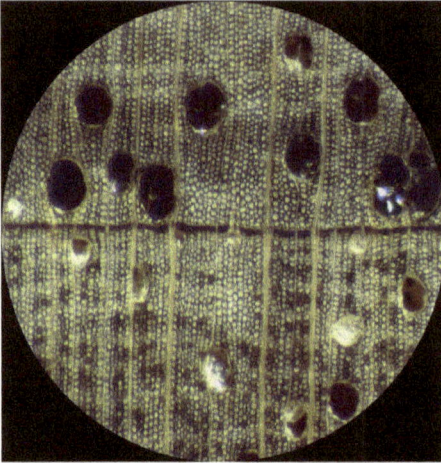

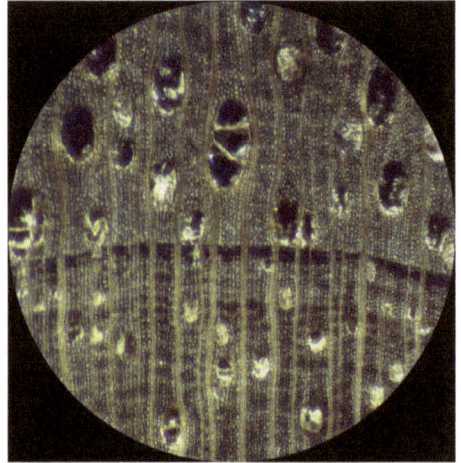

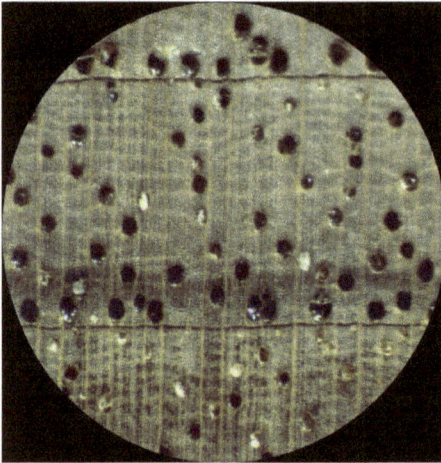

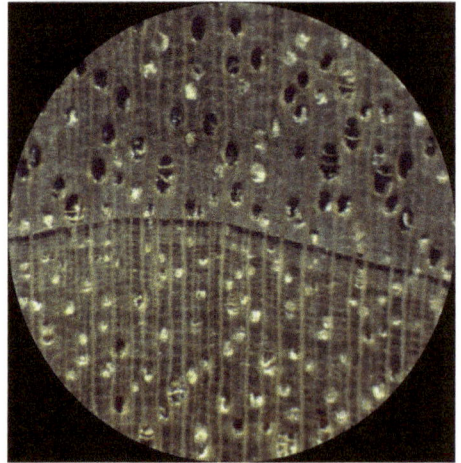

Juglans mandshurica
Manchurica walnut

Juglans nigra
Black Walnut

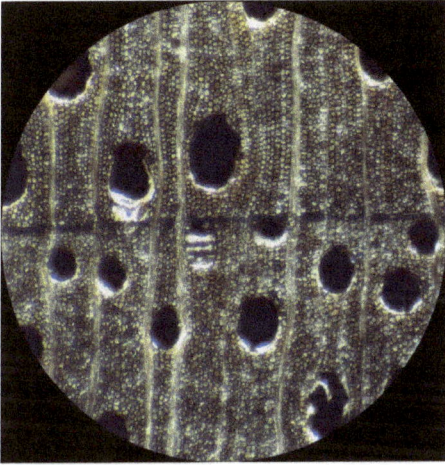

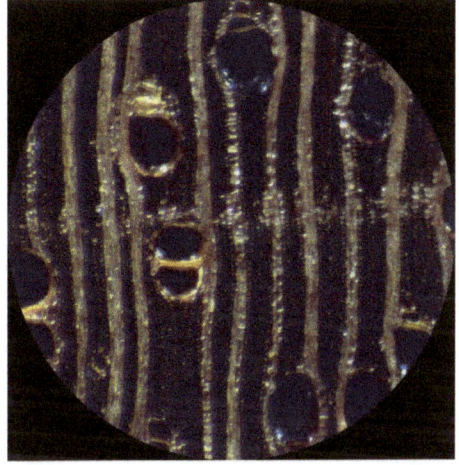

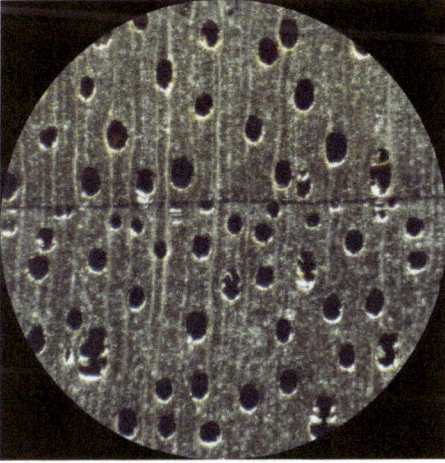

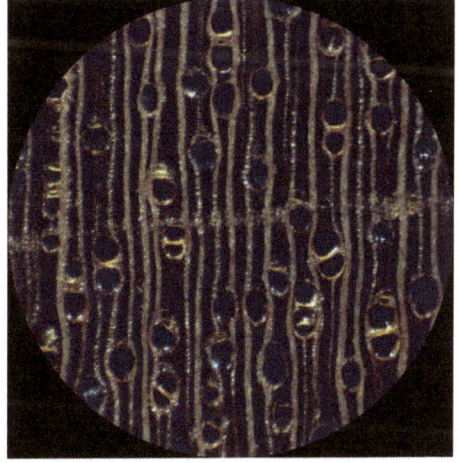

Juglans olanchana
Central America Walnut

Khaya anthotheca
East African Mahogany

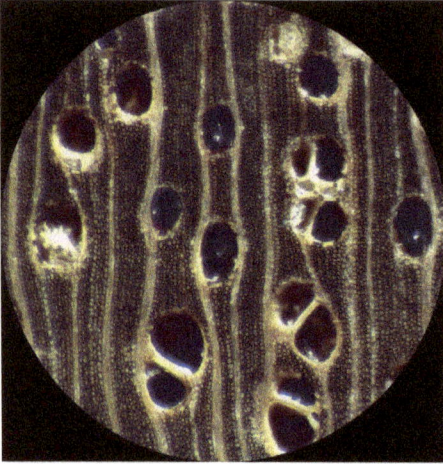

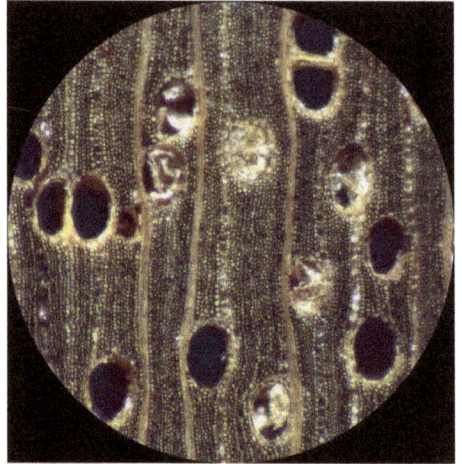

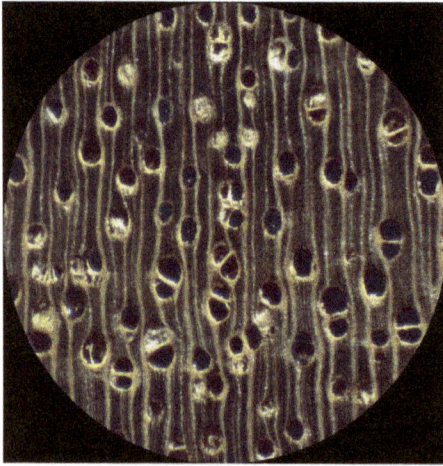

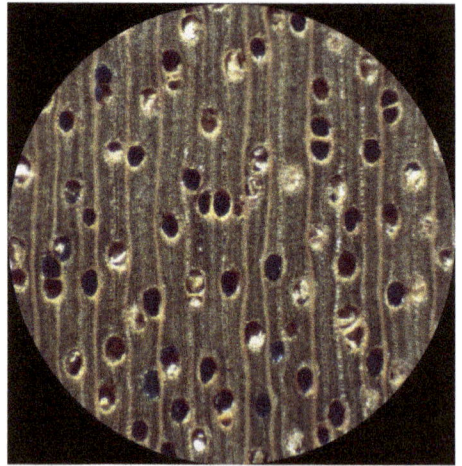

Khaya grandifoliola
African mahogany

Khaya ivorensis
African mahogany

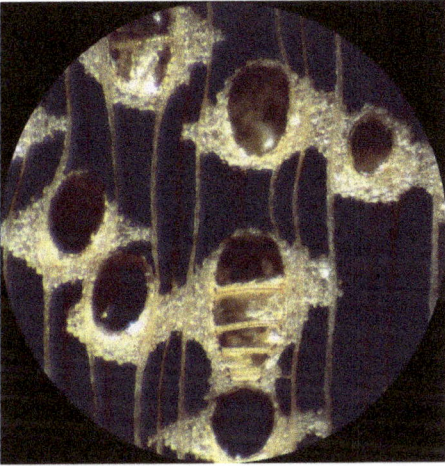

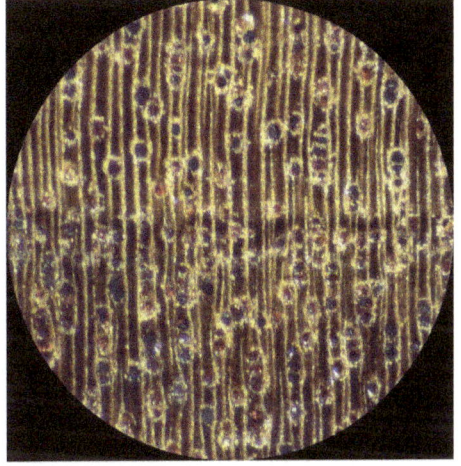

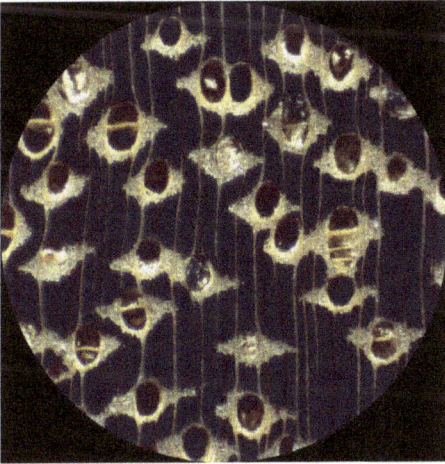

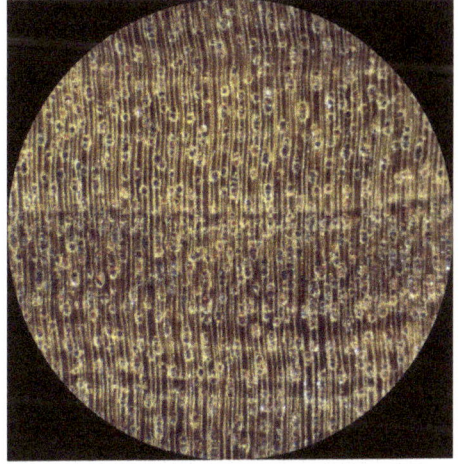

Koompassia
     malaccensis
Kempas

Krugiodendron ferreum
Black Ironwood

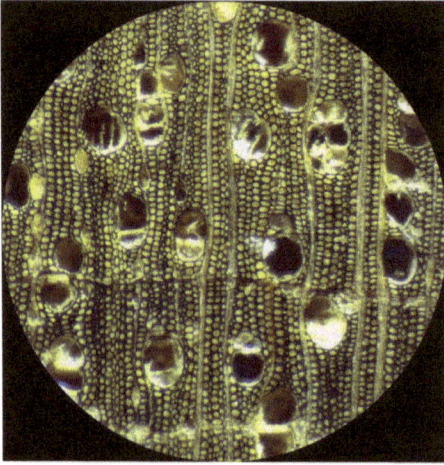

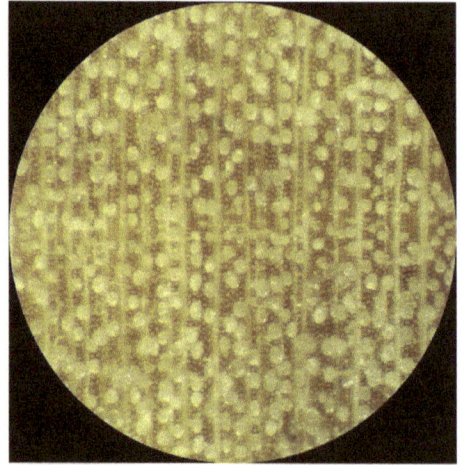

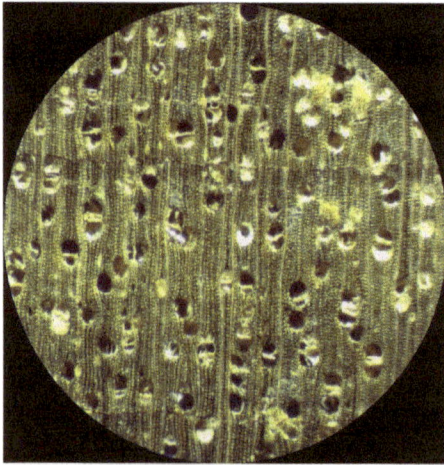

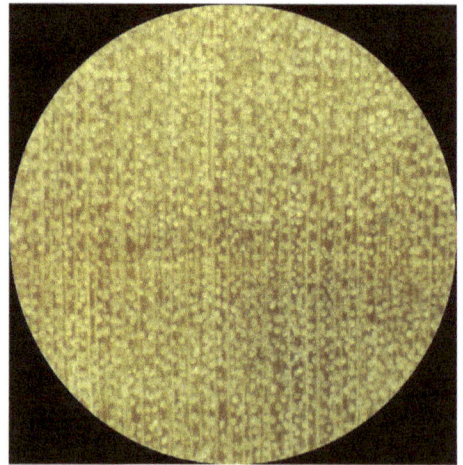

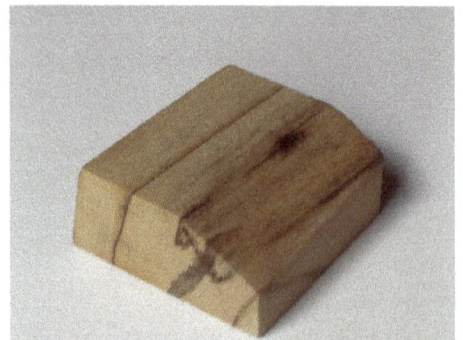

Lindera metcalfiana
Shan Hu Jiao

Liquidambar formosana
Chinesee Sweet Gum

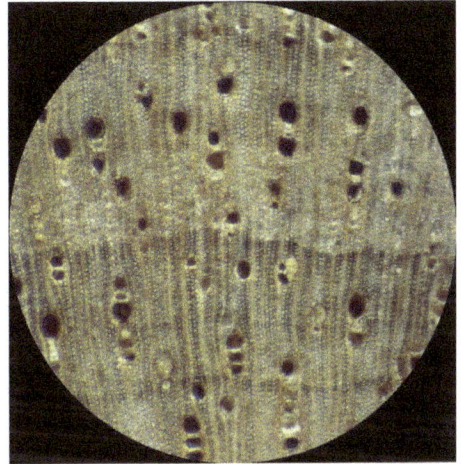

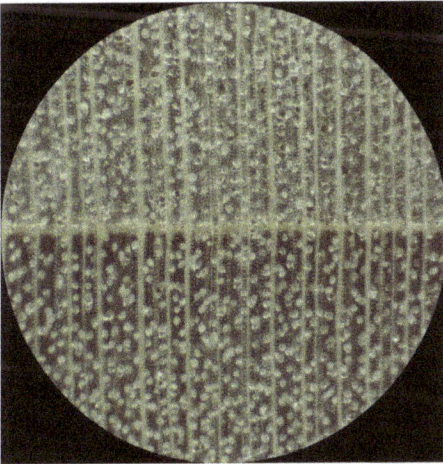

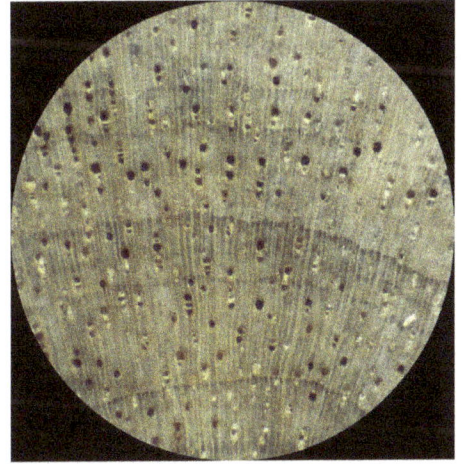

*Liriodendron
    tulipifera*
Tulip Poplar

Litchi chinensis
Lychee

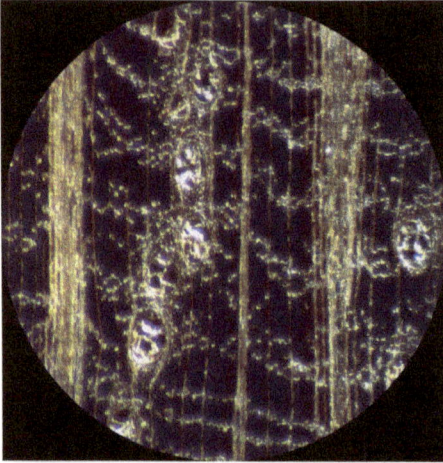

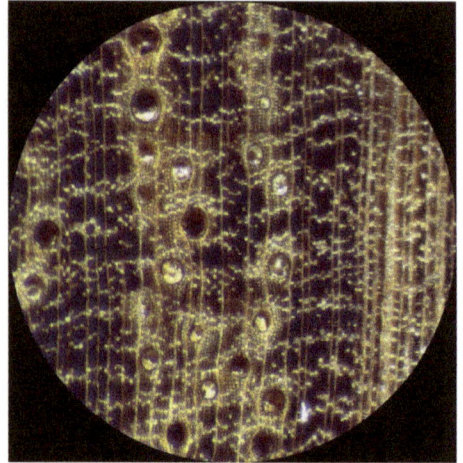

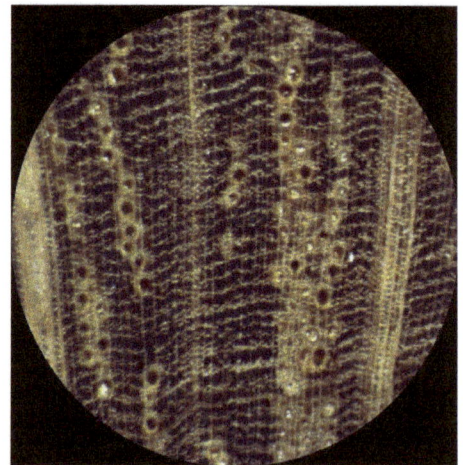

Lithocarpus amygdalifolius
Almon-leaved Tan Oak

Lithocarpus glaber
Hong chou

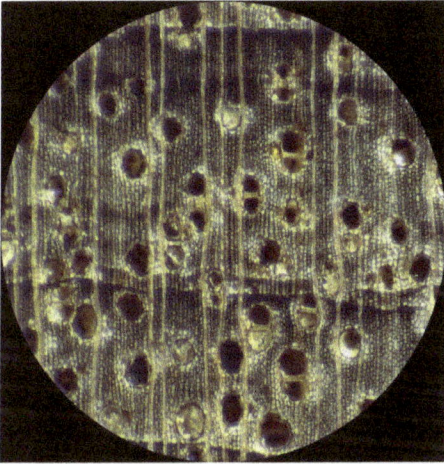

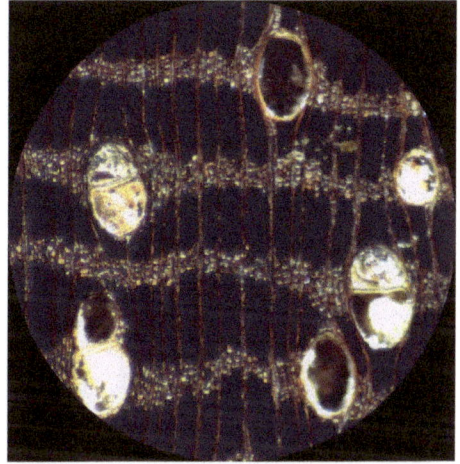

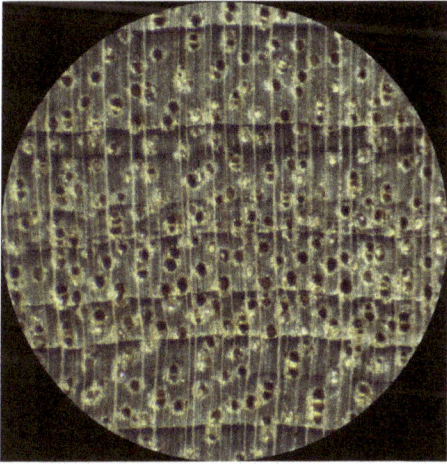

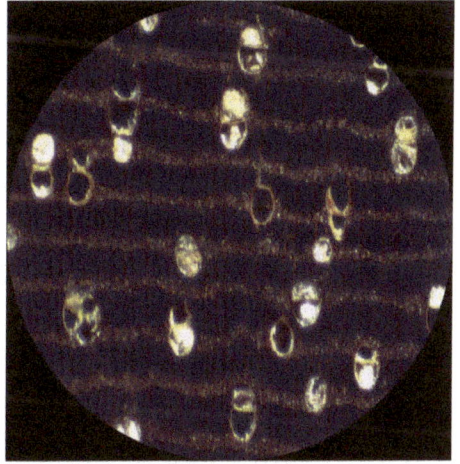

Litsea coreana
Bao Pi Zhang

Lophira alata
Ekki

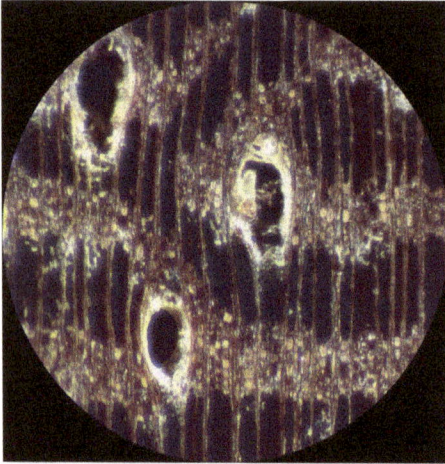

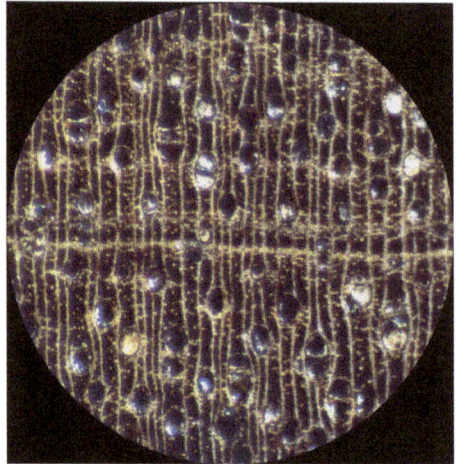

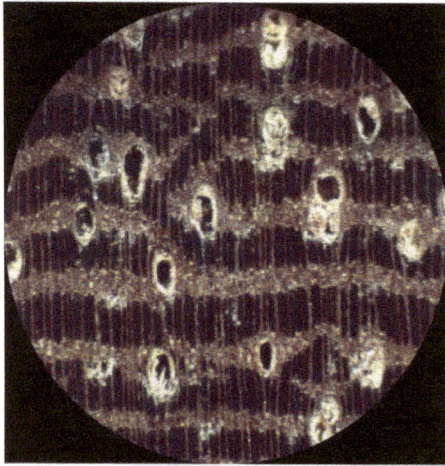

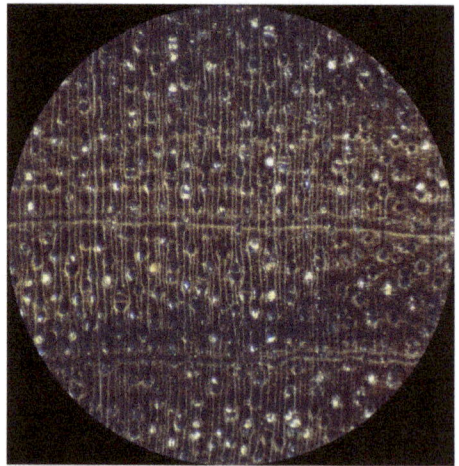

Lophira lanceolata
Dwarf Red Ironwood Tree

Machaerium scleroxylon
Santos Palisander

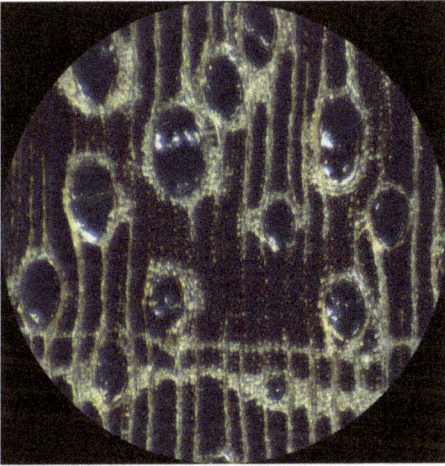

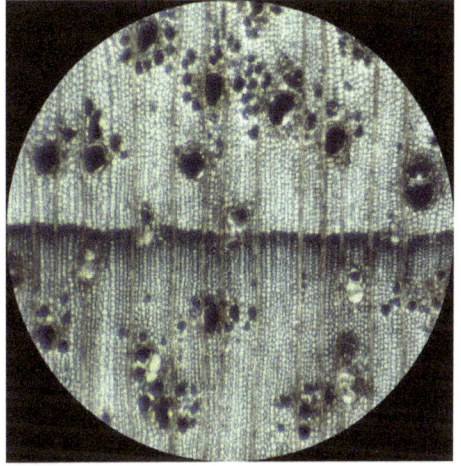

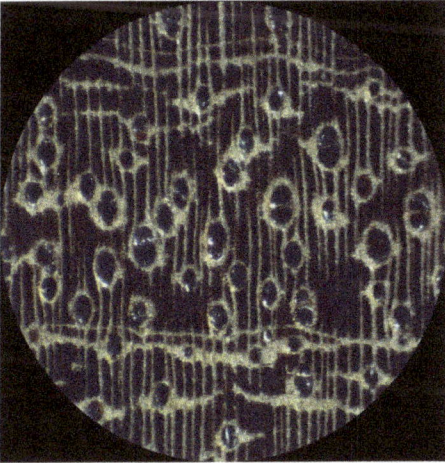

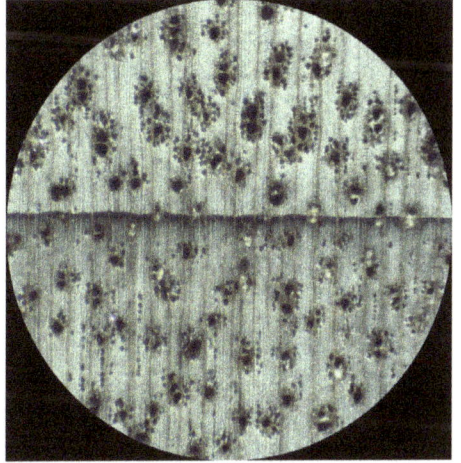

Machaerium villosum
Jacarandá-pardo

Machilus pauhoi
Bao Hua Nan

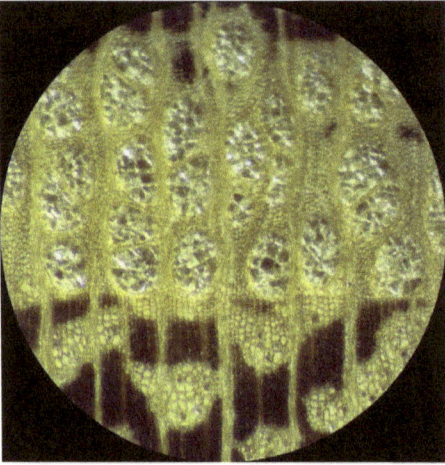

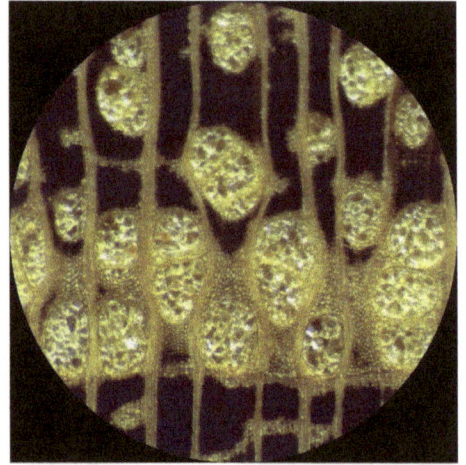

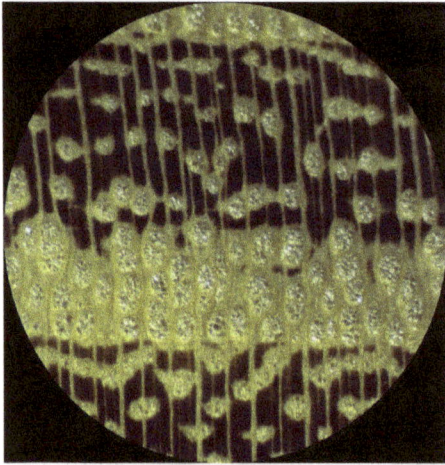

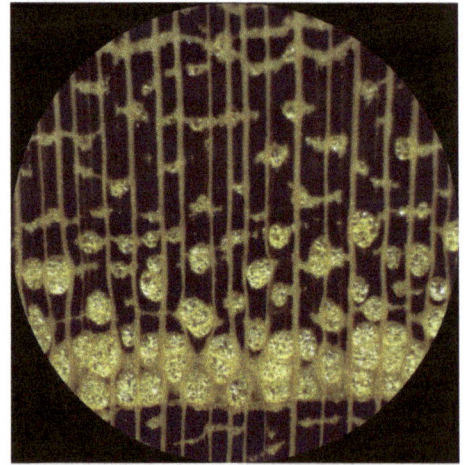

Maclura pomifera
Osage orange

Maclura tricuspidata
Zhe mu

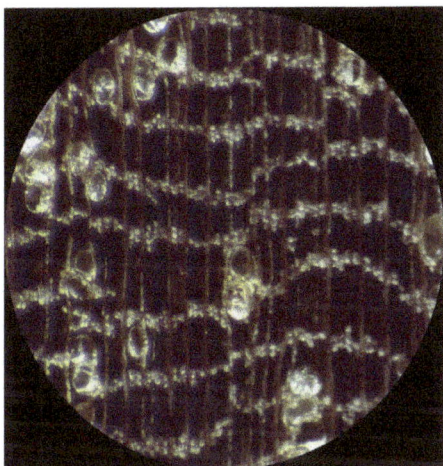

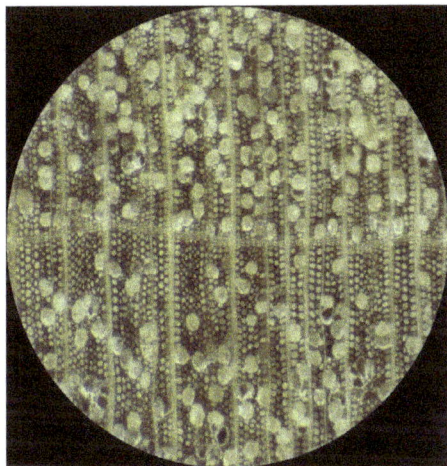

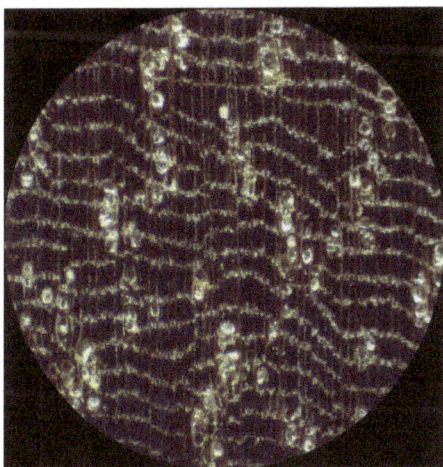

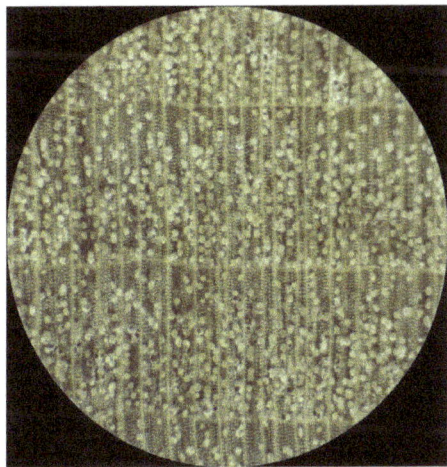

Madhuca hainanensis
Hainan butter-tree

Magnolia virginiana
Sweetbay

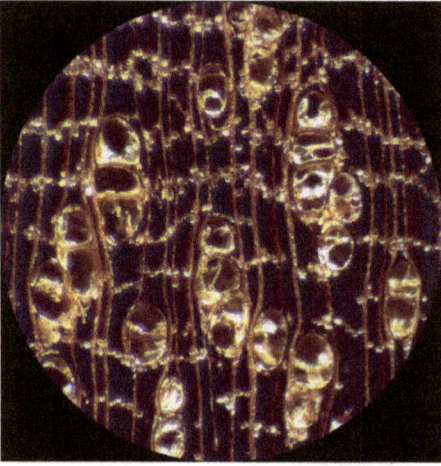

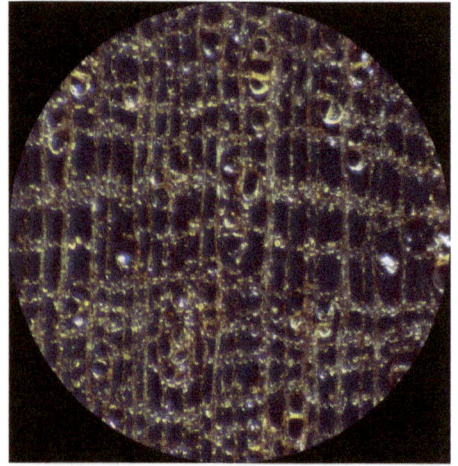

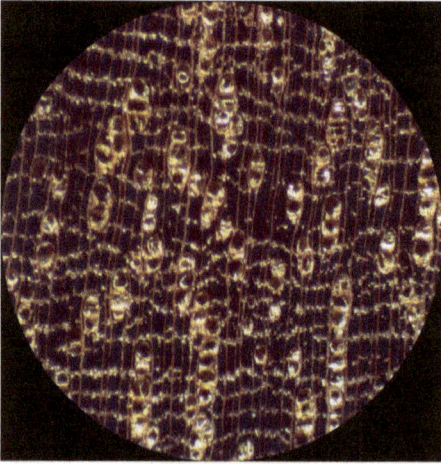

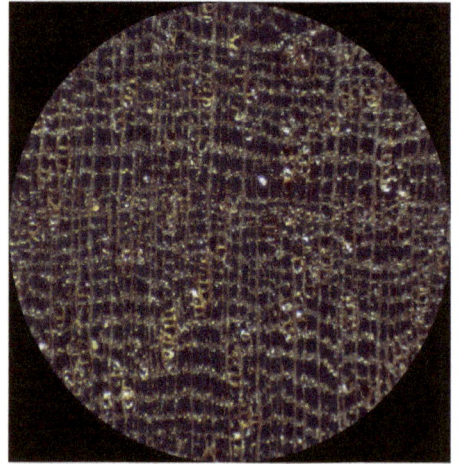

Manilkara bidentata
Bulletwood

Manilkara huberi
Massaranduba

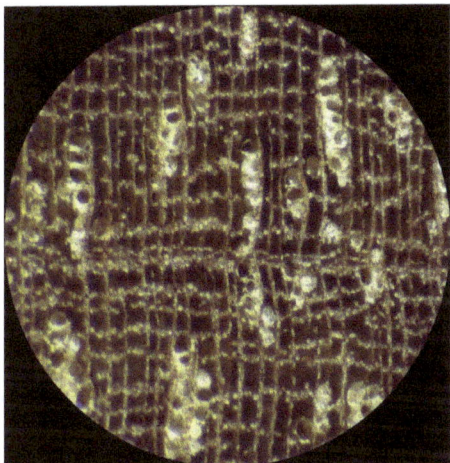

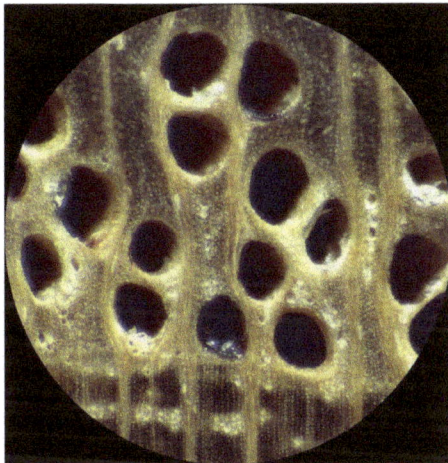

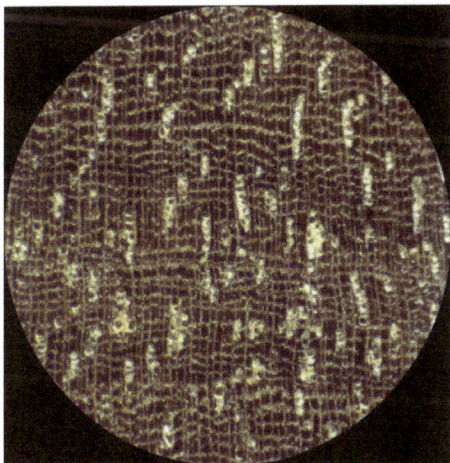

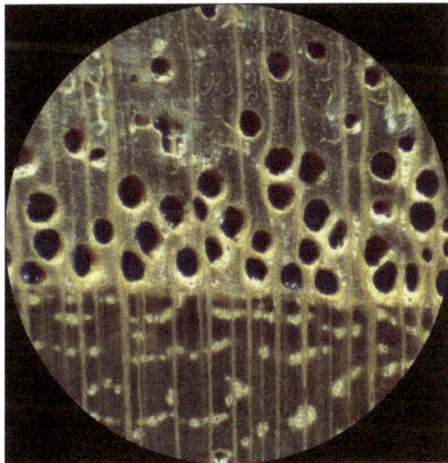

Manilkara zapota
Sapodilla

Melia azedarach
China-berry

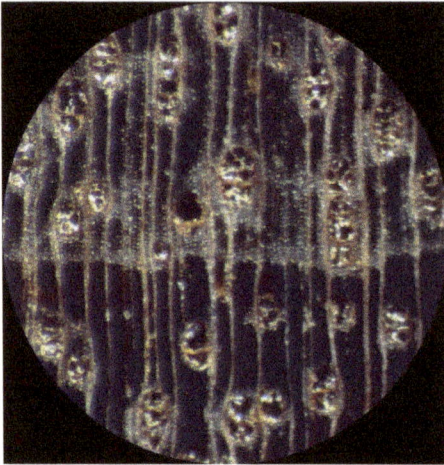

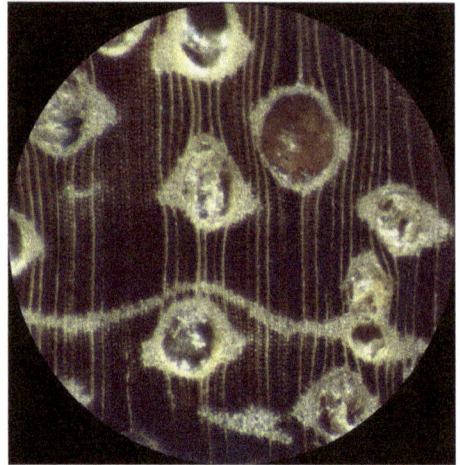

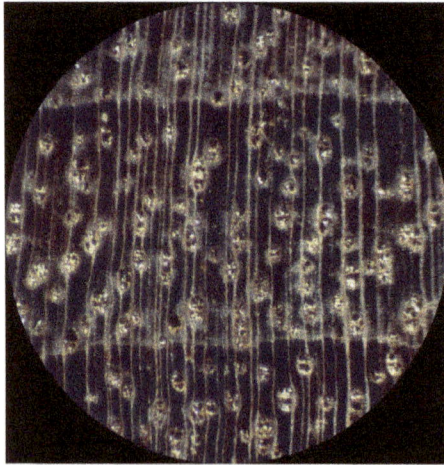

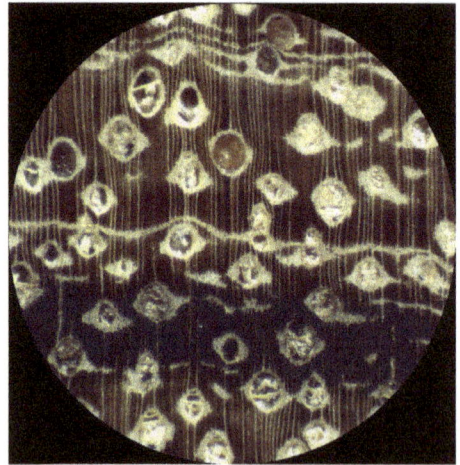

Metopium brownei
Chechem

Microberlinia bisulcata
Zebrawood

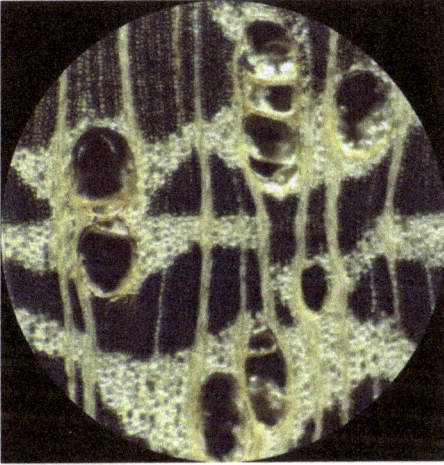

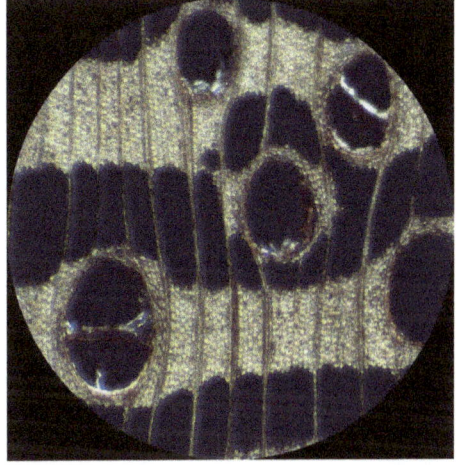

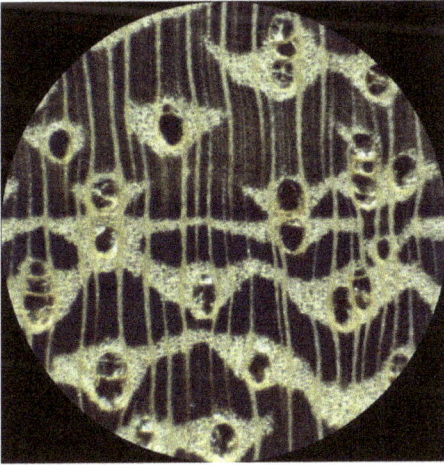

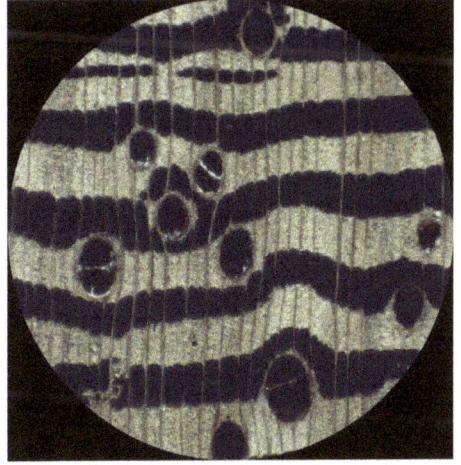

Milicia excelsa
Iroko

Millettia laurentii
Wenge

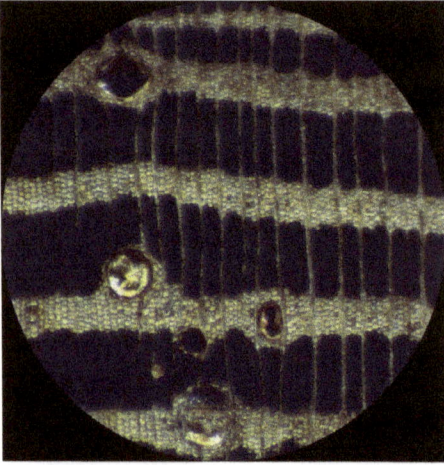

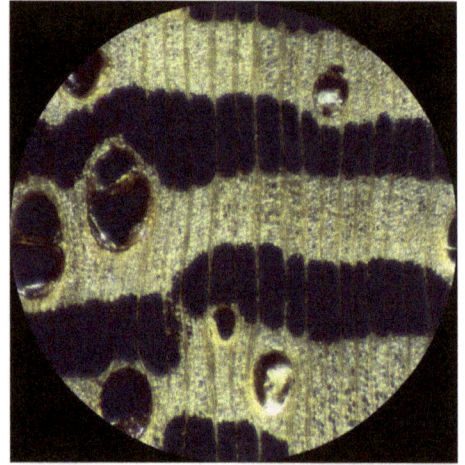

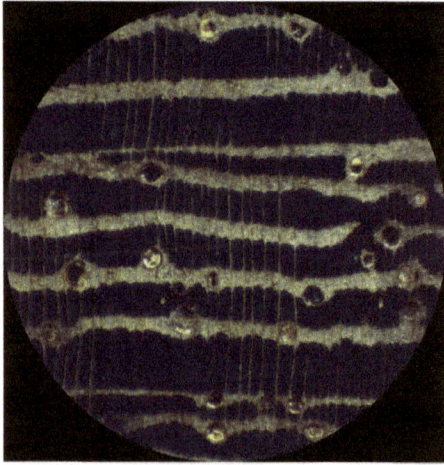

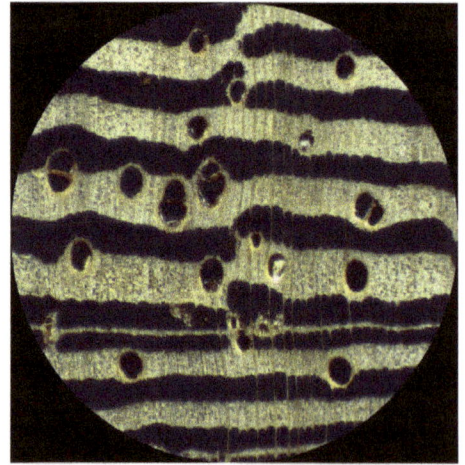

Millettia leucantha
Thinwin

Millettia stuhlmannii
Panga Panga

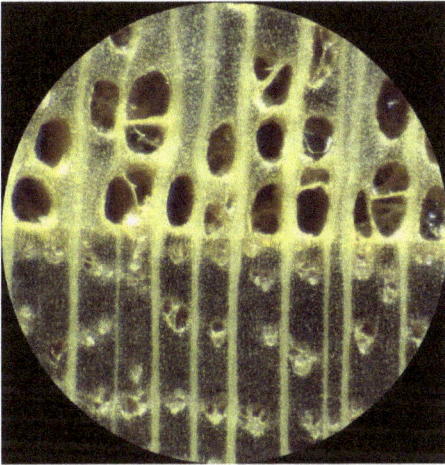

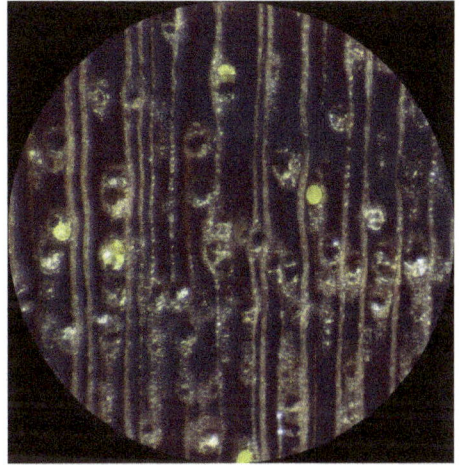

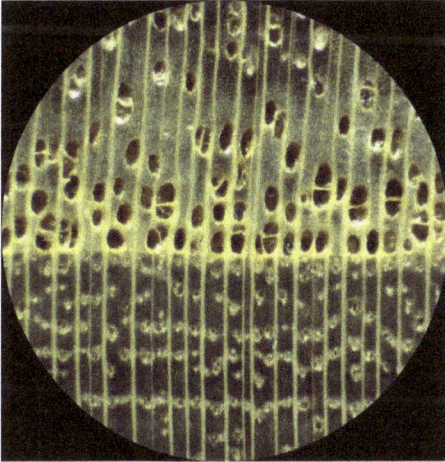

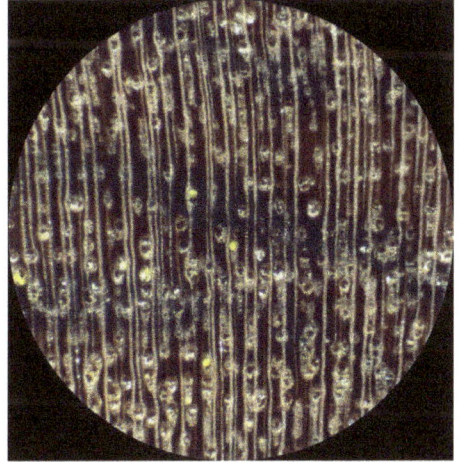

Morus alba
Mulberry

Myracrodruon balansae
Uranday

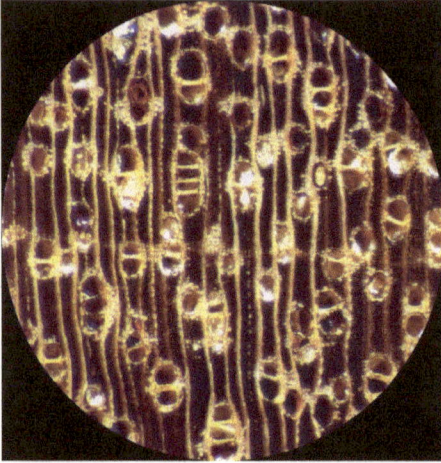

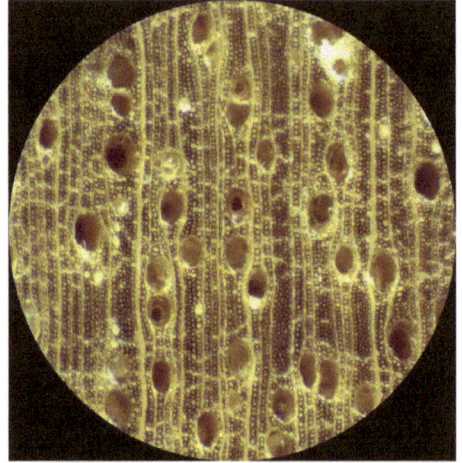

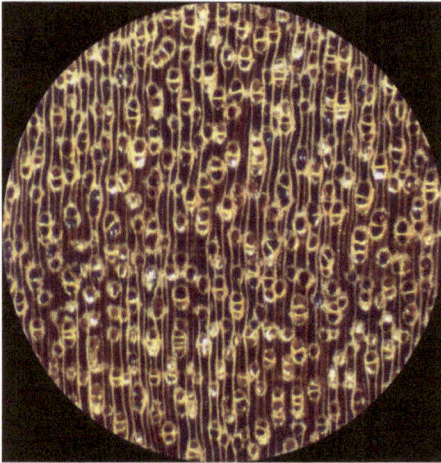

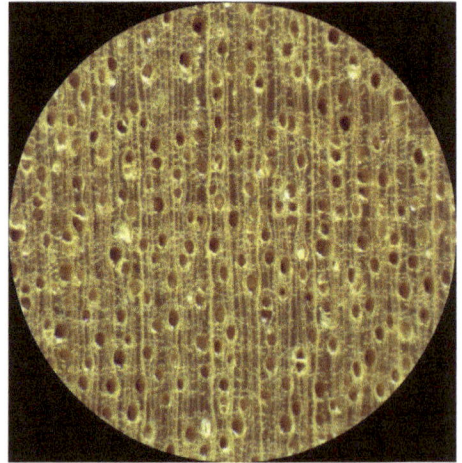

Myroxylon balsamum
Balsamo

Nauclea orientalis
Yellow Cheesewood

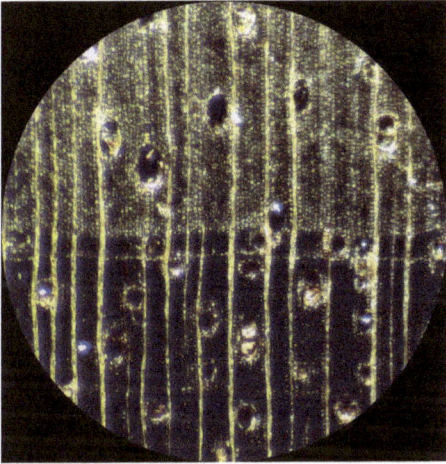

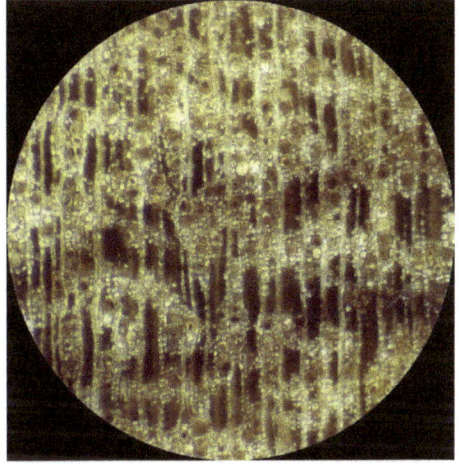

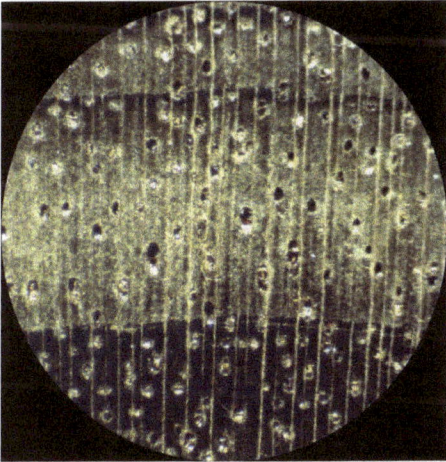

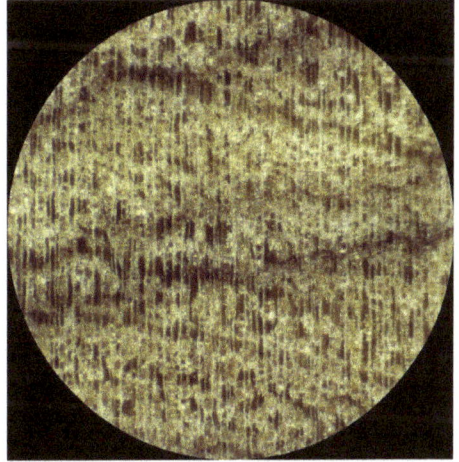

Ocotea bullata
Stinkwood

Olea hochstetteri
Olmasi

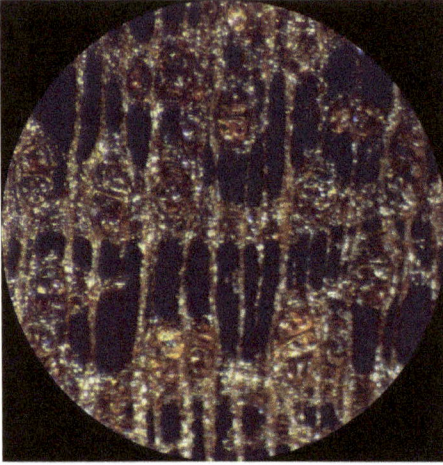

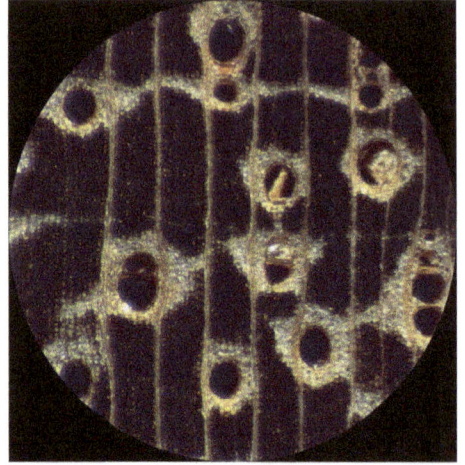

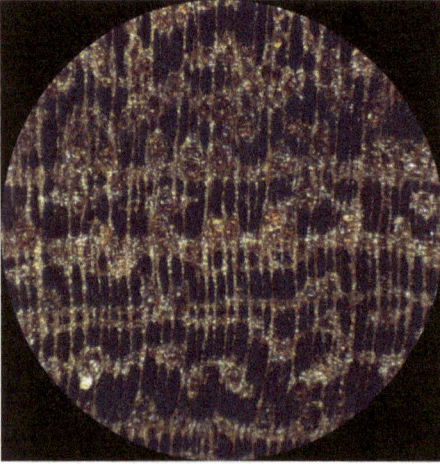

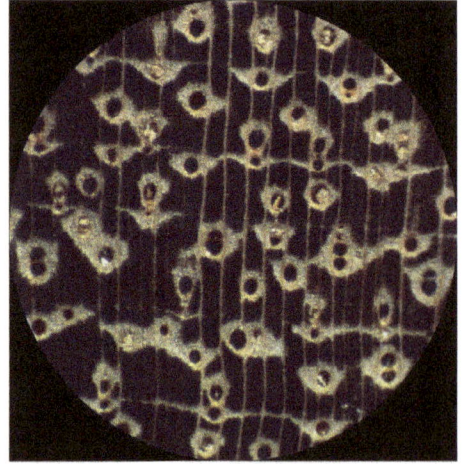

Olneya tesota

Desert Ironwood

Ormosia xylocarpa

Mujia hong dou

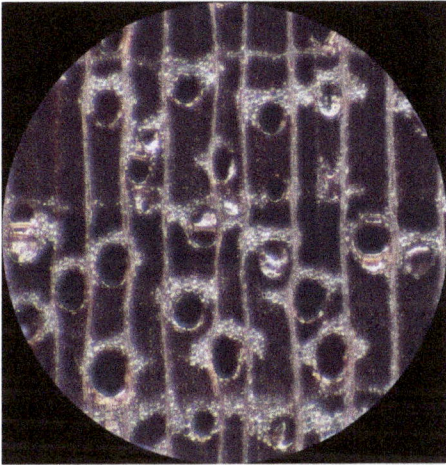

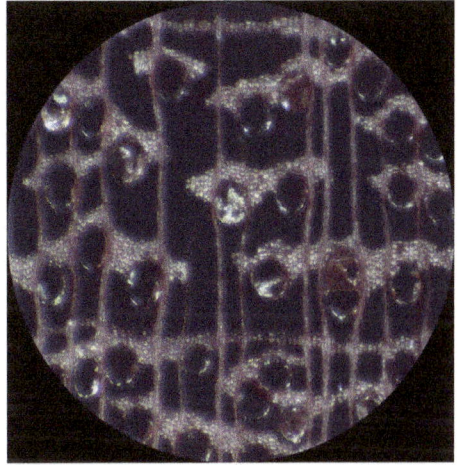

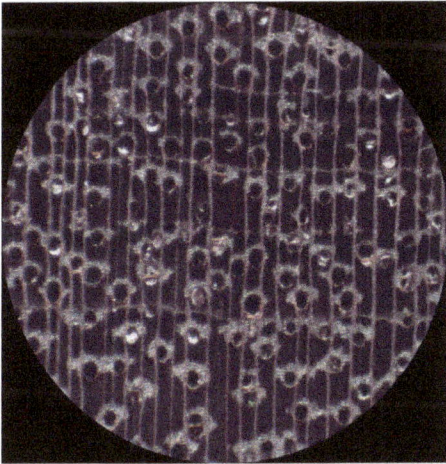

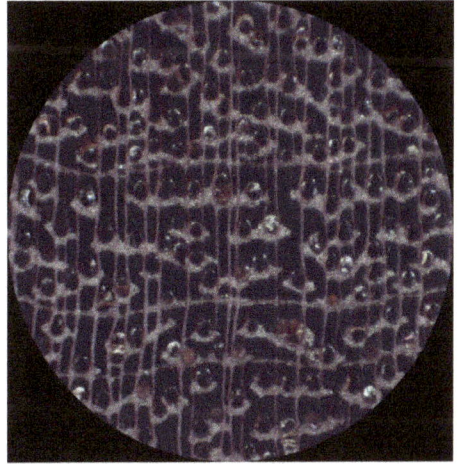

Peltogyne paniculata
Purpleheart

Peltogyne pubescens
Pau-roxo

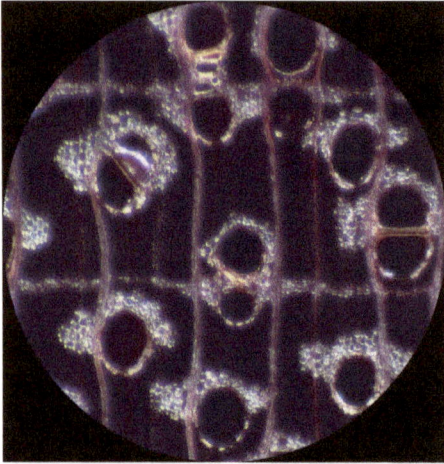

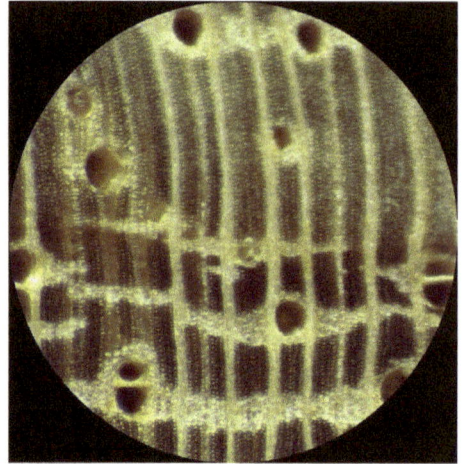

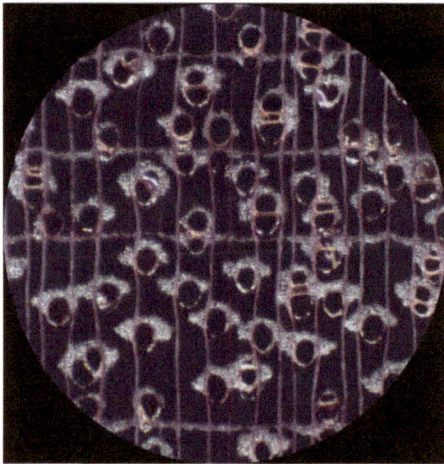

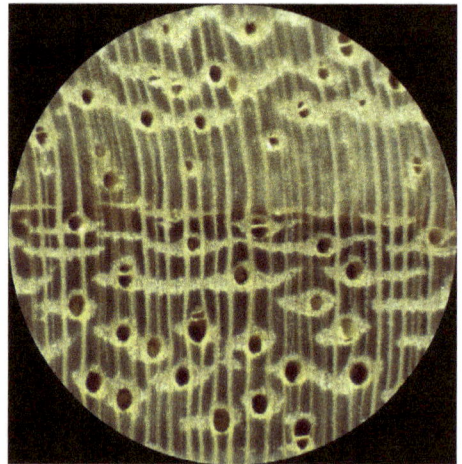

Peltogyne venosa
Amaranto

Pericopsis elata
African Teak

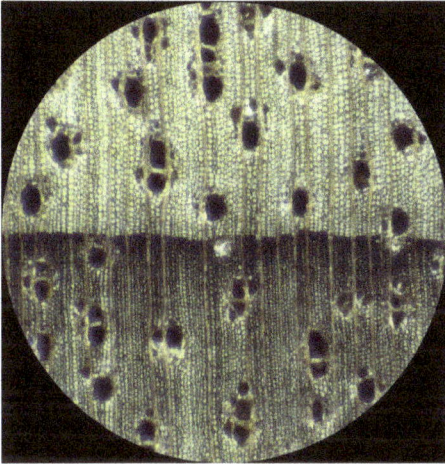

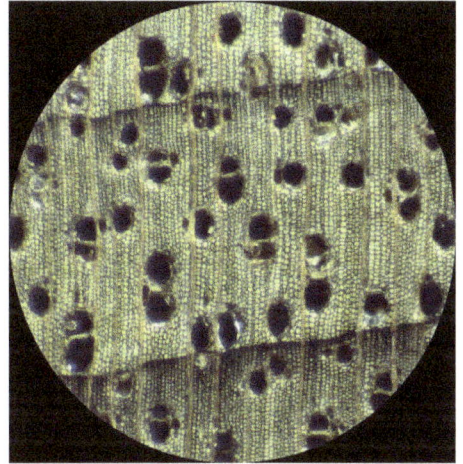

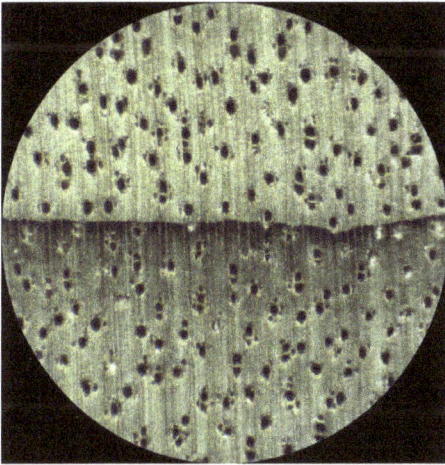

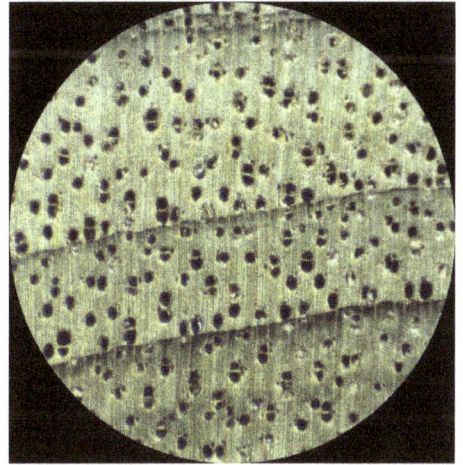

Phoebe bournei
Min nan

Phoebe sheareri
Zi nan

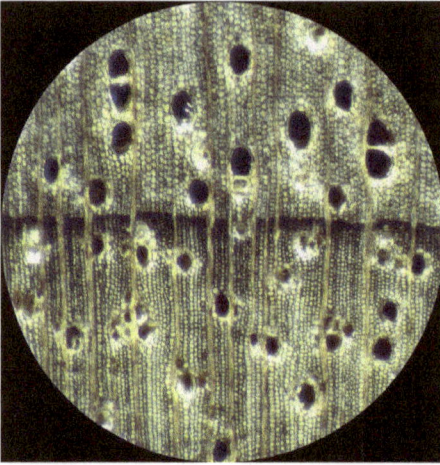

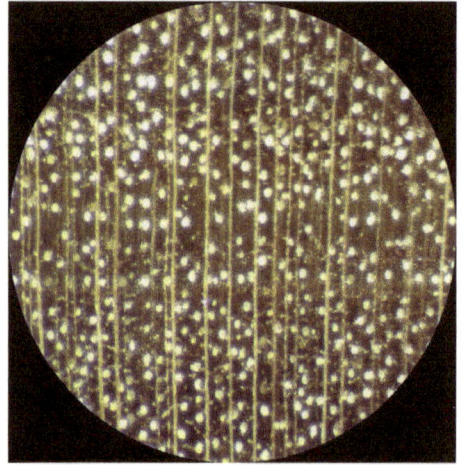

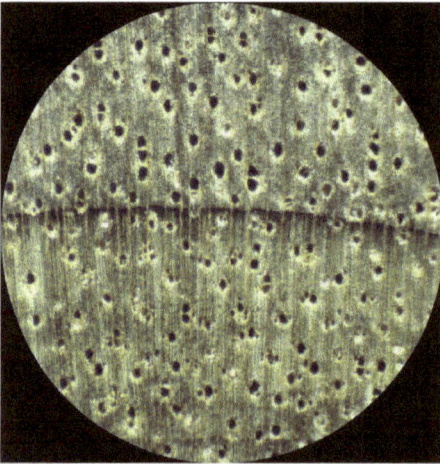

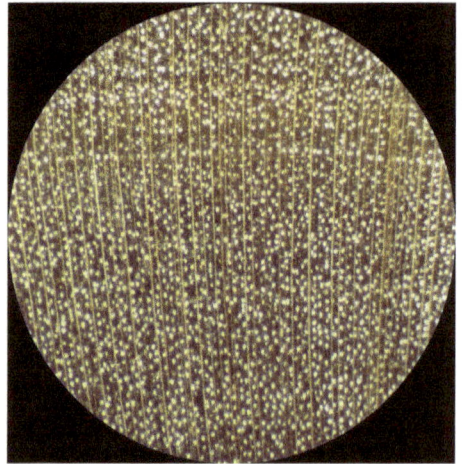

Phoebe zhennan

Zhen nan

*Photinia
davidasoniate*

Luo mu shi nan

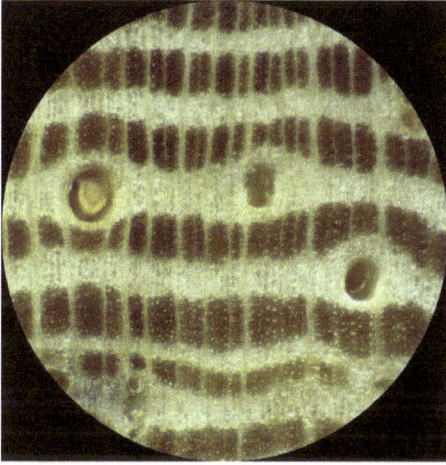

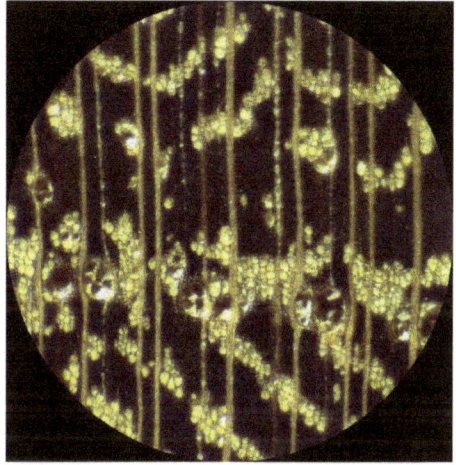

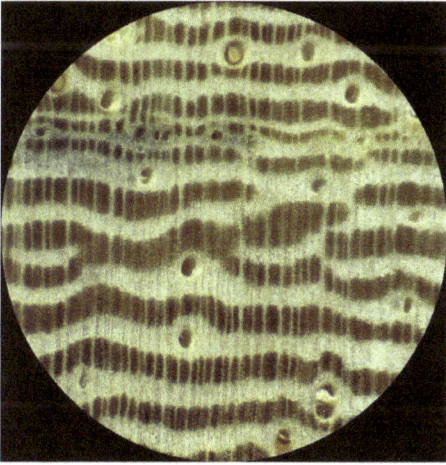

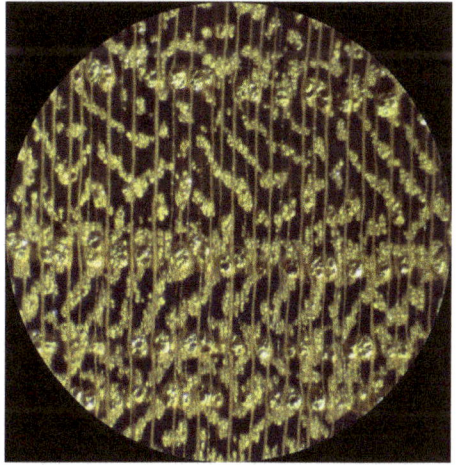

Piscidia communis
Jamaica Dogwood

Pistacia chinensis
Chinese Pistachio

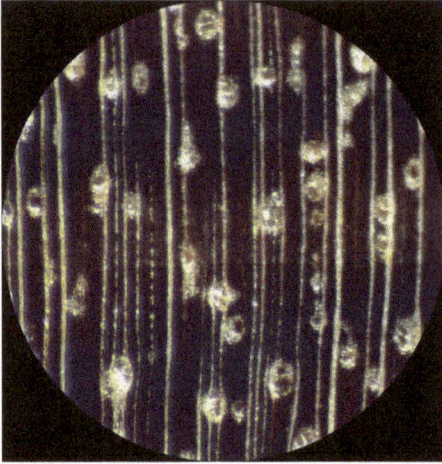

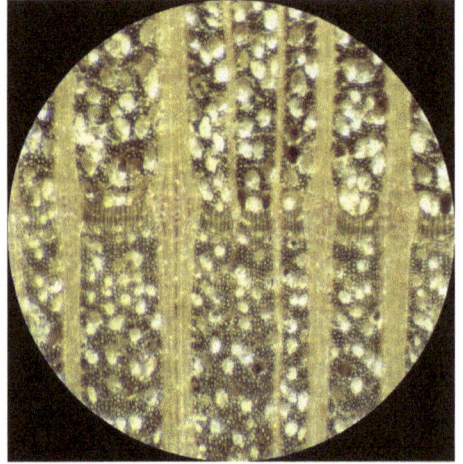

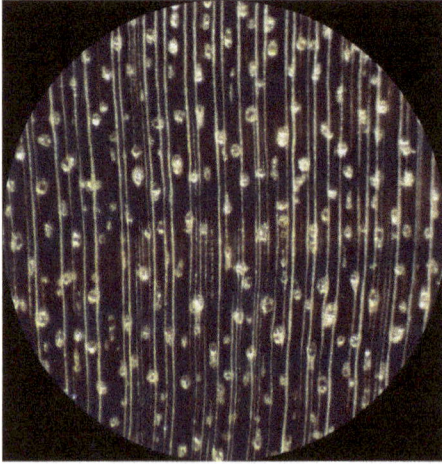

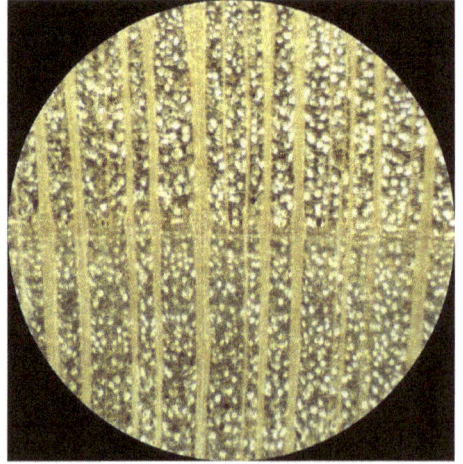

Pistacia weinmannifolia

Zi you mu

Platanus acerifolia

Plane-Tree

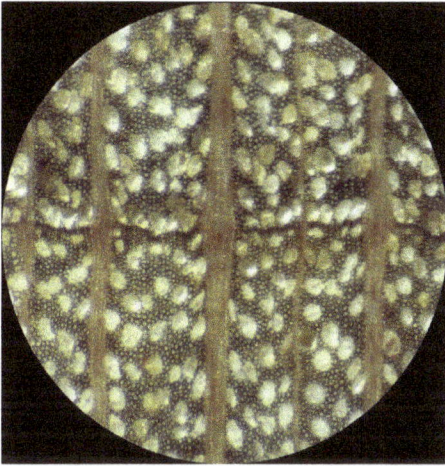

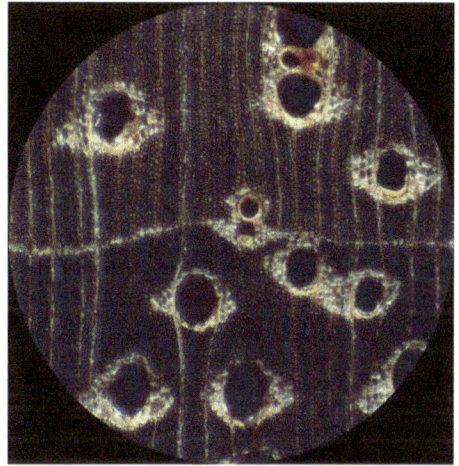

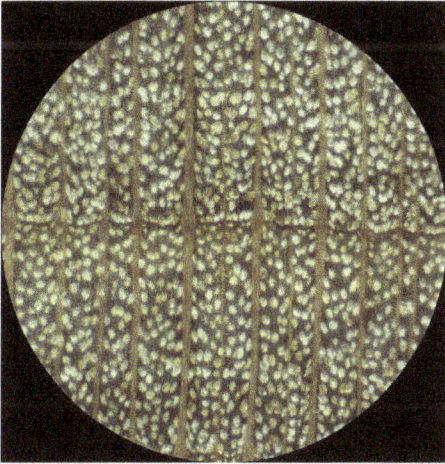

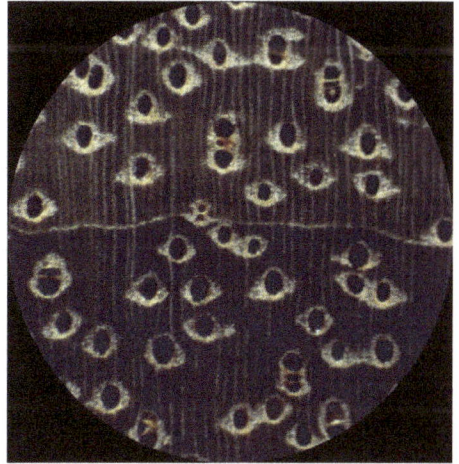

Platanus occidentalis
Sycamore

*Platymiscium
dimorphandrum*
Macawood

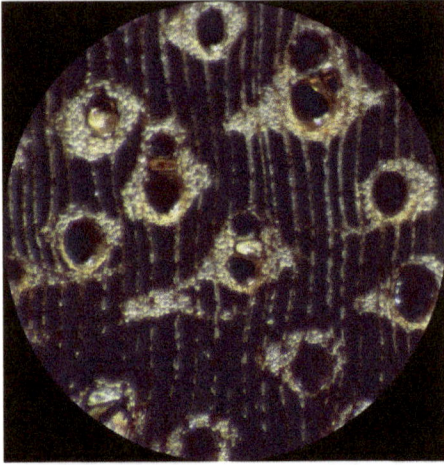

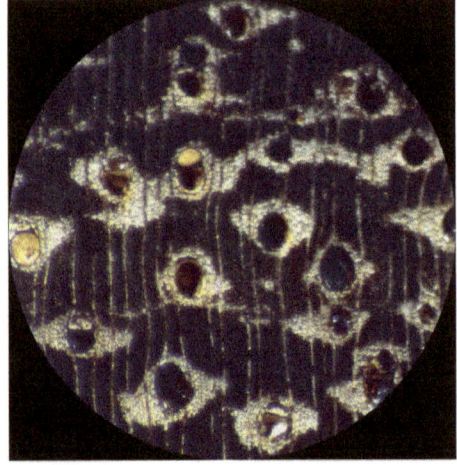

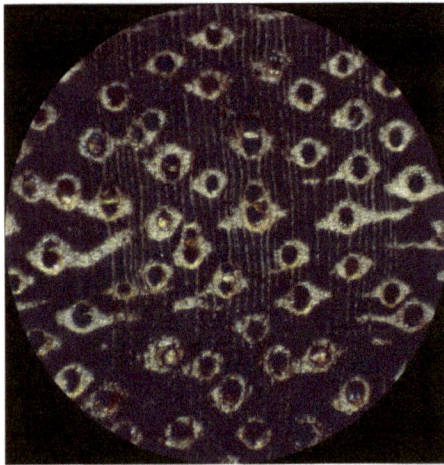

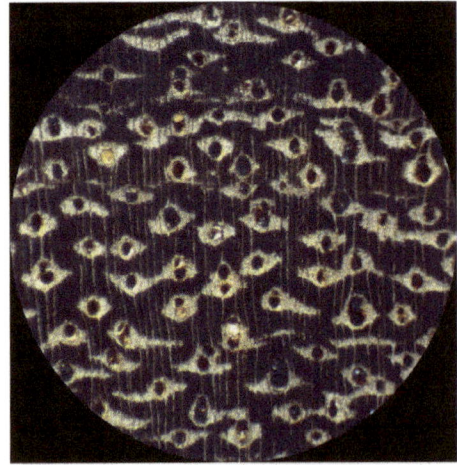

Platymiscium pinnatum
Granadillo

Platymiscium yucatanum
Macawood

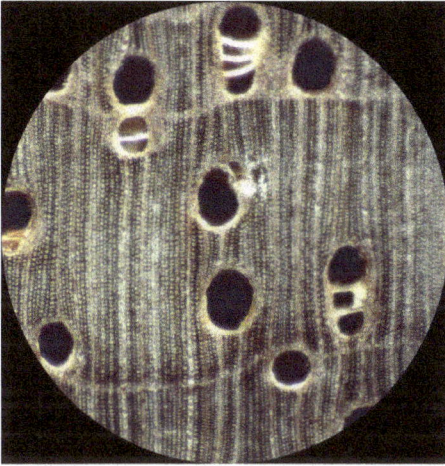

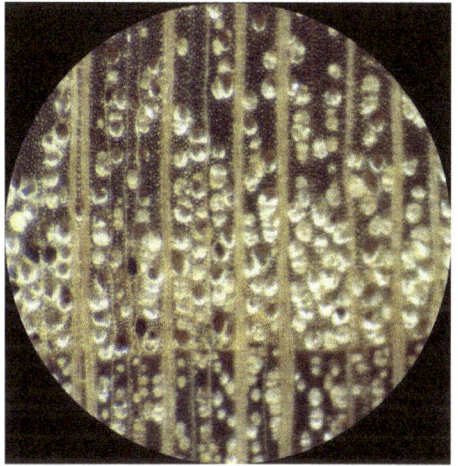

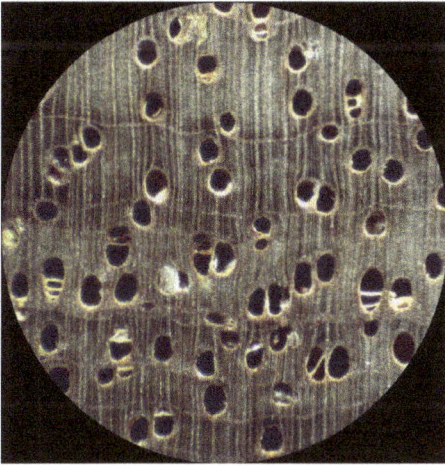

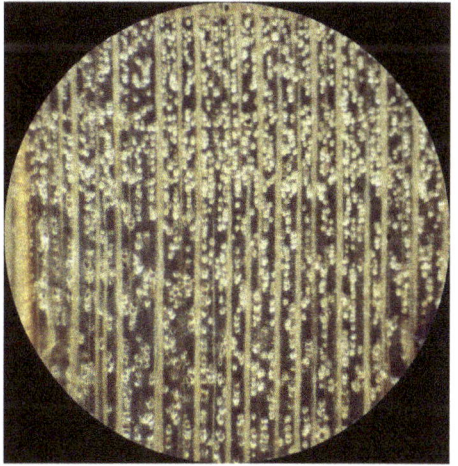

Pometia pinnata
Island Lychee

Prunus avium
Sweet Cherry

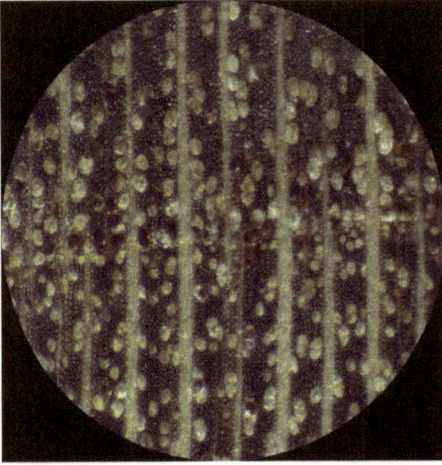

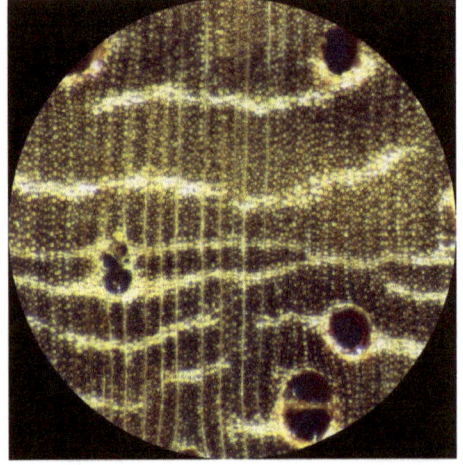

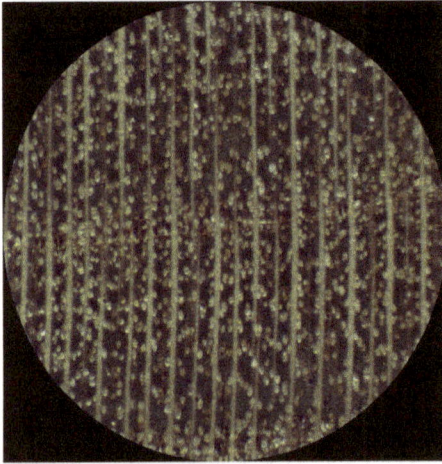

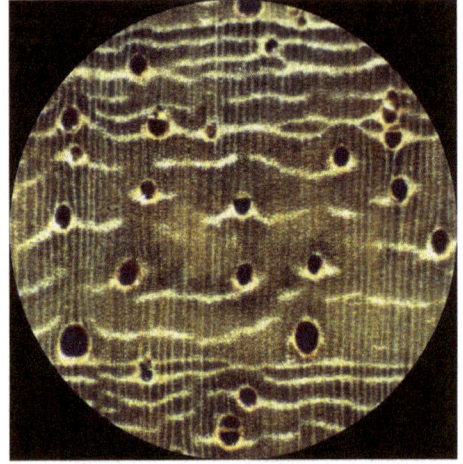

Prunus serotina
Black Cherry

Pterocarpus angolensis
Muninga

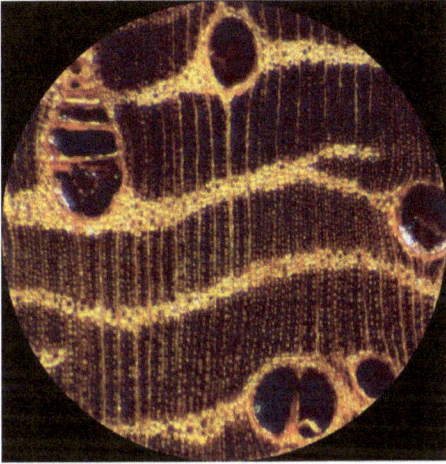

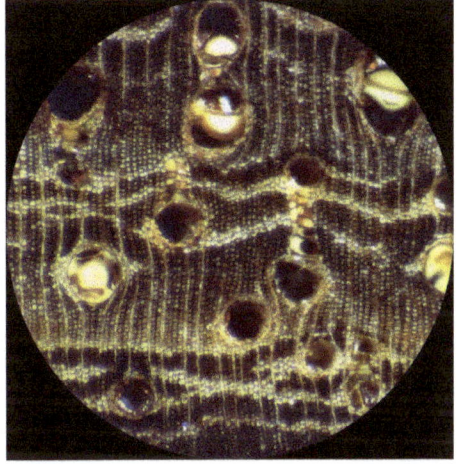

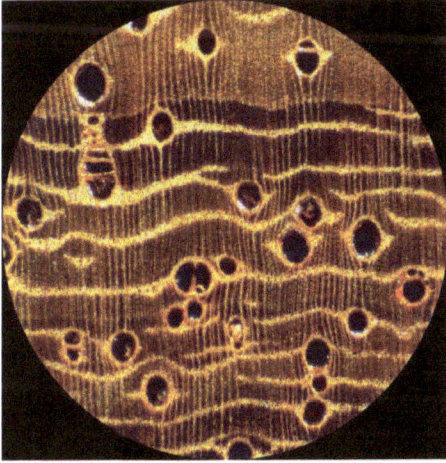

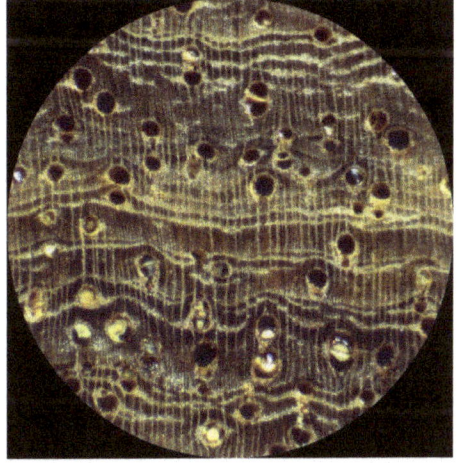

Pterocarpus angolensis
African Bloodwood

Pterocarpus antunesii
Chiviri

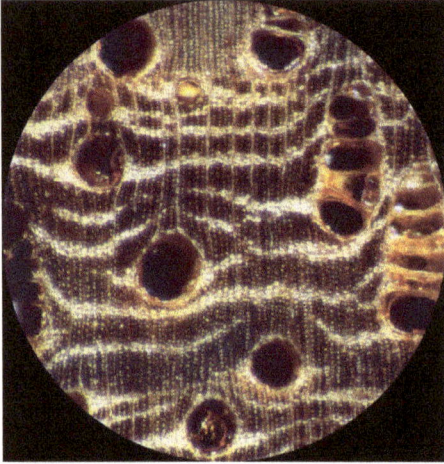

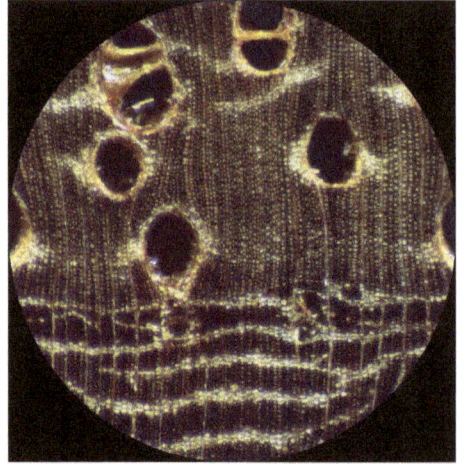

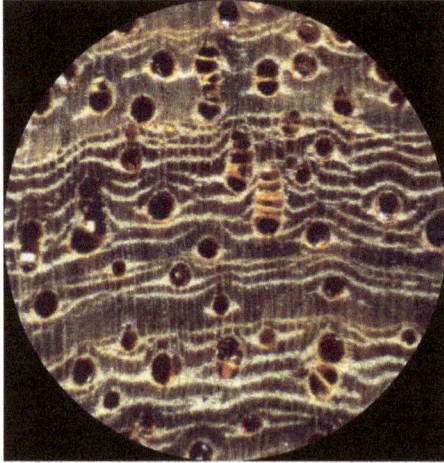

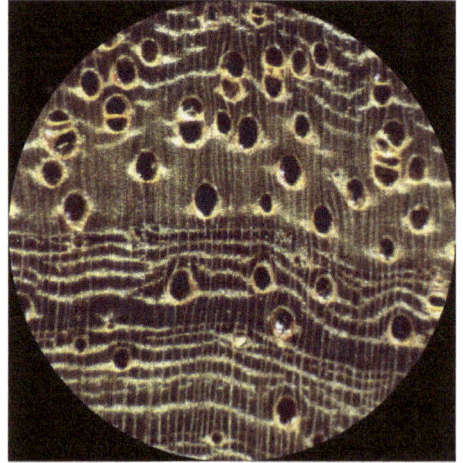

*Pterocarpus
    cambodianus*
Vietnam Padauk

*Pterocarpus
    dalbergioides*
Andaman Padauk

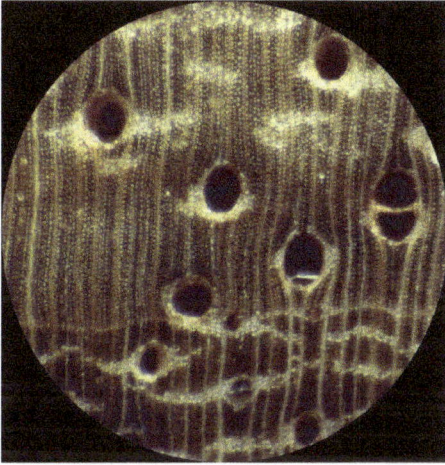

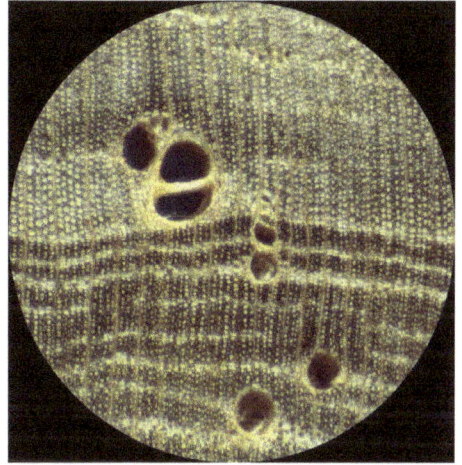

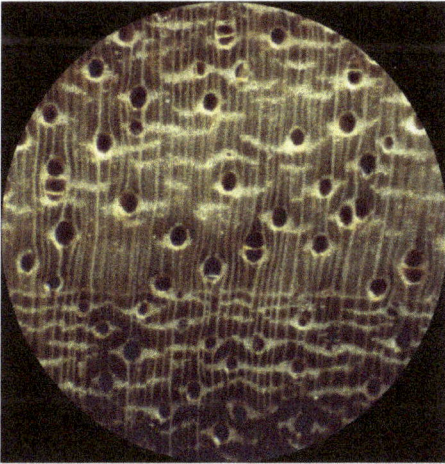

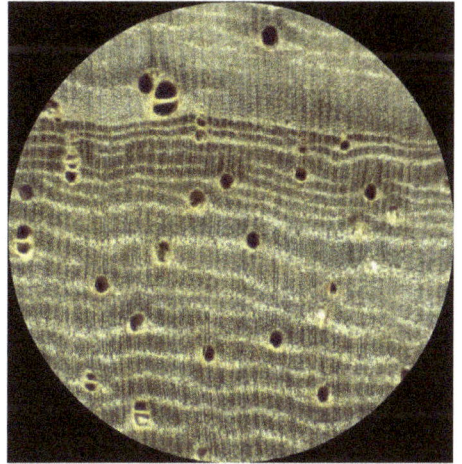

Pterocarpus erinaceus

Ambila

Pterocarpus indicus

Narra

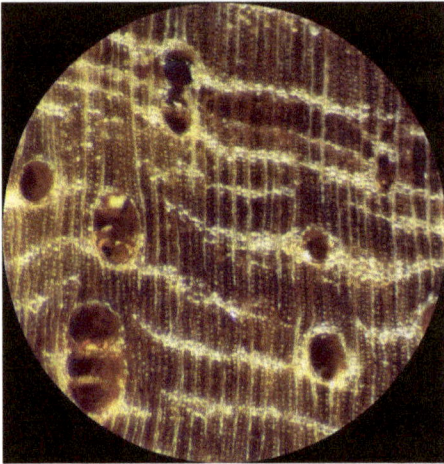

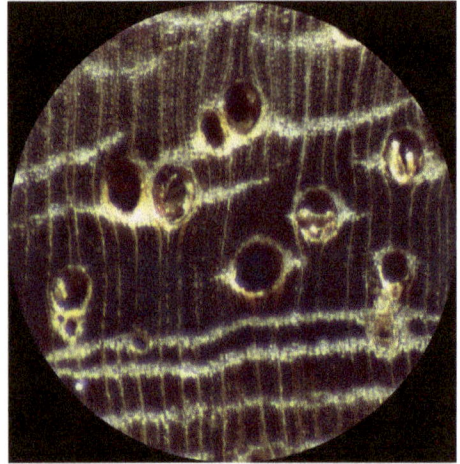

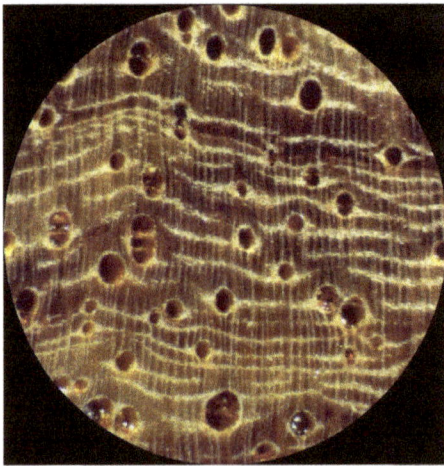

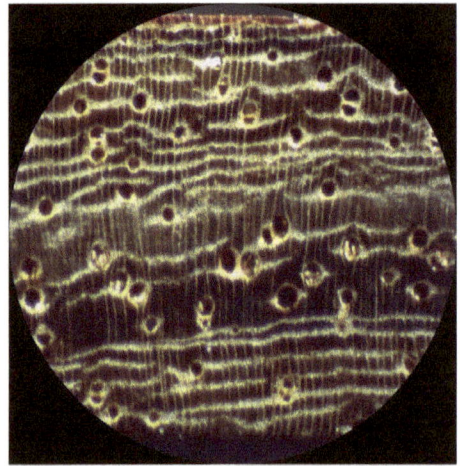

Pterocarpus indicus

Amboina

Pterocarpus macrocarpus

Burma padauk

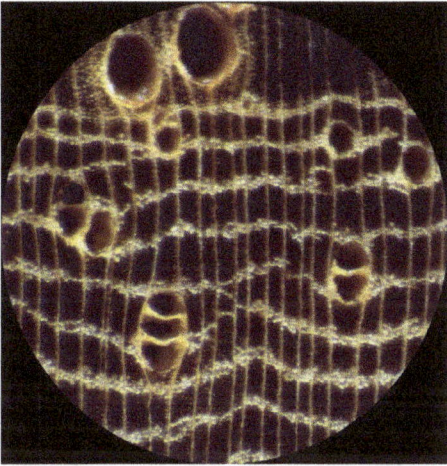

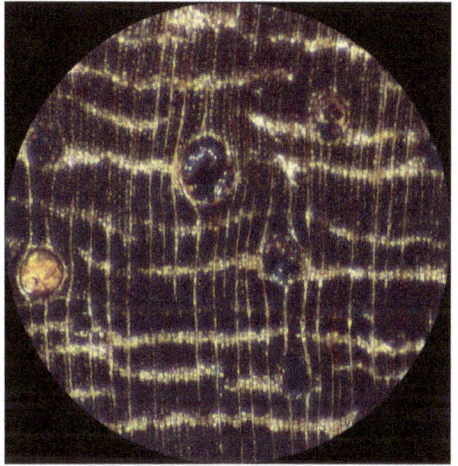

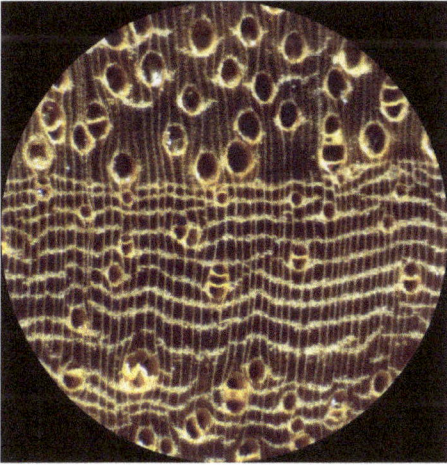

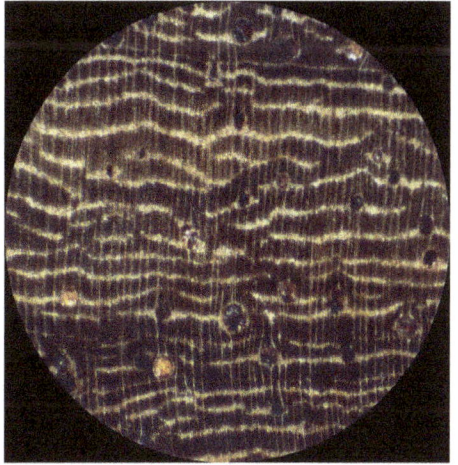

Pterocarpus marsupium

Bijasal

Pterocarpus pedatus

Maidu

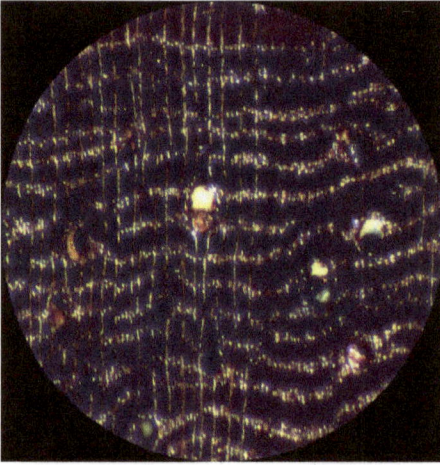
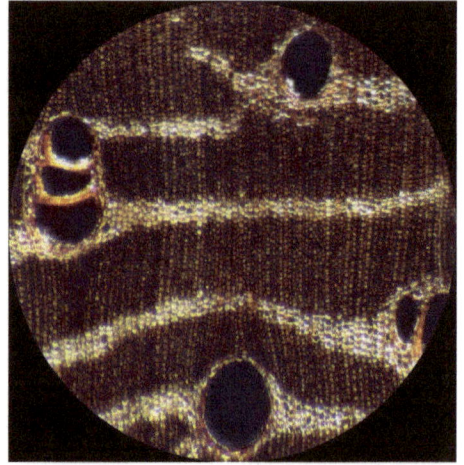

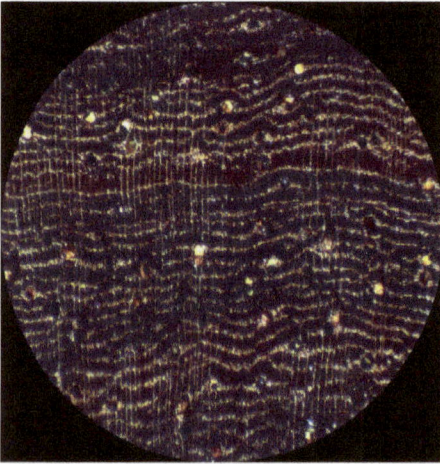
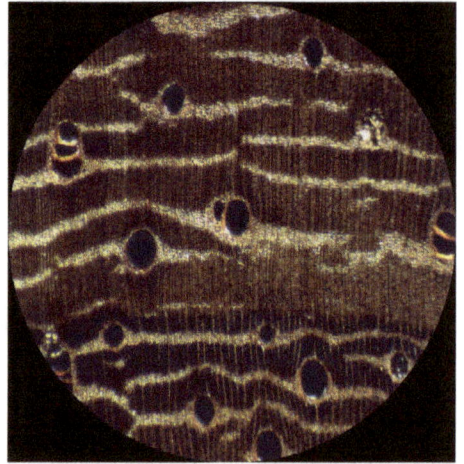

Pterocarpus santalinus

Red Sandalwood

Pterocarpus soyauxii

African Padauk

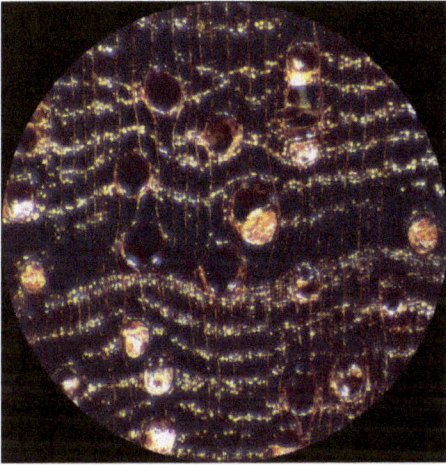

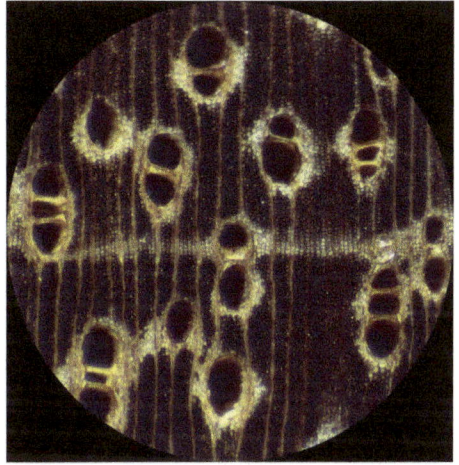

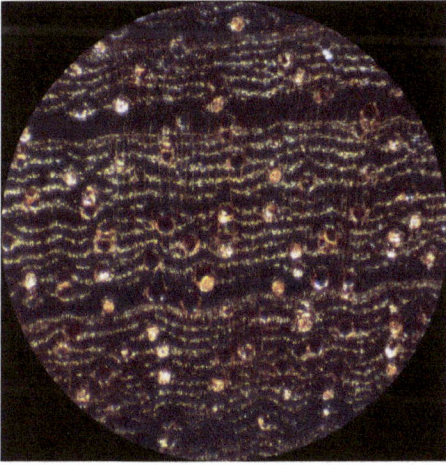

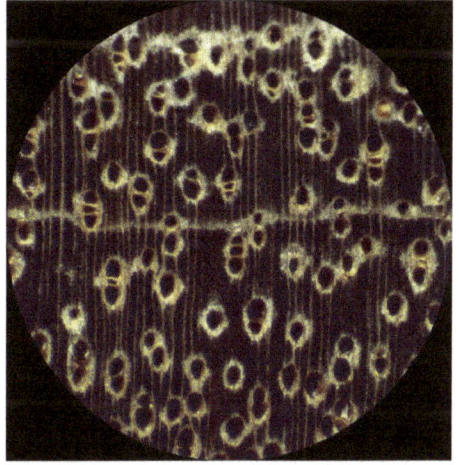

*Pterocarpus
  tinctorius*
Mukula

Pterogyne nitens
Amendoin

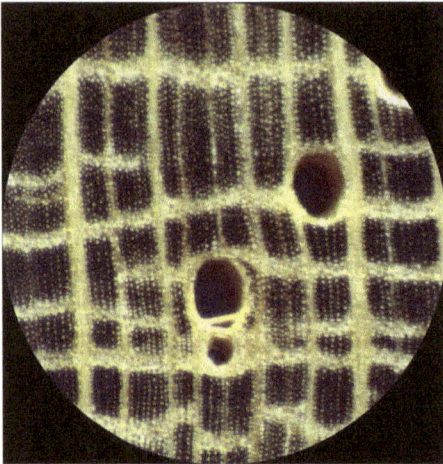

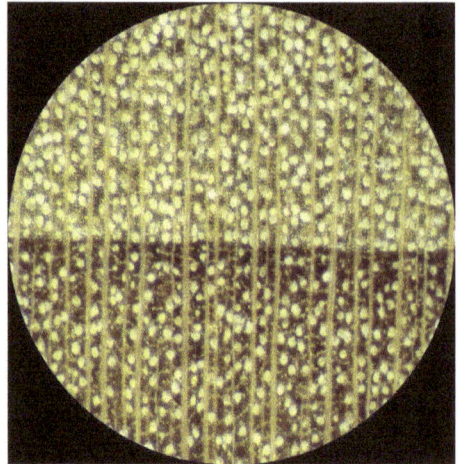

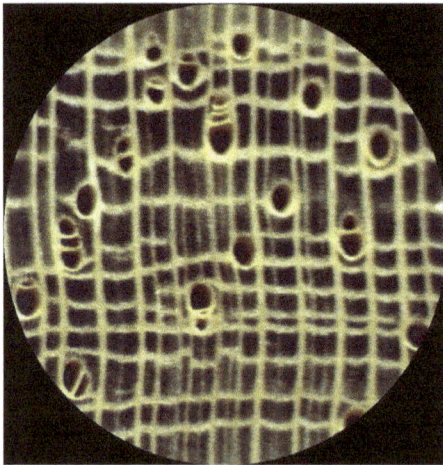

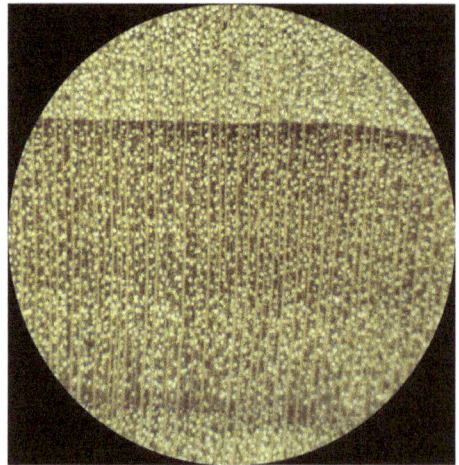

Pterygota horsfieldii
White Tulip Oak

Pyrus calleryana
Callery pear

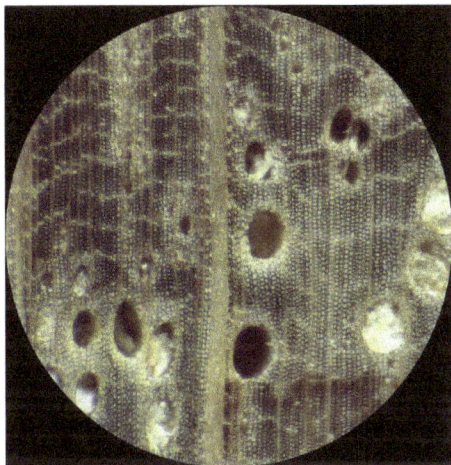

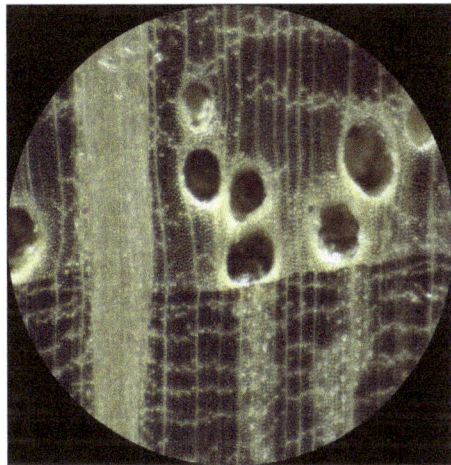

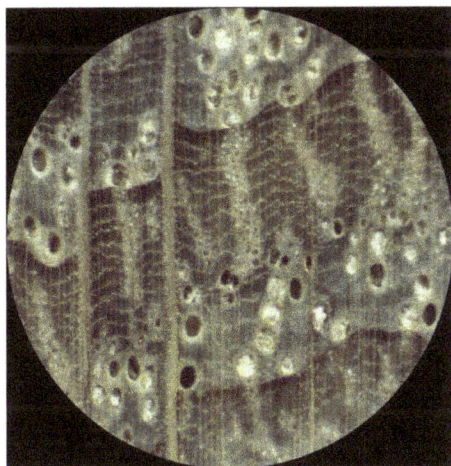

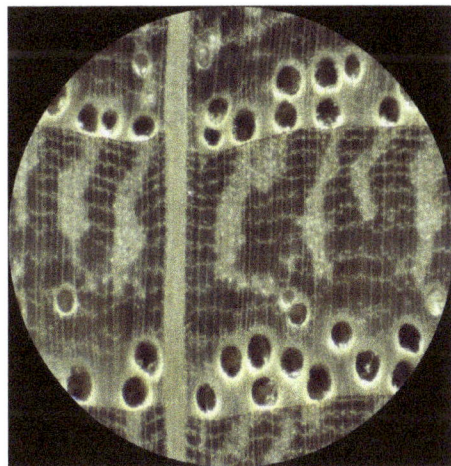

Quercus acutissima
Sawtooth Oak

Quercus alba
White Oak

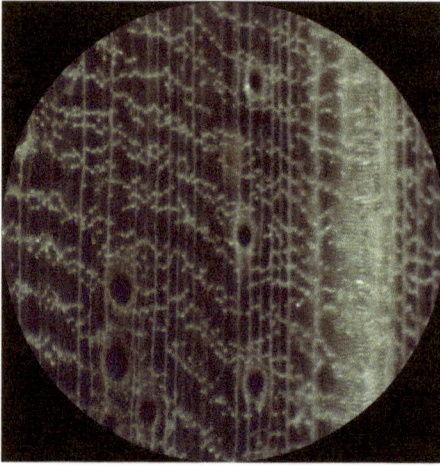

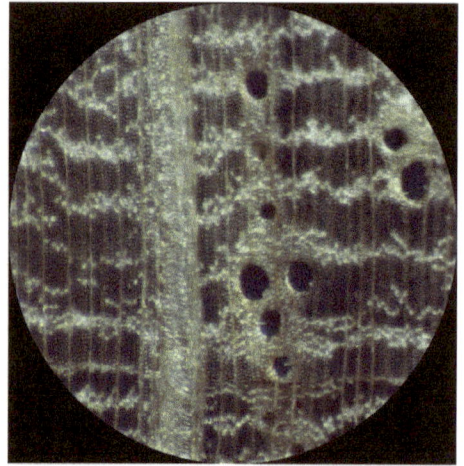

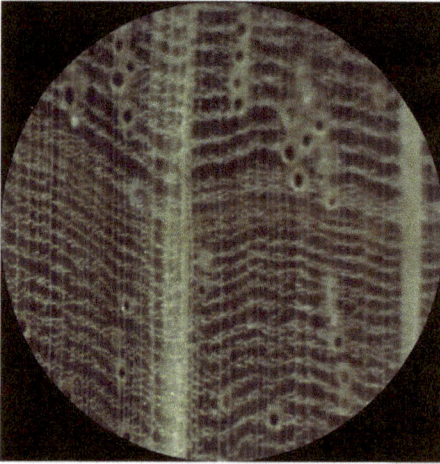

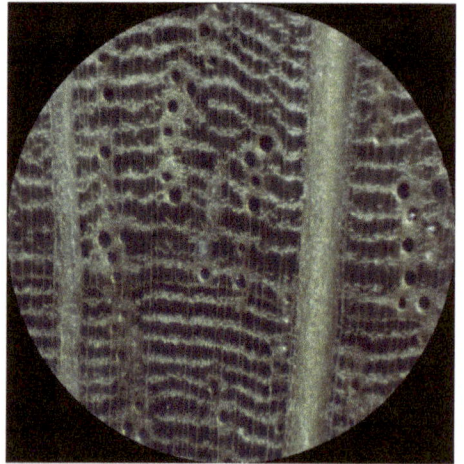

Quercus glauca
Qing gang

Quercus pachyloma
Mao guo qing gang

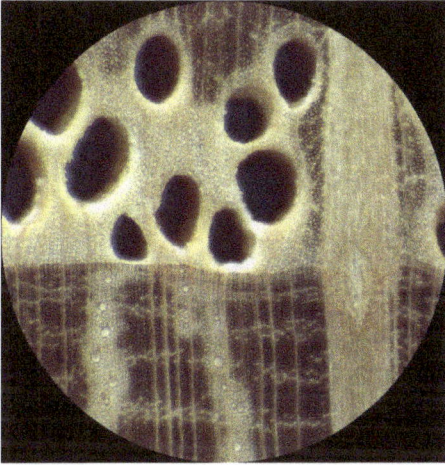

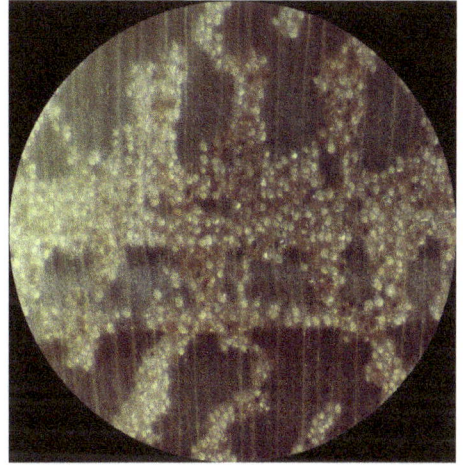

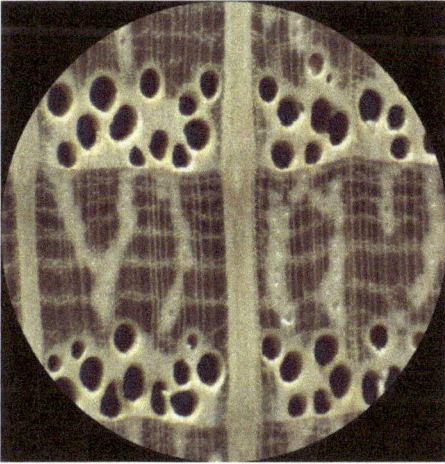

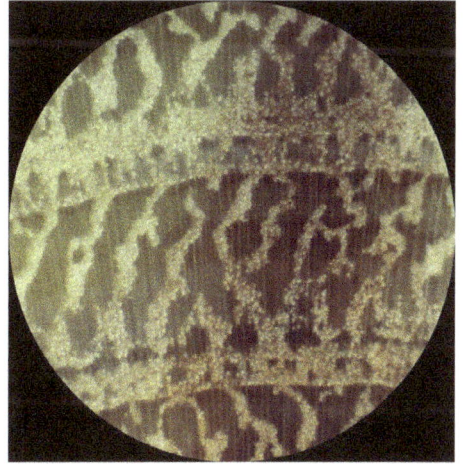

Quercus rubra
Northern Red Oak

Rhamnus cathartica
European Buckthorn

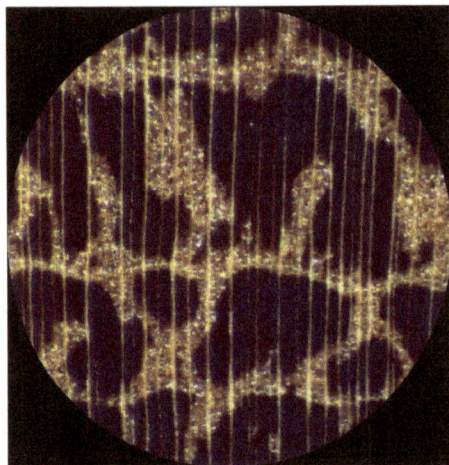

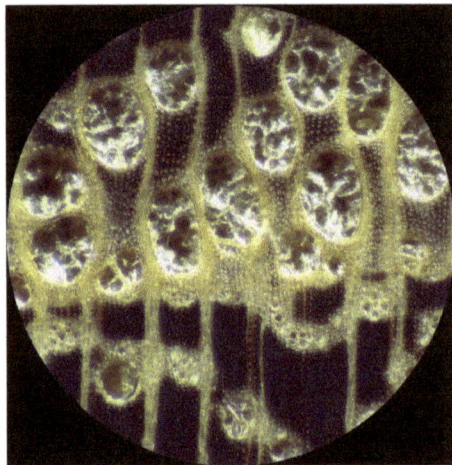

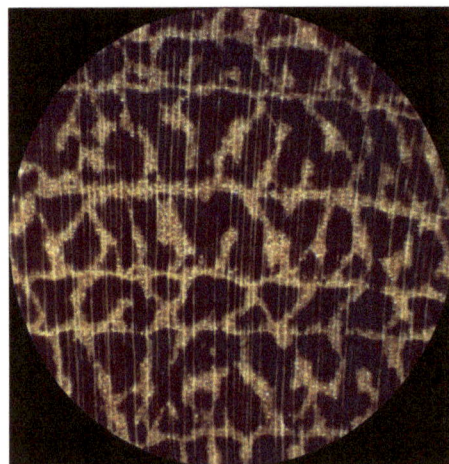

Rhamnus parvifolia
Xiao ye shu li

Robinia pseudoacacia
Black Locust

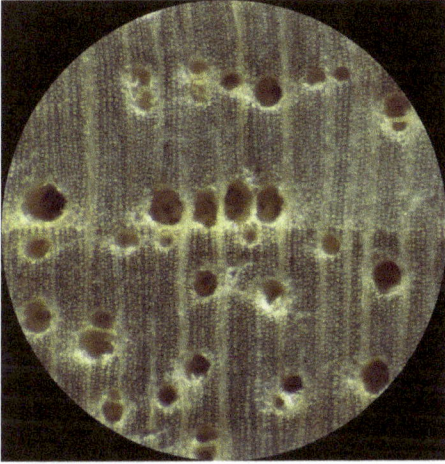

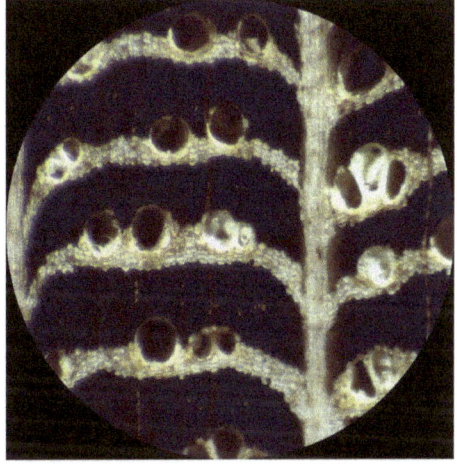

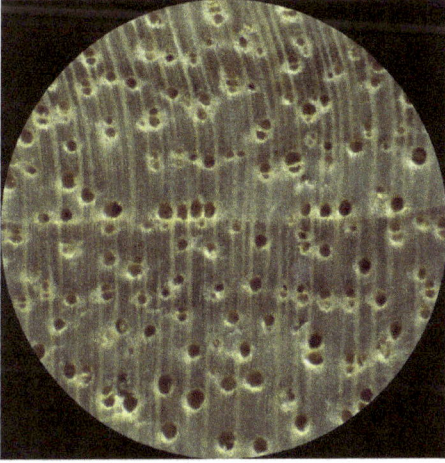

*Roseodendron
    donnell-smithii*
  Primavera

Roupala montana
  Leopardwood

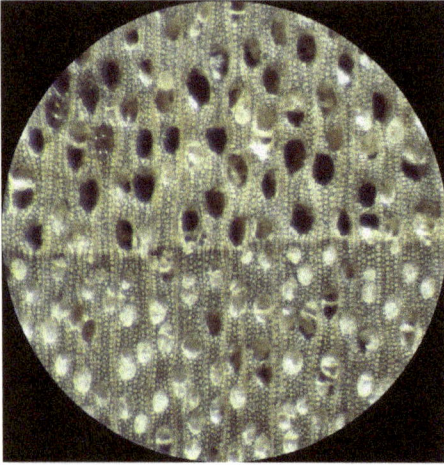

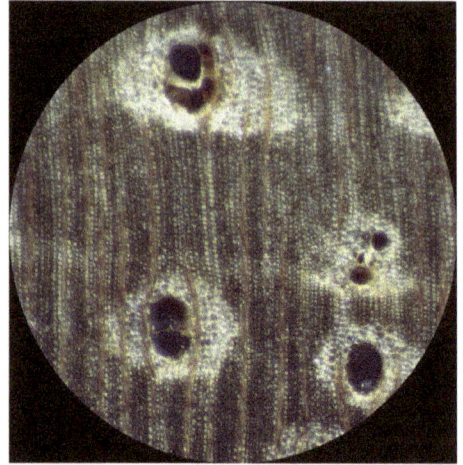

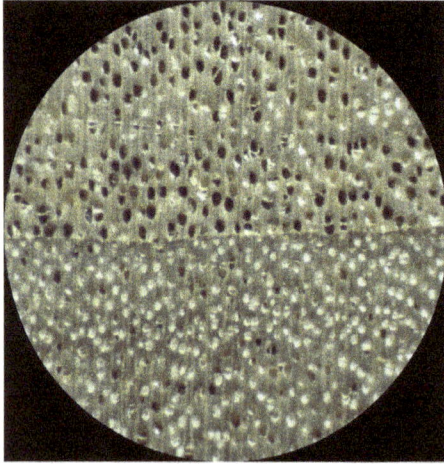

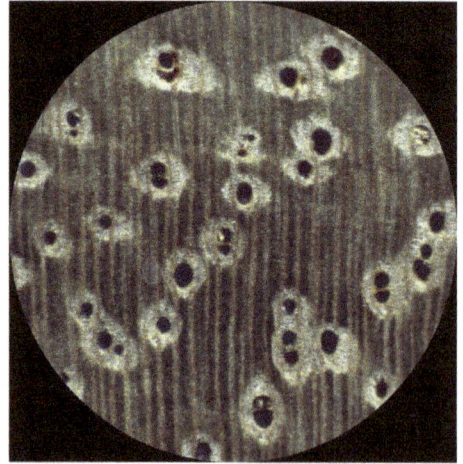

Salix babylonica
Weeping Willow

Samanea saman
Rain tree

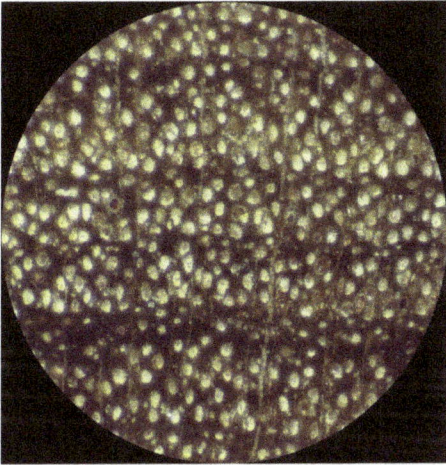

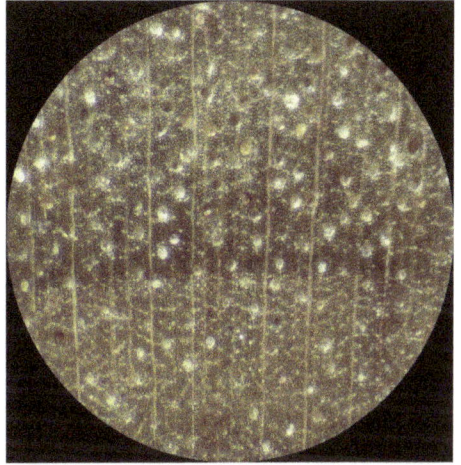

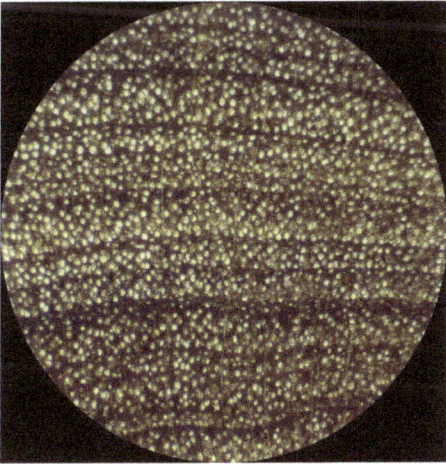

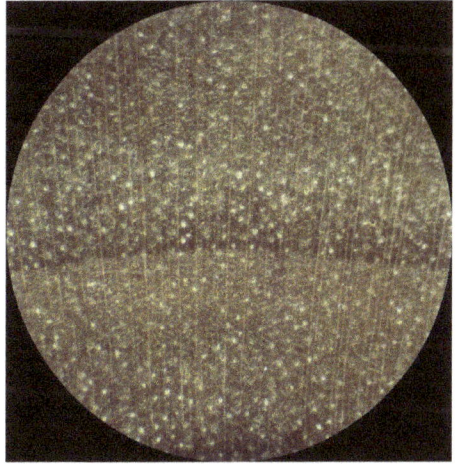

Santalum acuminatum
Sweet Quandong

Santalum album
Sandalwood

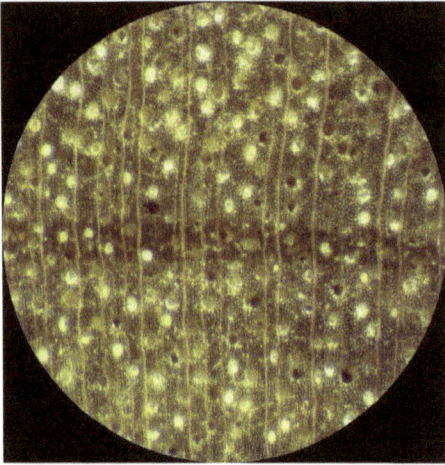

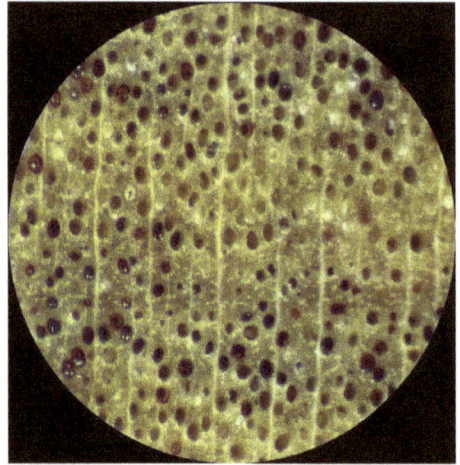

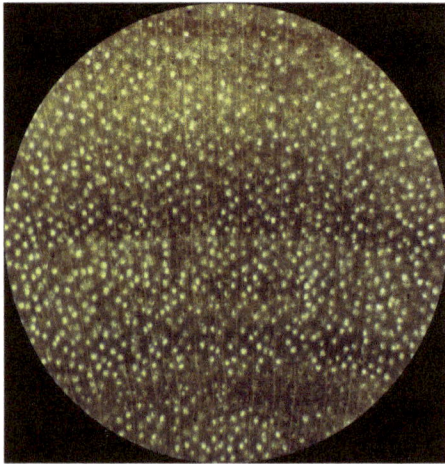

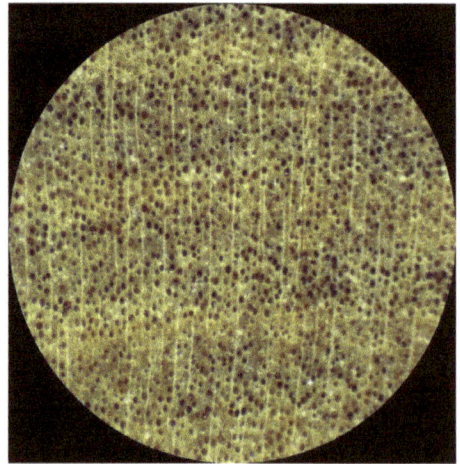

Santalum
freycinetianum
Freycinet Sandalwood

Santalum lanceolatum
Northern Sandalwood

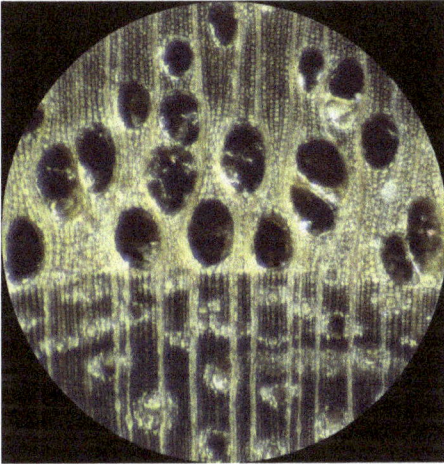

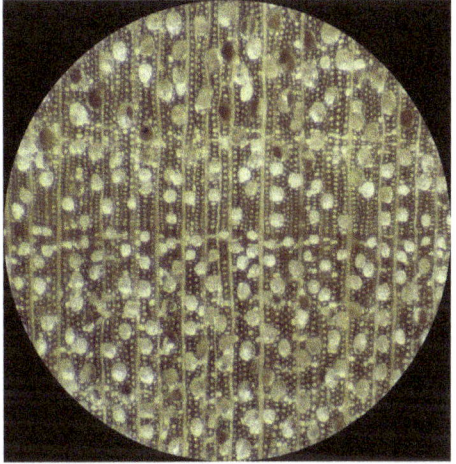

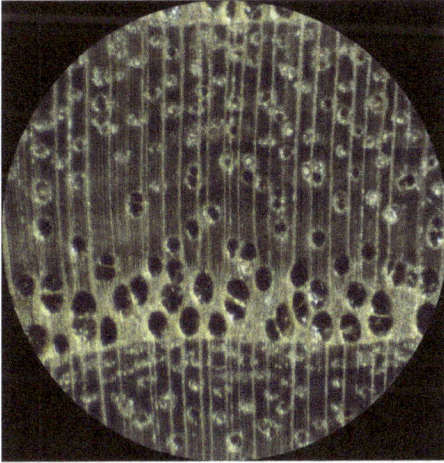

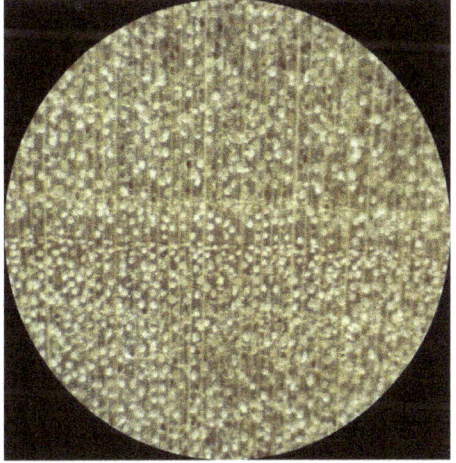

Sassafras tzumu
Chinese Sassafras

Schima superba
Chinese Guger Tree

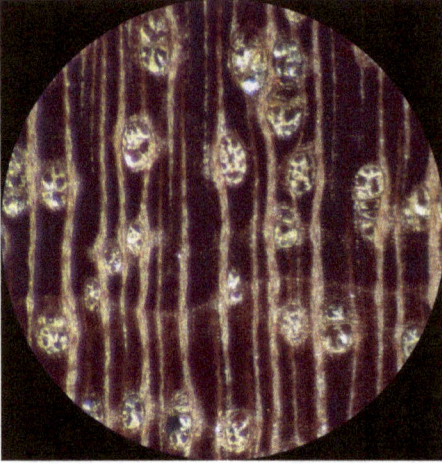

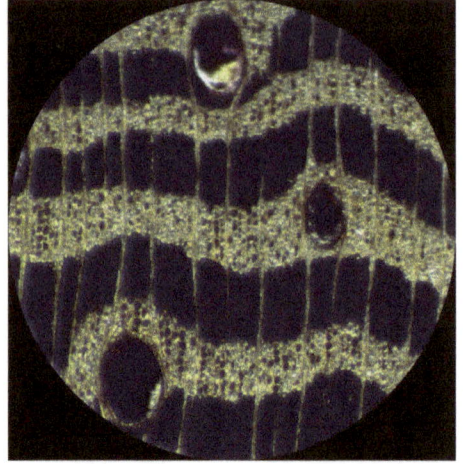

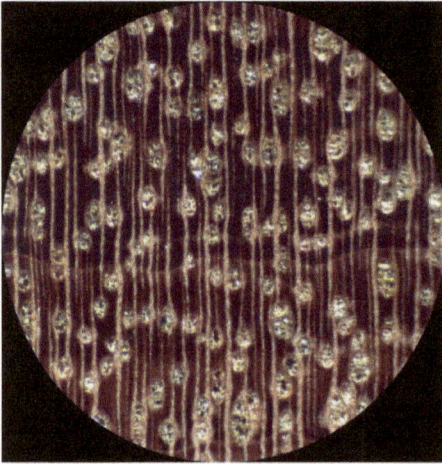

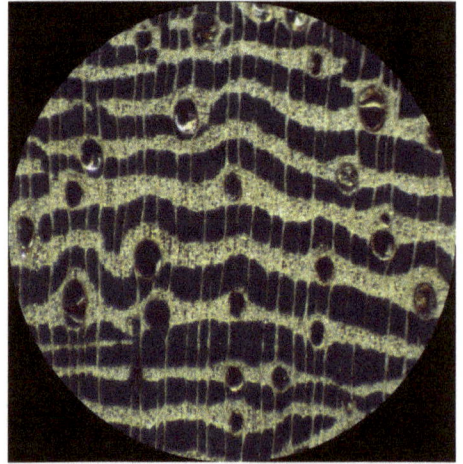

Schinopsis balansae
Quebracho coloeado

Senna siamea
SiameseI Senna

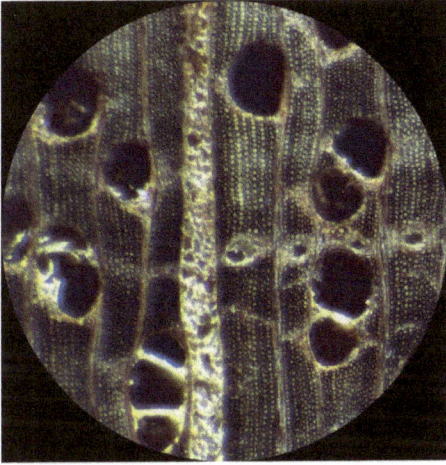

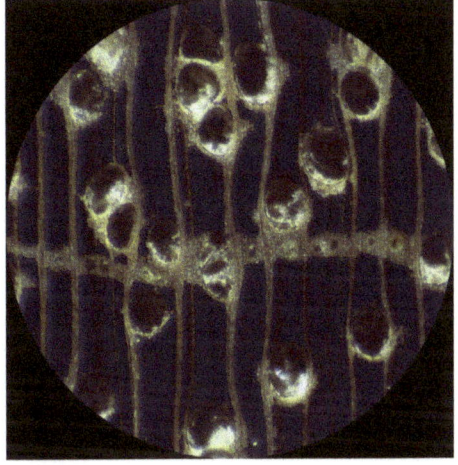

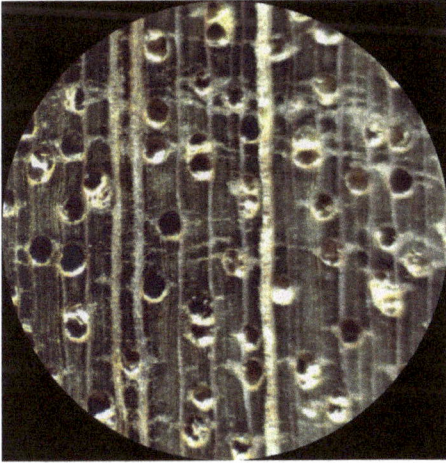

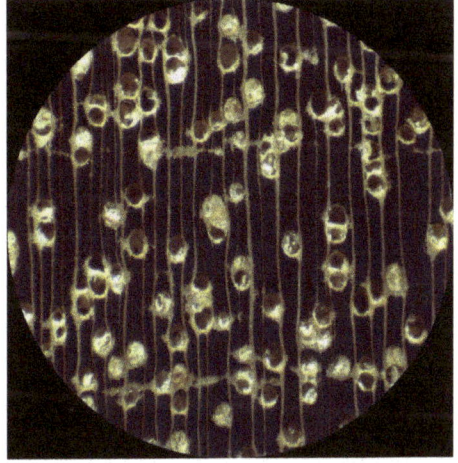

Shorea almon
Almon

Shorea glauca
Balau laut

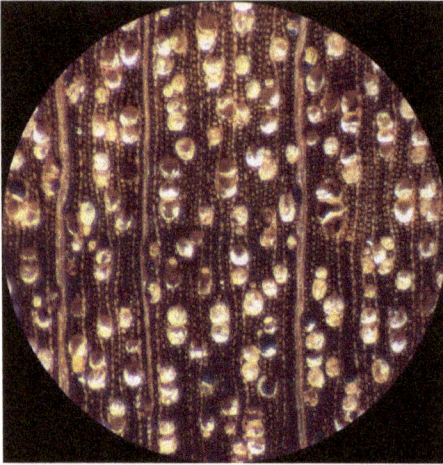

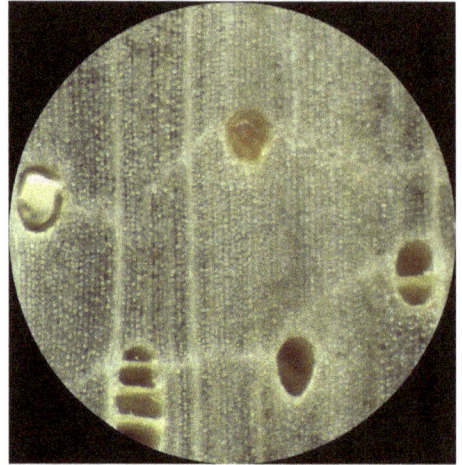

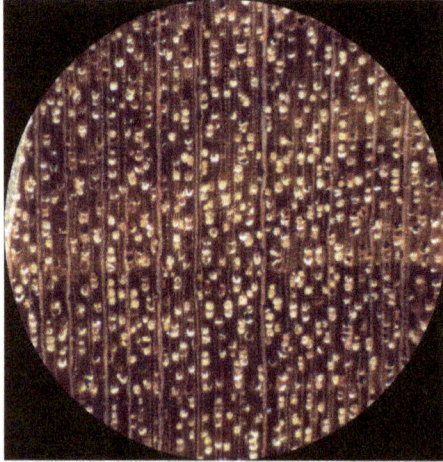

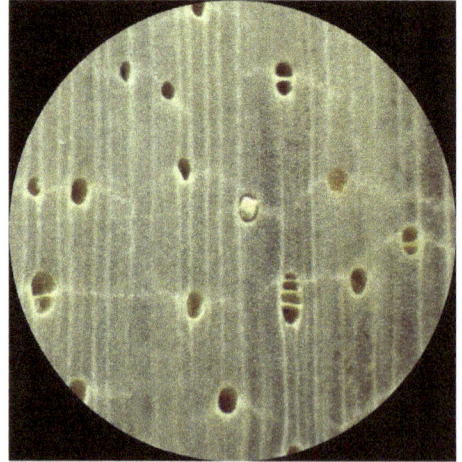

*Sickingia
    salvadorensis*
Redheart

Simarouba amara
Bitterwood

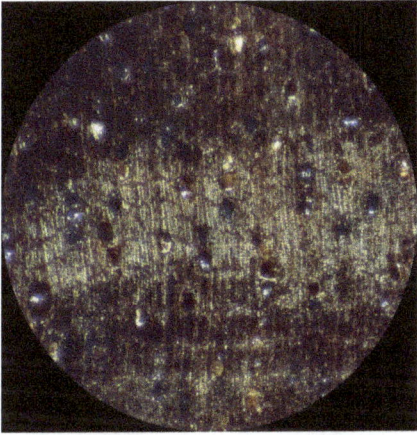

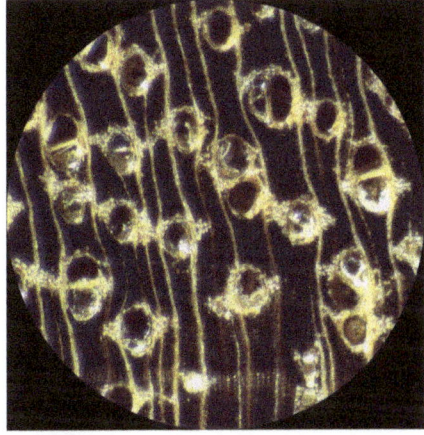

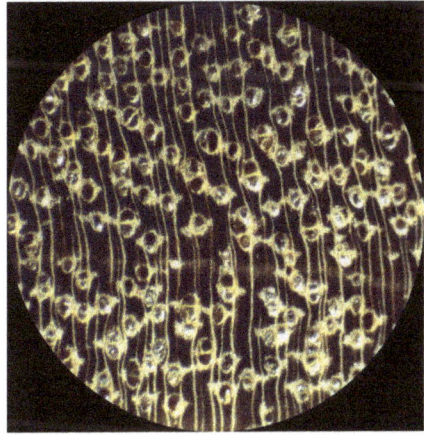

*Spirostachys
       africana*
Tanbotie

Streblus elongatus
Tempinis

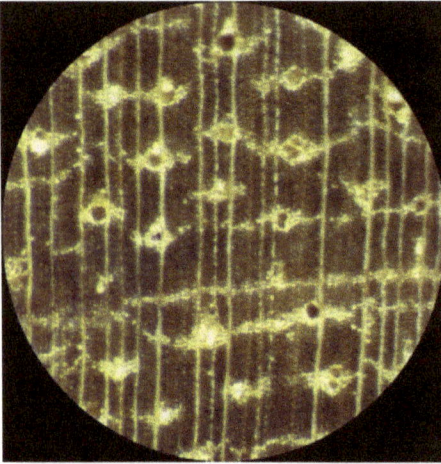

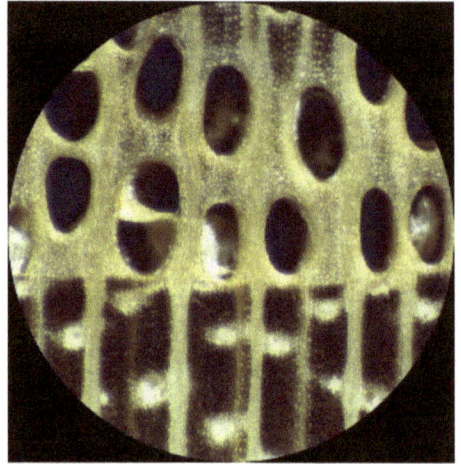

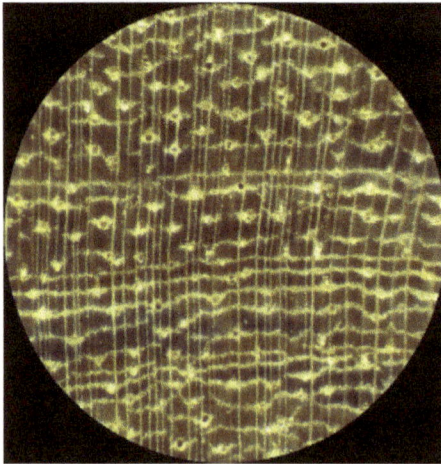

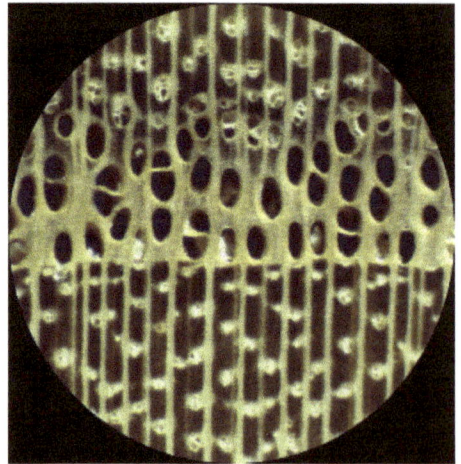

Streblus indicus
Shui Polei

Styphnolobium japonicum
Pagoda Tree

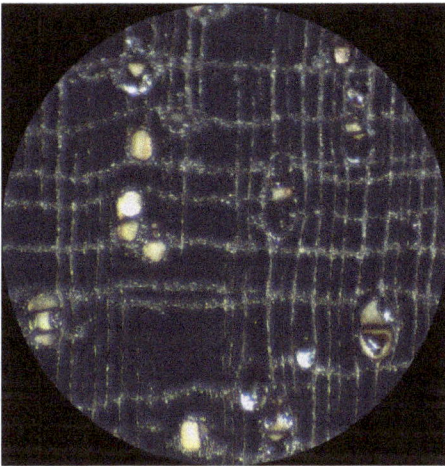

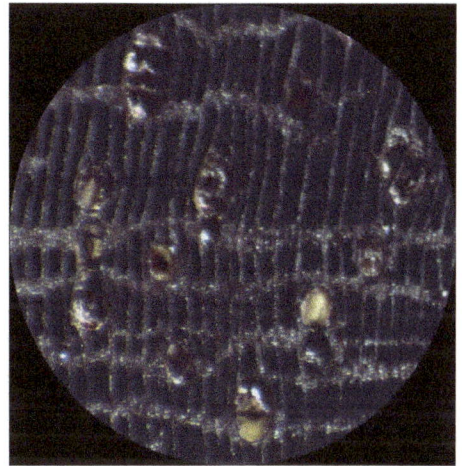

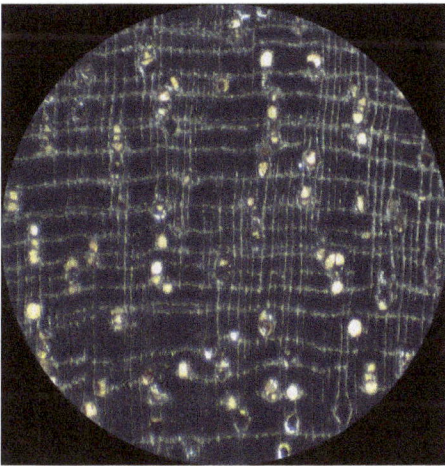

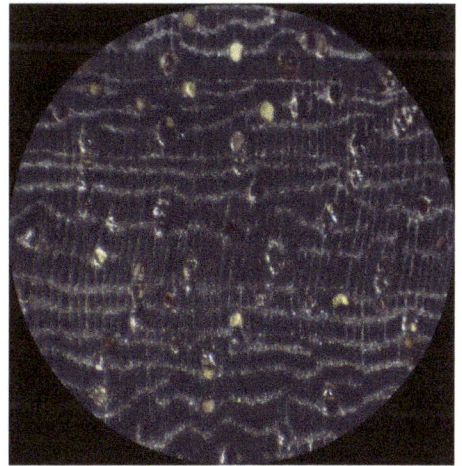

Swartzia bannia
Bannia

Swartzia cubensis
Katalox

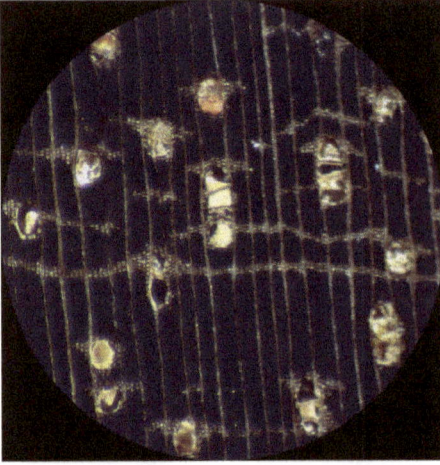

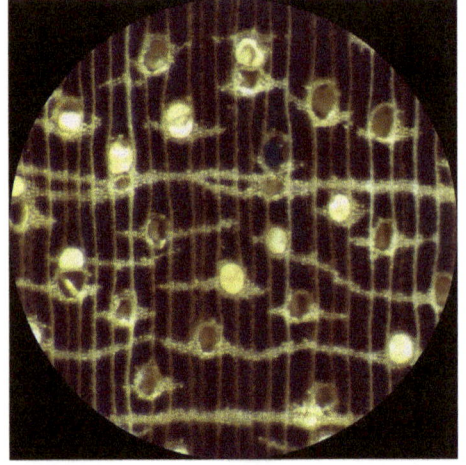

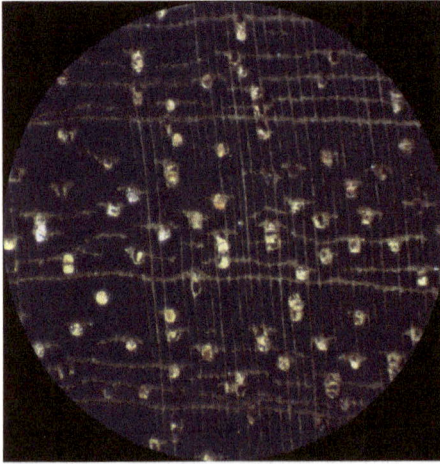

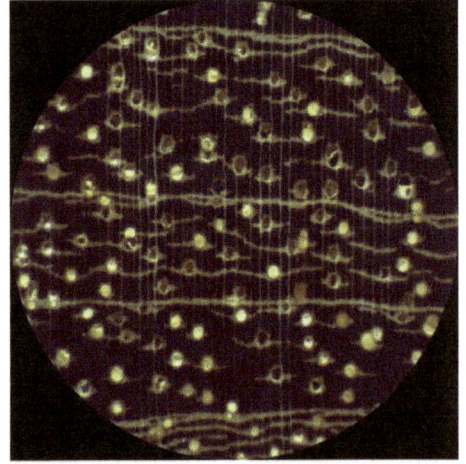

Swartzia leiocalycina
Wamara

Swartzia sprucei
Sprucei

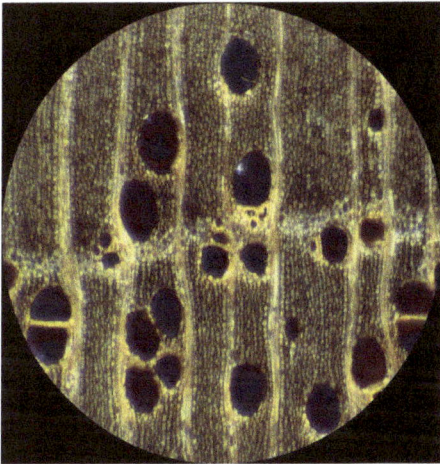

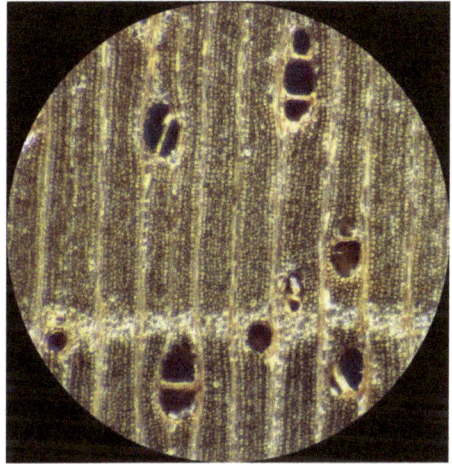

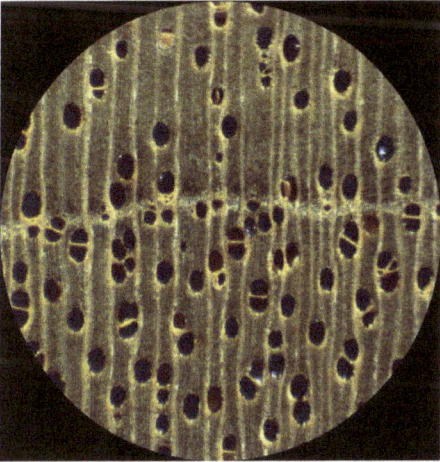

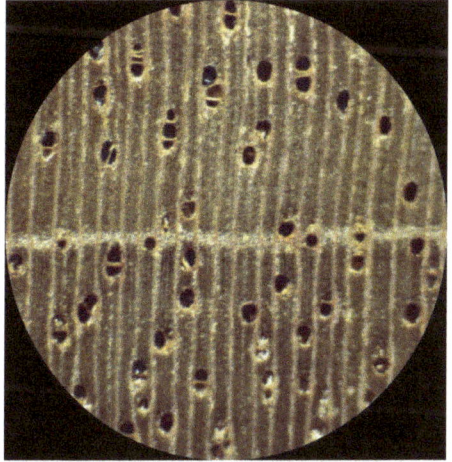

Swietenia humilis

Mexican Mahogany

Swietenia macrophylla

Bigleaf Mahogany

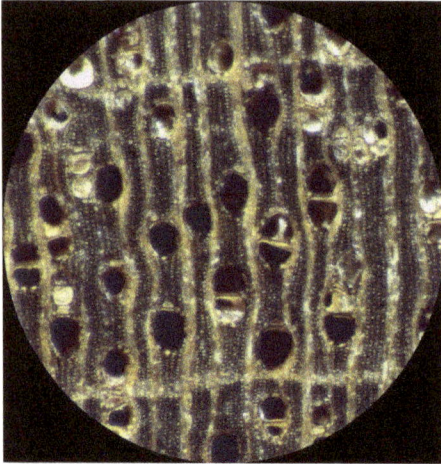

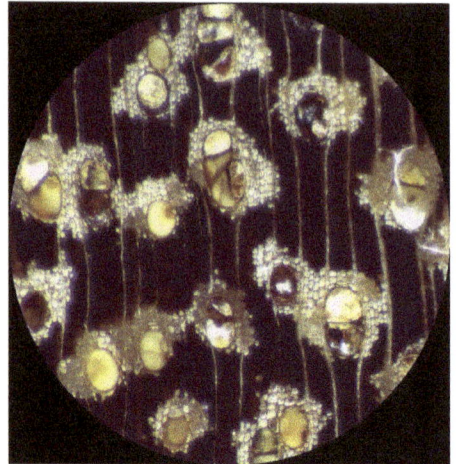

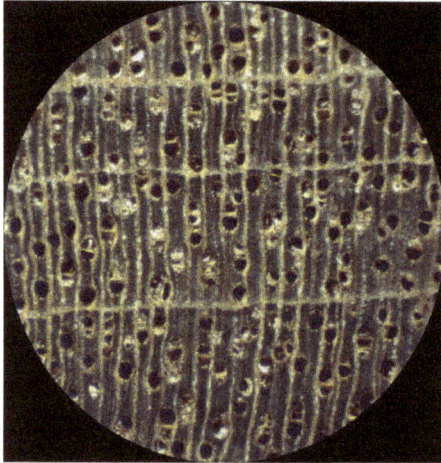

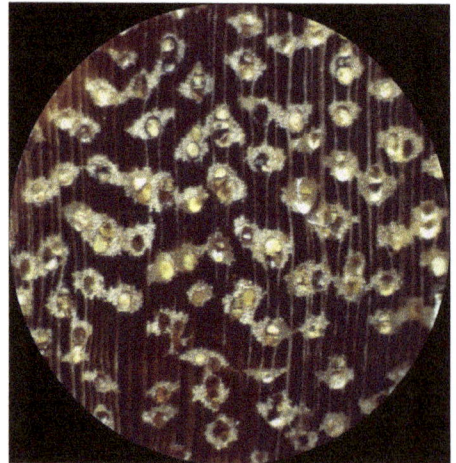

Swietenia mahagoni

Caribbean Mahogany

Tabebuia insignis

White cedar

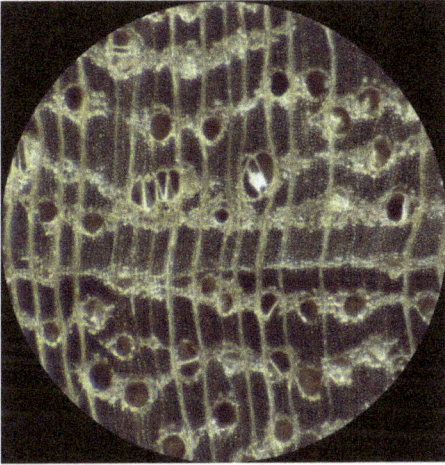

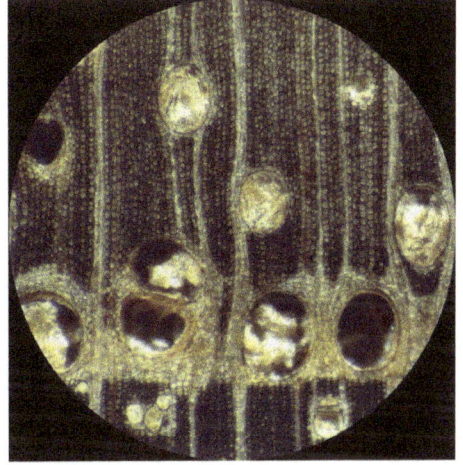

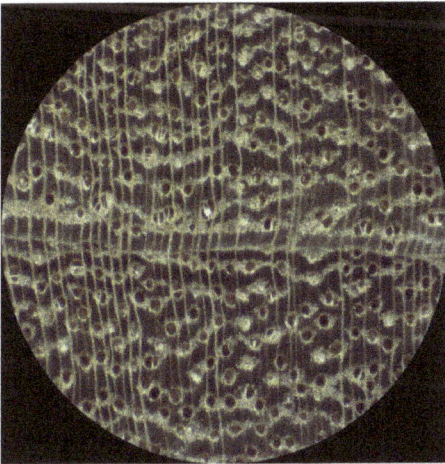

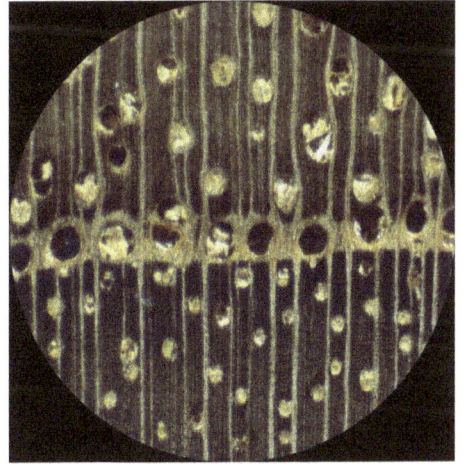

Tabebuia rosea
Apamate

Tectona grandis
Teak

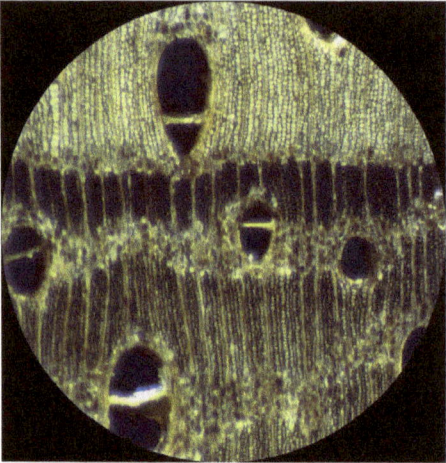

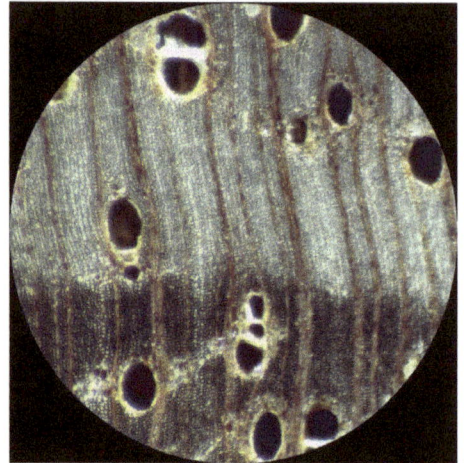

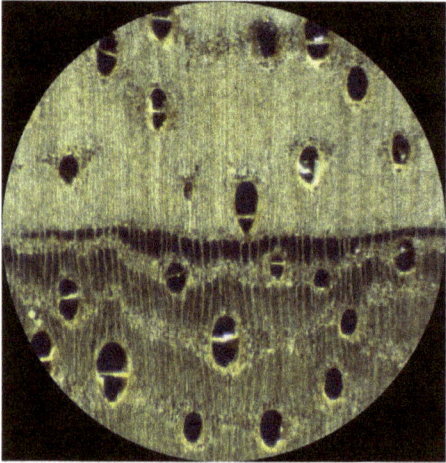

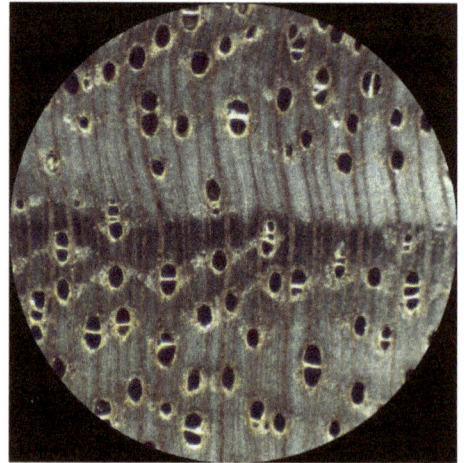

Terminalia bialata

White Chuglam

Terminalia catappa

Tropical Almond

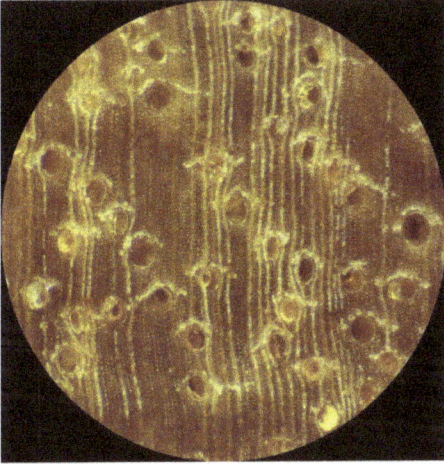

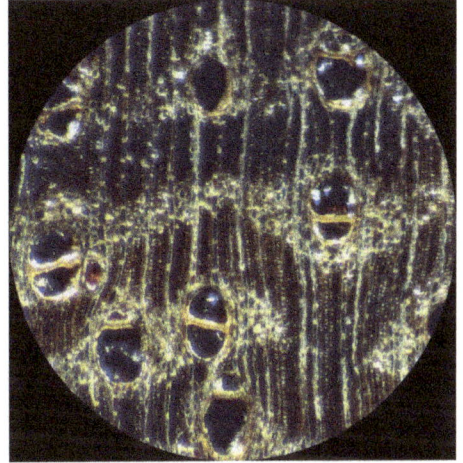

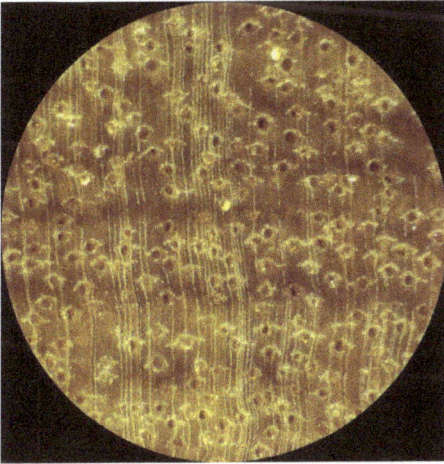

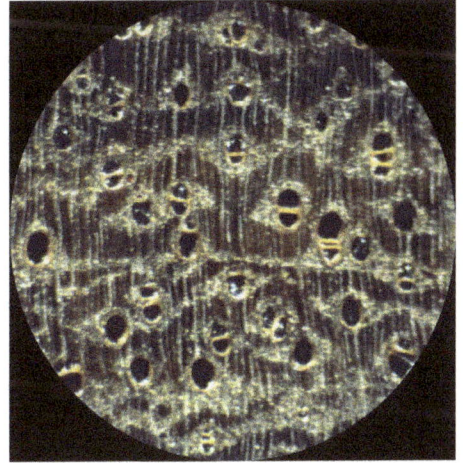

Terminalia mantaly

Madagascar Almond

Terminalia tomentosa

E. Indian Walnut

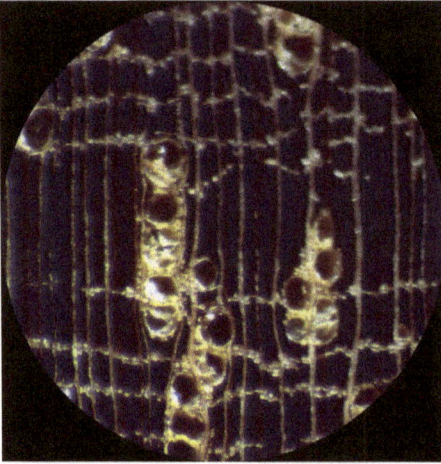

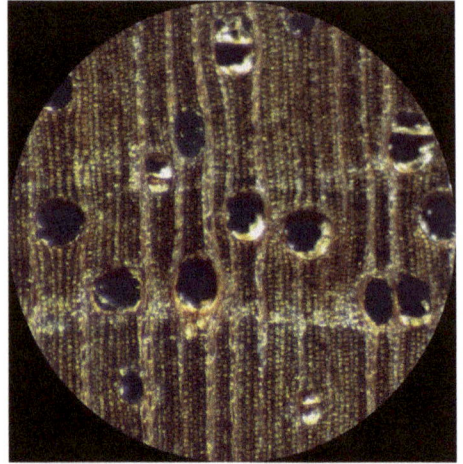

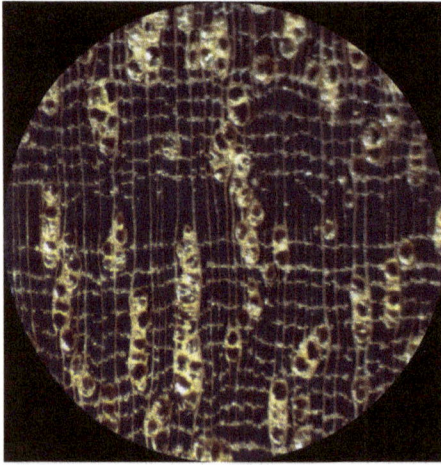

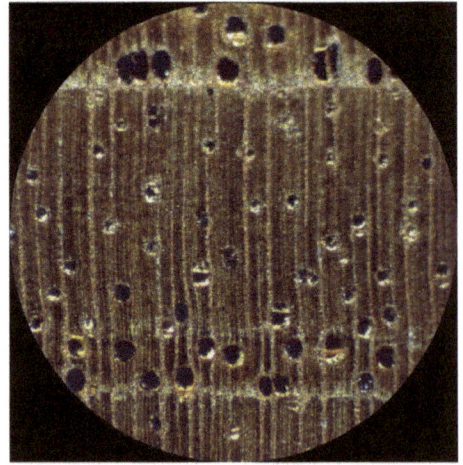

Tieghemella heckelii
Makore

Toona ciliata
Indian mahogany

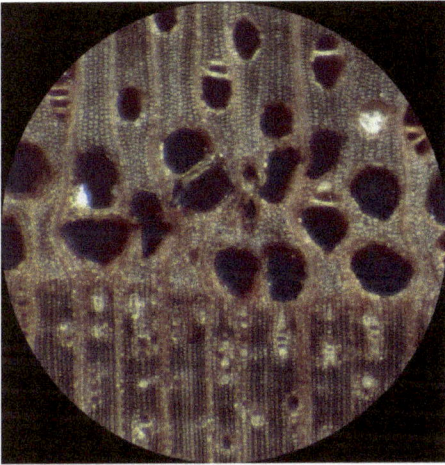

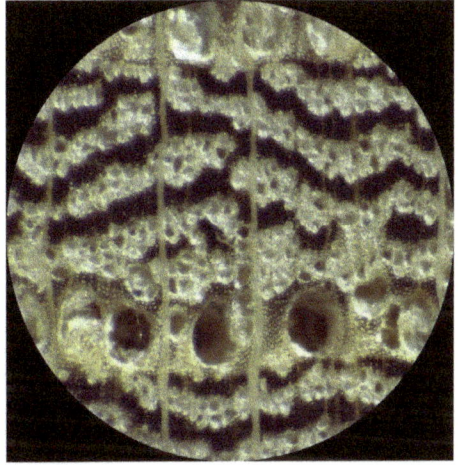

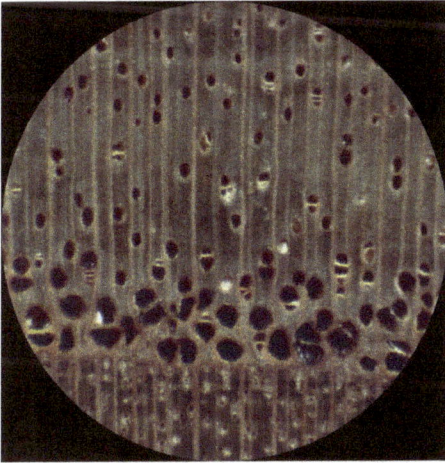

Toona sinensis
Chinese Toon

Ulmus americana
American Elm

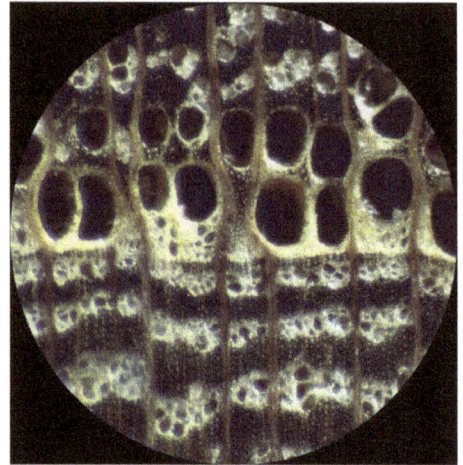

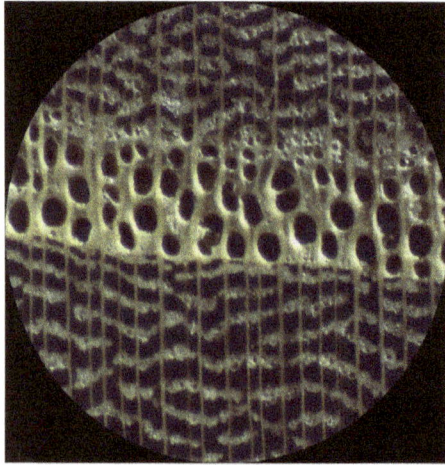

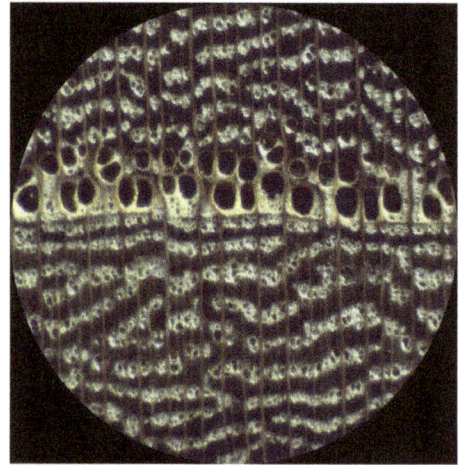

Ulmu carpinifolia
Smooth-leaf Elm

Ulmus japonica
Japanese Elm

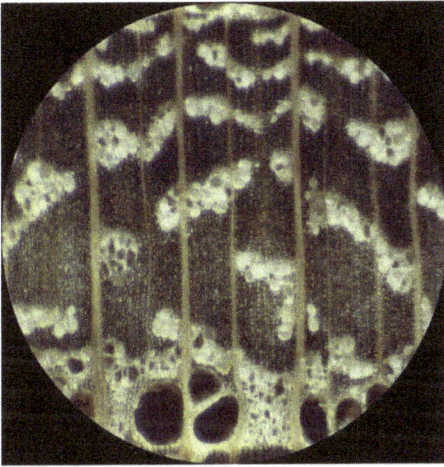

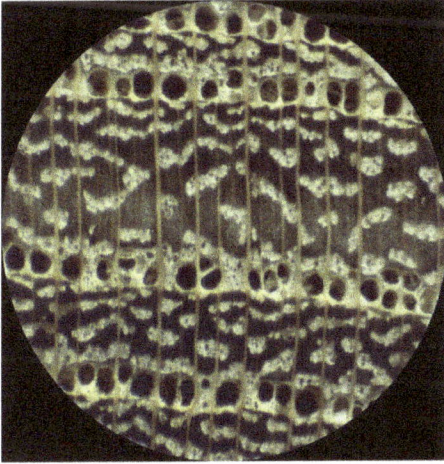

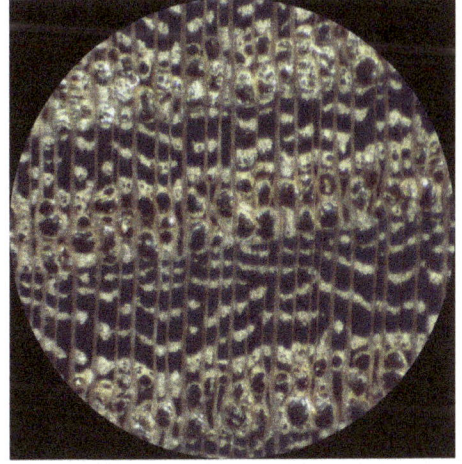

Ulmus laciniata

Lie Ye Yu

Ulmus parvifolia

Chinese Elm

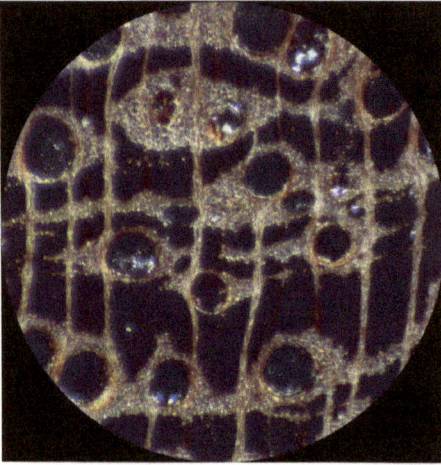

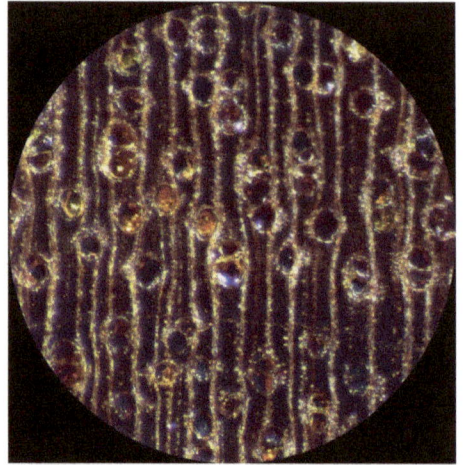

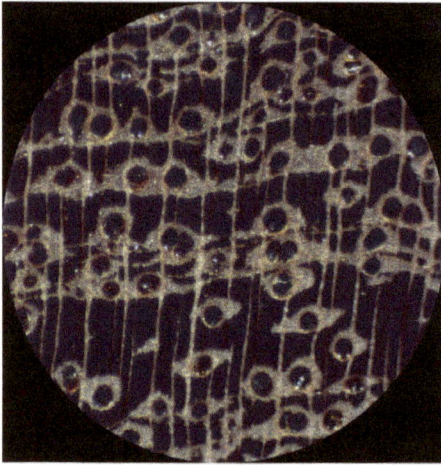

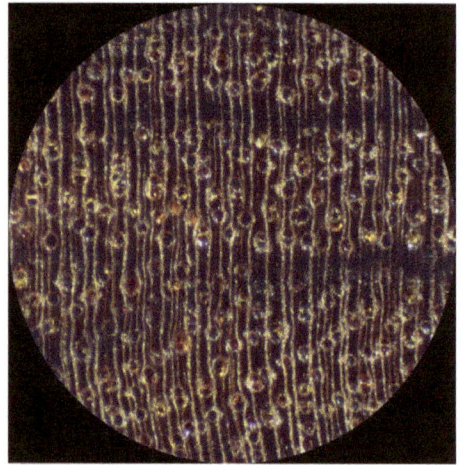

Vachellia erioloba
Camel thorn

Xylia xylocarpa
Pyinkado

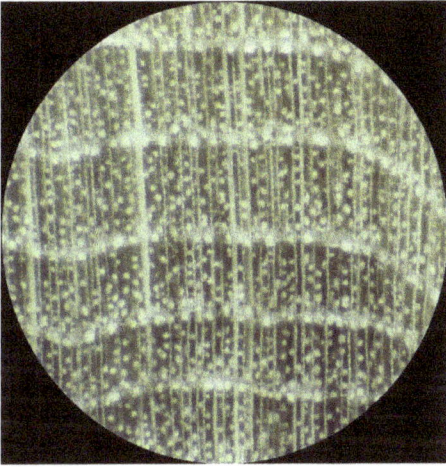

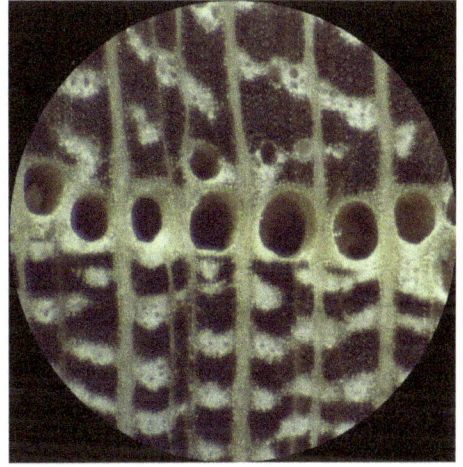

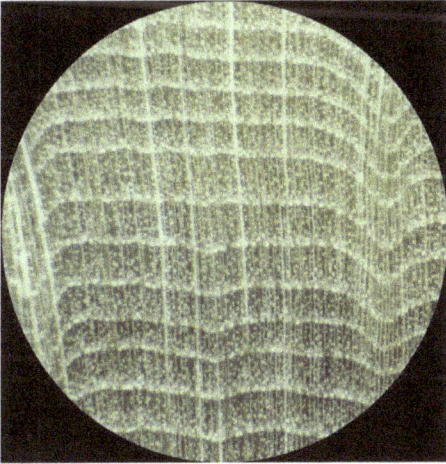

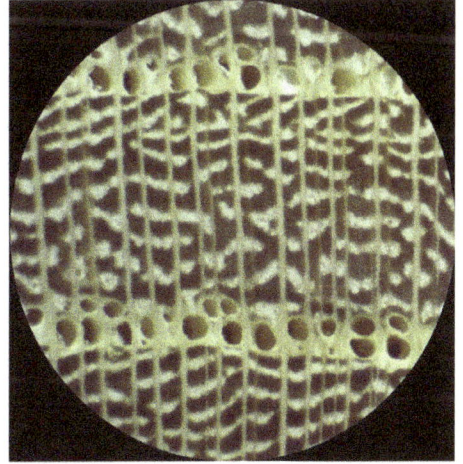

Zabelia biflora

liu dao mu

Zelkova schneideriana

Ju Mu

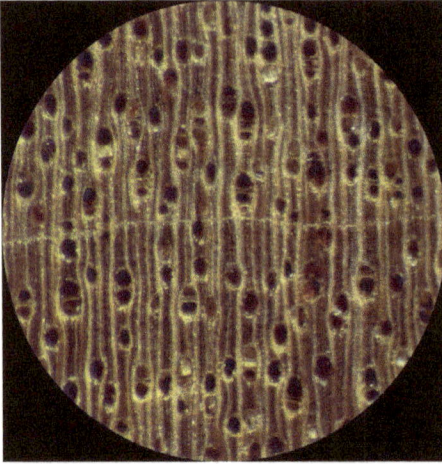

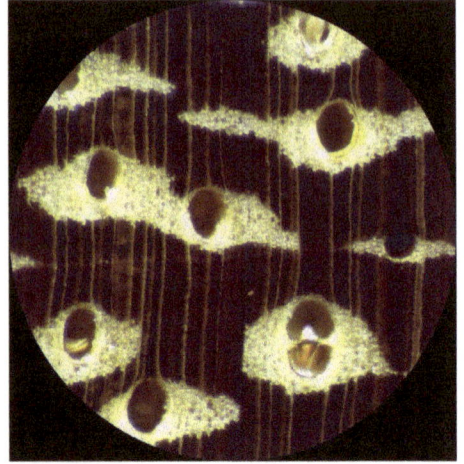

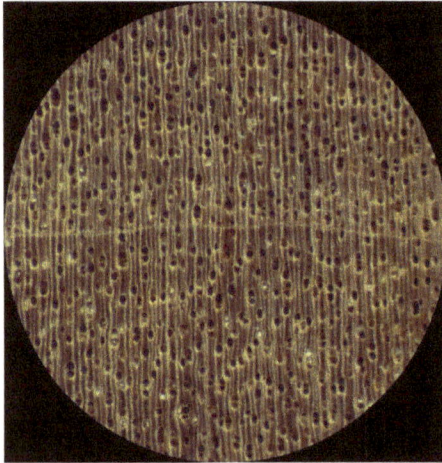

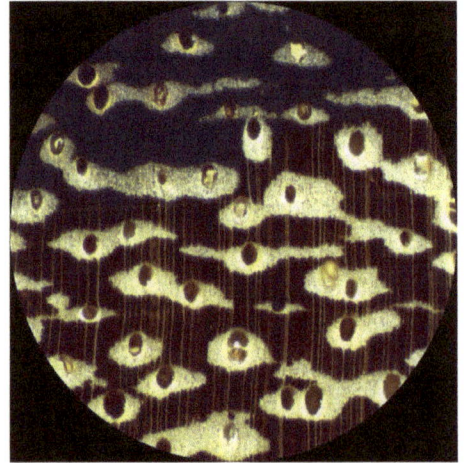

Ziziphus jujuba
Chinese Date

Zygia racemosa
Marblewood

Index

Main Literature Cited

Ruling Tian, Ruyan Tian, Rusong Tian. Aug, 2021. Atalas Hardwood Identification Three Sections Microphptograph. Amazon.

Flavio Ruffinatto, Alan Crivellaro 2020.The Hardwood Cross-sections Book. Endgrain Macroscopic Images of the Most Common Timbers. Kessel Publishing House.

Flavio Ruffinatto, Alan Crivellaro 2019. Atlas of Macroscopic Wood Identification With a Special Focus on Timbers Used in Europe and CITES-listed Species. Kindal e-Books: Springer.

Jean Gerard, Daniel Guibal. Sebastien Paradis, Jean-Claude Cerre 2017. Tropical Timber Atlas Technological Characteristics and Uses. Versailles: Editions Quae.

Habil Gerald koch 2017 CITES wood ID (Control of CITES wood protected Timber). Thunen: Institute of Wood Research.

UNODC 2016. Best Practice Guide for Forensic Timber Identification. United Nation.

Bhikhi, C.R., P.J.M. Maas, J. Koek-Noorman, T.R. van Andel. 2016. Timber Trees of Suriname. An Identification Guide. Volendam, The Netherland, LM Publishers

Morris Lake, 2015. Australian Rainforest Woods. CSIRO Publishing.

Alex C Wiedenhoeft. 2011 Identification of Central American Woods. Madison: Forest Product Society.

Paul Corbineau. Jean-Michel Flandin. 2009 Wood Identification. Turin: Editions Vial.

Ken Ogata, Tomoyuki Fujii, Hisashi Abe, Pieter Baas 2008. Idetification of the timbers of Southeast Asia and The Western Pacific. Tsukuba: Kaiseisha Press.

Bruce H R. 1995 Identifying Wood-Accurate Results with Simple tools. Newtown: The Tauntonpress.

Jugo Ilic 1991 CSIRO Atlas of Hardwood. New York: Springer.

Wheeler, E.A., P. Baas and P. E. Gasson, eds. 1989 IAWA List of Microscopic Features for Hardwood Identification. Leiden, The Netherland: IAWA.

Ruling T, Ruyan T, Rusong T, 2018. Micrographic Illustrated redwood. Beijing: Chemistry Industry Press.

Xu F, Liu H Q, 2016, Atlas of Wood Identification by Comparison. Beijing: Chemistry Industry Press.

Yin Y F, Jiang X M, 2015. Atlas of Identification Endangered and Precious Tropical wood. Beijing: Science Press.

Hai L C, Xu F. 2010. Atlas of Identification Rosewood and Precious Hardwood Furniture. Beijing: Chemistry Industry Press.

Jiang X M, Cheng Y M, Yin Y F, et al. 2010. Atlas of Gymnosperms Wood of China. Beijing: Science Press.

Guo X L, Ran J X, 2004. Atlas of True Color Imported Wood. Shanghai: Shanghai Science and Yang J J, Lu H J, 2003. Wood of Dipterocarpaceae. Beijing Construction Industry Publishing House.

Jiang X M, Zhang l F, Liu P. 1999. Tropical wood Imported from Latin America. Beijing; China Forestry Industry Press.

Liu P, Jiang X M, Zhang L F. 1996. Tropical wood Imported from Africa. Beijing; China Forestry Industry Press.

Liu P, Yang J J, Lu h J, 1993. Tropical wood Imported from Southeast Asia. Beijing; China Forestry Press.

Cheng j Q, Yang J J, Liu P. 1992. Atlas of Chinese Wood. Beijing: China Forestry Industry Press.

Ahmed Abdrabou. Feburary 2021 Non-invasiv wood identification on parts of king Horemheb's ritual couches (New kingdom) Conservar Patrimonio 36(1) DOI: 10.14568/cp2019038 Research Gate.

Peter Kitin, John C. Hermanson, Hisashi Abe, Satoshi Nakaba, Ryo Funada. 06, May 2021 Light microscopy of wood using sanded face instead slides. IAWA Journal.

Prabo Raviindran, Blaise J.Thompson, Richard K. Soares, Alex C. Wiednhoeft. 10, July 2020 The XyloTron: Flexible, Open-source, Image-based, Marcroscopy Field Identification of wood Products. Front Plant Sci. Doi.org/10.3389/fpls.2020.01015

Antonio C. F. Barbosa, Caian S. Gerolamo, Andre C. Lima, Veronica Angyalossy, Marcelo R. Pace 2021. Polishing entire stems and roots sandpaper under water. An alternative method for macroscopic analyses: Application in Plant science 2021 9 (5): e11421.

Prabu Ravindran,Frank C. Owens, Adam C. Wade, Patricia Vega, Rolando Montenegro, Rubin Shmulsky and Alex C. Wiedenhoeft, 2021 Field-Deployable Computer Vision Wood Identification of Peruvian Timbers. Front. Plant Sci., 02 June 2021.

Tuo He, Joao Marco, Richard Soares, Yafang Yin, Alex C. Wiedenhoeft. 2020. Machine Learing Models With Quantitative Wood Anatomy Data Can Discriminate between Swietenia macrophylla and Swietenia mahagoni, Forests 2020, 11(1), 36.

Paloma de Palacios, Luis G. Esteban, Peter Gasson, Francisco Garcia-Femandez, Antonio de Marco, Alberto Garcia-Iruela, Lydia Garcia-Esteban, David Gonzalez-de-Vega, 2020 Using Lenses Attached to a Smartphone as a macroscopic Early Warning Tool in the Illegal Timber Trade, in Particular for CITES-Listd Species. Forests 2020, 11(11).

Andre R. De Geus, Sergio Francisco da Silva, Alexandre B, Gontijo, Flavio O. Silva 2020. An analysis of timber sections and deep learning for wood species classification Multimedia Tool and Appliication 79(1) Springer.

Wheeler, E.A.,P. E. Gasson, and P. Baas. 2020 Using the InsideWood web site: Potentials and pitfalls IAWA Journal 0 (0), 2020: 1–51.

Veronica De Micco, Angela Balzano, Elisabeth A. Wheeler, Pieter Baas, 2016 Tyloses and gums: a review of structure, function and occurrence of vessel occlusions. IAWA Journal 37 (2), 2016: 186–205.

http://www.insidewood.lib.ncsu.edu

http://www.wood-database.com

http://www.prota4u.org/database

https://www.gbif.org/species/search?

http://www.xycol.net

http://www.tropicaltimber.info

http://www.woodanatomy.ch/species

https://www.delta-intkey.com/wood/index.htm

www.ingramcontent.com/pod-product-compliance
Lightning Source LLC
Chambersburg PA
CBHW041220030426
42336CB00024B/3399